MW01168985

Competing Memories

The aftermath of modern conflicts, deeply rooted in political, economic, and social structures, leaves pervasive and often recurring legacies of violence. Addressing past injustice is therefore fundamental not only for societal well-being and peace but also for future conflict prevention. In recent years, Truth and Reconciliation Commissions have become important but contentious mechanisms for conflict resolution and reconciliation. This book fills a significant gap, examining the importance of context within transitional justice and peace-building. It lays out long-term and often unexpected indirect effects of formal and informal justice processes. Offering a novel conceptual understanding of "procedural reconciliation" on the societal level, it features an in-depth study of Commissions in Peru and Sierra Leone, providing a critical analysis of the contribution and challenges facing transitional justice in societies recovering from conflict. It will be of interest to scholars and students of comparative politics, international relations, human rights, and conflict studies.

Dr. Rebekka Friedman is Associate Professor in International Relations in the Department of War Studies at King's College London. Her teaching and research focus on the intersection of transitional justice, peace-building, reconciliation, memory, and gender. She is a former editor of *Millennium: Journal of International Studies.*

Competing Memories

Truth and Reconciliation in Sierra Leone and Peru

Rebekka Friedman

King's College London

CAMBRIDGE
UNIVERSITY PRESS

University Printing House, Cambridge CB2 8BS, United Kingdom

One Liberty Plaza, 20th Floor, New York, NY 10006, USA

477 Williamstown Road, Port Melbourne, VIC 3207, Australia

4843/24, 2nd Floor, Ansari Road, Daryaganj, Delhi – 110002, India

79 Anson Road, #06–04/06, Singapore 079906

Cambridge University Press is part of the University of Cambridge.

It furthers the University's mission by disseminating knowledge in the pursuit of education, learning, and research at the highest international levels of excellence.

www.cambridge.org
Information on this title: www.cambridge.org/9781107185692
DOI: 10.1017/9781316874950

First published 2017

A catalogue record for this publication is available from the British Library.

Library of Congress Cataloging-in-Publication Data
Names: Friedman, Rebekka, author.
Title: Competing memories : truth and reconciliation in Sierra Leone and Peru / Rebekka Friedman.
Description: Cambridge, United Kingdom ; New York, NY : Cambridge University Press, 2017. | Includes bibliographical references and index.
Identifiers: LCCN 2017000014 | ISBN 9781107185692 (hardback)
Subjects: LCSH: Truth commissions – Sierra Leone. | Truth commissions – Peru. | Sierra Leone. Truth and Reconciliation Commission. | Peru. Comisión de la Verdad y Reconciliación. | Reconciliation – Political aspects – Sierra Leone. | Reconciliation – Political aspects – Peru. | Transitional justice – Sierra Leone. | Transitional justice – Peru. | Sierra Leone – Politics and government – 1961– | Peru – Politics and government – 2000– | BISAC: POLITICAL SCIENCE / General.
Classification: LCC DT516.826 .F75 2017 | DDC 966.4/0441–dc23
LC record available at https://lccn.loc.gov/2017000014

ISBN 978-1-107-18569-2 Hardback

Contents

Figures

Acknowledgments

I am deeply thankful for the many people who took an interest in my research and encouraged me while working on this book. This manuscript would not have been possible without their tremendous support.

I want to thank the colleagues, friends, and academics who supported my research. First and foremost, I am deeply grateful to Chris Brown and Kirsten Ainley for their continuous support and helpful guidance and suggestions at every stage of this project. The LSE International Relations Department provided a stimulating and supportive atmosphere and funded my research. At the LSE, Mark Hoffman, Nicholas Sims, Jens Meierhenrich, and Chris Alden were particularly helpful. The late William Wechsler, Rex Brynen, Michael Brecher, and Jean-François Drolet have been very supportive. Leslie Vinjamuri and Leigh Payne provided helpful comments on an early version of this book. I also thank two anonymous peer reviewers for their invaluable suggestions on the draft manuscript.

The War Studies Department at King's College London provided an immensely stimulating and welcoming environment to complete this manuscript. I am very grateful to Ned Lebow, Theo Ferrell, Mervyn and Lola Frost, Natasha Kuhrt, Guglielmo Verdirame, Mike Rainsborough, Vivienne Jabri, Claudia Aradau, Jan Willem Honig, Rachel Kerr, Nicholas Michelson, James Gow, Christine Cheng, Mats Berdal, Walter Ladwig, Frank Foley, Thomas Rid, Nicola Palmer, and Jana Krause for their encouragement and support. A special thank you goes to the students of my Transitional Justice and International Criminal Law course whose enthusiasm and insights have been enriching and inspiring. The War Crimes Research Group and Conflict, Security and Development have provided a highly engaging intellectual home. I also thank Jenna Marangoni, Paola Ferrero, John Gugiere, and Jasmine Mitchell for their invaluable assistance with this manuscript. I am most grateful to my CUP editor, John Haslam, my content manager, Neil Ryan, and Puviarassy Kalieperumal for their helpful and thorough preparation of this manuscript.

Many people in Sierra Leone and Peru welcomed me and actively supported my research. In Freetown, I am grateful to the Human Rights Commission and the Interreligious Council for providing access to Truth and Reconciliation Commission material. The staff at Forum of Conscience allowed me to travel with them and gave me unique insight into community reconciliation in war-affected areas. Kieran Mitton, Laura Martin, Jessica Lincoln, Gearoid Millar, and Saleem Vahidy provided valuable insights and support. I am especially grateful to Pel Koroma and my late friend Coco Lakish.

In Lima, Salomón Lerner Febres and Rosemary Lerner Rizo Patron supported my research and opened their home and archives to me. The staff and researchers at El Instituto de Democracia y Derechos Humanos de la Pontificia Universidad Católica del Perú were very generous, particularly Rolando Ames Cobián, Félix Reátegui, and Orietta Perez Barreto. I also thank Luis Rebaza-Soraluz at King's College London and the Bas family. It is with sadness that I thank the late Pilar Coll Torrente for her generosity and interest and introducing me to Shining Path and Movimiento Revolucionario Túpac Amaru women, and the late Carlos Iván Degregori, whose scholarship informed my research on the Shining Path and who insisted on going forward with our meetings in Lima even when he was very ill.

In Ayacucho, Sister Anne Carbon provided immense support, hospitality, and friendship. I thank the staff at La Comisión de Salud Mental de Ayacucho for allowing me to join them on trips to villages in Ayacucho and their assistance with my research. I am especially indebted to Ruth Moises and Juana García Blásquez and her family, for their valuable insights and close friendship. Our conversations have shaped many of my views and have stayed with me.

I am very grateful to my family for their assistance and enthusiasm. I thank my father, Henry, particularly for his continuous support of this project especially during difficult periods. I also want to acknowledge my mother, Sabine; my cousin, Roy Benedek; and siblings, Jonah, Marcia, Zohar, and Ascher, who read parts of the book and provided a kind yet critical eye. I thank the Aiello-Johnson-Garlach family for their continuous and generous interest and support, particularly my "adopted" grandfather, the late George Garlach. I am also grateful to Flora and Tony Jacobs, who invited me to stay with them on numerous occasions and provided a home in London between field research. I am also grateful to Benjamin Wolf, Clare McIntyre, Carmen Gayoso, Kristine Behm, Tsetsi Kgama, Rahwa Fessehaye Caplan, Andrew Jillions, Kristine Behm, Joseph Brown, Jenny Kagan Gelfand, Simone Datzberger, and Kristin Annexstad for their comments on sections of this manuscript.

Lastly and most importantly, I am deeply touched by the warmth and generosity of my interviewees in different parts of the world and from many walks of life who invited me into their homes and communities and enthusiastically and generously engaged with my research. Their faith in the research project and encouragement offered tremendous inspiration. I thank them for continuously reminding me of the significance of this subject matter.

The remote village of Uchuraccay, Ayacucho, was deserted during Peru's decades of political violence, following severe attacks from the Shining Path and military. At the right is the Santuario de la Paz y Reconciliación (Sanctuary of Peace and Reconciliation), commemorating the attack on eight journalists, mainly from the capital, and their guide on January 26, 1983. Although subject to high-level investigations, responsibility for the attack remains disputed and many have criticized the little attention generated by villagers' experiences of violence before and since the attack. Where women head many of the homes in the village, the photo signifies resilience and hope in the women's rebuilding of life and community. It also highlights the politics of voice and representation, where residents of the region remain isolated and struggle to navigate the difficult realities of daily life. Photo taken by author in October 2010.

Abbreviations and Definitions

Afectado	Individual affected by political violence (Peru)
AFRC	Armed Forces Revolutionary Council (Sierra Leone)
ANC	African National Congress (South African political party)
ANFASEP	Asociación Nacional de Familiares de Secuestrados, Detenidos y Desaparecidos del Perú (Organization in Ayacucho for relatives of victims, Peru)
APC	All People's Congress (Political party, Sierra Leone)
APRA	Alianza Popular Revolucionaria Americana (Political party, Peru)
Campesinos	Peasants (Spanish)
CDCs	Civil defense committees (Sierra Leone)
COSMA	La Comisión de Salud Mental de Ayacucho (Mental health organization in Ayacucho, set up as a follow-up to the CVR's mental health reparations plan, Peru)
CVR	Comisión de la Verdad y Reconciliación (Truth and Reconciliation Commission, Peru)
DDR	Disarmament, Demobilization, and Reintegration
ECOMOG	Economic Community of West African States
EPAF	Equipo Peruano Antropológico Forénsico (Forensic anthropology organization, Peru)
Fambul Tok	Family Talk (Translated from Krio. Community-level reconciliation project, run by Forum of Conscience, Sierra Leone)
ICC	International Criminal Court
ICTR	International Criminal Tribunal for Rwanda

ICTY	International Criminal Tribunal for the former Yugoslavia
IDEHPUCP	El Instituto de Democracia y Derechos Humanos de la Pontificia Universidad Católica del Perú (Institute of Democracy and Human Rights, Peru)
IPAC	Instituto de Promoción Agropecuaria y Comunal (Agrarian and development NGO, Peru)
Kamajor	Traditional Mende hunters (Sierra Leone)
La Colina	Death squad made up of armed forces under President Fujimori and National Intelligence Director, Vladimiro Montesinos (Peru)
MOVADEF	Movimiento Por Amnistía y Derechos Fundamentales (Movement for Amnesty and Fundamental Rights, Peru)
MRTA	Movimiento Revolucionario Túpac Amaru (Tupac Amaru Movement, Peru)
NACSA	The National Commission for Social Action (Reparations Commission, Sierra Leone)
NFHR	National Forum for Human Rights (Sierra Leone)
NGO	Non-governmental organization
NPRC	National Provisional Ruling Council
PUCP	Pontificia Católica del Perú (Catholic University, Peru)
Pueblos Jóvenes	Shanty Towns (Peru)
Rondas Campesinas	Peasant patrol groups (Peru)
RUF	Revolutionary United Front (Sierra Leone)
Sendero Luminoso	Shining Path (Peru)
SCSL	Special Court for Sierra Leone
SLA	Sierra Leone Army
SLPP	Sierra Leone People's Party
TRC	Truth and Reconciliation Commission
UNSCH	Universidad Nacional de San Cristóbal de Huamanga

1 Justice and Reconciliation in Enduring Conflicts

In March 2011, rural women from the conflict-devastated department of Ayacucho, Peru, traveled to the Peruvian capital to organize a *Chalina de la Esperanza* (Scarf of Hope) exhibition to raise awareness for survivors of political violence. The centerpiece of the occasion, a kilometer-long quilt, made by the women, documented their experiences and those of their still-missing family members. Originally scheduled to take place in the upscale Lima neighborhood of San Isidro, the mayor canceled the event days before the women's arrival, on the allegation that the event was pro-Shining Path, prompting both outrage among human rights organizations and close media scrutiny. Under public pressure, the Lima municipality moved the event to the capital's town hall, hanging the quilts in a display around the municipal square. The attempt to censor the event resulted in a much bigger and higher-profile ceremony, with Nobel Prize laureate and political figure Mario Vargas Llosa giving a keynote speech and candidates in Peru's upcoming elections in attendance. While the controversy surrounding the event revealed deep divisions in Peruvian society, outrage over its censorship is also testament to victims' increased visibility in an era of increased attention to state violence.

Since Peru's large-scale and controversial truth-seeking process was launched, historical memory has come to play a prominent role in Peruvian social politics. Two decades of political violence at the hands of the Shining Path and the Movimiento Revolucionario Túpac Amaru (MRTA), mirrored by violence on the part of state actors, sharply divided the country. In 2001, Peru's large-scale truth-seeking process, the Comisión de la Verdad y Reconciliación (CVR), was set up by presidential decree counter to a strong discourse among Peru's coastal middle classes and elites saying that it was time to "*voltear la página*" (turn the page) and focus on the future. The CVR was the only Latin-American commission to use public hearings – a practice it adopted from South Africa's Truth and Reconciliation Commission (TRC) – yet it also consciously distanced itself from the South African restorative model. Where a large percentage of victims represented a historically marginalized and largely indigenous rural population, the Commission focused on two main goals: first, to acknowledge and dignify victims and historically marginalized communities as citizens, and thereby advance civic nation- and state-building, and, second, to raise awareness of the state's role in the conflict and the effects of political violence among Peru's coastal middle classes. The conflict's main protagonists – the military and the Shining Path – were largely absent from hearings and, unlike other truth commissions, the CVR was not tied to any official reintegration program.

In Sierra Leone, following a violent and destructive eleven-year civil war, a heavy-handed international intervention in the country's post-conflict reconstruction process unleashed a different dynamic. A long history of colonial rule and external interference before and during the war had further politicized external interference, unleashing a debate over the appropriate ends, means, and agents of post-conflict peace-building. Although some worked in support of the UN-established TRC and the Special Court for Sierra Leone (SCSL), sectors of Sierra Leonean civil society also distanced themselves from global justice, emphasizing localism and a decentralization of politics. Despite criticisms that internationally supported transitional justice had sidelined local culture and civil society, global justice also mobilized local actors and grassroots processes. The emergence of the community-based reconciliation project Fambul Tok, established by the organization Forum of Conscience, illustrates a complex interplay between global and local accountability processes, with its founder, human rights activist John Caulker, eventually distancing himself from his earlier work at the TRC Working Group. Maintaining that the TRC had not generated ownership and had insufficiently engaged war-affected communities, Fambul Tok (meaning "family talk" in Krio) seeks to advance a locally driven restorative agenda, plugging into communities' own traditions and working through community authorities and representatives. While the project situates itself as a Sierra Leonean alternative to globalized transitional justice, it is also an outgrowth of formal mechanisms, plugging into an expectations crisis resulting from a loss of momentum and legitimacy surrounding global means.

In this book, I examine the nature and dynamics of justice and reconciliation in Peru and Sierra Leone and the challenges of reconciliation in societies recovering from complex and protracted societal conflicts. In many ways, the politics and controversy surrounding formal justice and memory described above indicate a clear lack of substantive reconciliation and evidence the raw and still unsettled natures of both conflicts. The challenges of reconciliation in societies recovering from complex and protracted societal conflicts are a major theme of this research and emerge strongly in both the theoretical and empirical chapters of the book. Whereas much of transitional justice theory and practice was consolidated in the aftermath of World War II at the Allied prosecutions at Tokyo and Nuremberg, and later in the context of regime transitions in the Cold War, in this manuscript I look closely at the difficulties in establishing transitional justice in different parts of the world, and particularly in divided societies following protracted and complex internal conflicts. Stressing endogeneity in transitional justice and peacebuilding, I maintain that the conditions that justice and reconciliation processes were set up to address also fundamentally constrained their reach and impact. The long-term political, social, and economic marginalization of remote regions, and highly concentrated experiences of violence in particular, generated profound mistrust and resentment and fundamentally shaped local experiences of justice and reconciliation. In both countries, a subsequent lack of follow-up, especially in reparatory justice, combined with political and public indifference further magnified popular frustrations and generated loss of momentum over time. The controversies surrounding transitional justice are expressions of these fractions, showing the unfinished and partial nature of conflict transitions.

Despite these problems, I argue that limited degrees of reconciliation and justice can take place even in deeply divided societies where the legacies and root causes of conflict remain unsettled. Looking at the intersection of formal and informal justice, I advance a view of justice and reconciliation as complex, dynamic, and temporally sensitive processes that can assume varying forms and degrees over time. While international theory and practice has frequently conceived of reconciliation as a concrete endpoint that individuals and societies reach, reconciliation, as I conceive of it in this book, principally involves the consolidation of a critical space that allows for political engagement and the contestation of ideas. I develop an understanding of what I call "procedural reconciliation" – a long-term and ongoing process of setting out and consolidating common parameters through which actors and communities can articulate grievances and pursue distinct (and often competing) grievances and claims. Procedural reconciliation is, by nature, contextually variable and open ended, yet what is important is the longer-term cumulative consolidation of effects over time. Individuals and groups may disagree over the past and the legitimacy of each other's claims, yet, through their disagreement, reinforce a normative and discursive framework of rights and responsibilities. This process places historical memory in the public sphere and by transferring conflict into political channels strengthens nonviolent norms and procedures.

Reconciliation in Protracted Social Conflicts

Reconciliation is pivotal to conflict transformation, yet it is often the least integrated dimension of peace-building theory and practice. Since World War II, intrastate wars have killed over 16.2 million people, five times the number caused by interstate warfare.[1] Some of the worst outbreaks of violence have occurred within protracted conflicts. Protracted conflicts tend to have deep roots in political, economic, and social structures, target and recruit civilians, and divide societies along identity lines.[2] Significantly, multiple cycles of violence characterize protracted conflicts, with 40 percent of countries that had civil wars experiencing a new civil war within a decade.[3] Unlike interstate wars, where victims and perpetrators did not have to come into contact after the military termination of violence, the demands of coexistence in today's intrastate conflicts mean that individuals must find ways to live not only with their histories but also with each other.

Despite recognition of the importance of reconciliation, the field of transitional justice – the formal and informal measures used to address past abuses during transitions from violence or authoritarian rule – has uneasily integrated reconciliation as an objective. As I will detail in Chapter 3, reconciliation has been difficult to theorize and empirically assess. Academic literature has often approached it with caution, criticizing it for its conceptually nebulous, vague, and subjective nature.[4] Despite a longer intellectual concern with forgiveness and justice following mass atrocity, within transitional justice, reconciliation has had a specific historical foundation. As I will argue in Chapter 2, the historical trajectory and experience of transitional justice as a field is significant and continues to bear relevance. Transitional justice consolidated as a set of global epistemic practices and ideas during Cold War "third wave" democratization in South America. In the Southern Cone, as in Uruguay (1985) and Argentina (1983–1984), sustained civil society activism and strong leadership bolstered the legitimacy of accountability processes, linking them to democratization and popular struggles against oppressive regimes. In these early instances of transitional justice,

[1] James D. Fearon and David Laitin, "Ethnicity, Insurgency, and Civil War," *American Political Science Review* 97 (2003), p. 75.

[2] Edward Azar, *The Management of Protracted Social Conflict: Theory and Cases* (Dartmouth: Aldershot, 1990); Louis Kriesberg, "Reconciliation: Aspects, Growth, Sequences," *International Journal of Peace Studies* 12, no. 1 (2007), p. 1.

[3] Paul Collier, Anke Hoeffler, and Måns Söderbom, "Post-conflict Risks," *Journal of Peace Research* 45 (2008), pp. 461–478.

[4] Joanna Quinn, "What Is Reconciliation?" in *Reconciliation(s): Transitional Justice in Postconflict Societies*, ed. Joanna Quinn (Montreal and Kingston: McGill-Queen's University Press, 2009), p. 181.

scholars and practitioners focused often on vertical relationships between political authorities and citizens, and viewed reconciliation with suspicion as a political nation-building discourse and alternative to criminal justice. The development of transitional justice practices during this time thus further steered scholars and practitioners away from engagement with reconciliation and peace-building.

The South African TRC was, in fundamental ways, a turning point in transitional justice, and bolstered interest in reconciliation as a legitimate and necessary societal end. Its invocation of ideas of restorative justice and Christian themes of forgiveness, catharsis, and repentance, and its public and charged procedures, helped generate a distinct sociopsychological understanding of reconciliation, focused on forgiveness and the transformation of viewpoints and relationships. Unlike previous truth commissions in the Southern Cone, the South African TRC looked beyond state-sponsored abuses, bringing attention to horizontal ties and interracial dialogue and healing. In the post–Cold War period, dissatisfaction with criminal justice domestically and abroad and a concern with complex political emergencies again augmented interest in reconciliation. The technocratic and short-term global emphasis on criminal justice and individual accountability translated less straightforwardly to contexts marked, for instance, by forced recruitment of combatants, the widespread use of child soldiers, and the use of civilians as collaborators.[5] This, in many ways, has prompted critical scrutiny on the aims and priorities of transitional justice. It has also encouraged reassessment of the emphasis of global transitional justice on short-term formal and legalistic procedures over the longer-term and locally valued objectives of psychological healing, reconciliation, and structural justice.[6]

[5] Rami Mani, *Beyond Retribution: Seeking Justice in the Shadows of War* (Cambridge and Maldon, MA: Polity Press, 2007), p. 18. See also Harvey M. Weinstein, Laurel E. Fletcher, and Patrick Vinck, "Stay the Hand of Justice," in *Localizing Transitional Justice: Interventions and Priorities after Mass Violence*, ed. Rosalind Shaw, Lars Waldorf, and Pierre Hazan (Stanford, CA: Stanford University Press, 2010), pp. 27–48; Moses Chrispus Okello, "Afterword: Elevating Transitional Local Justice or Crystallizing Global Governance," in *Localizing Transitional Justice: Interventions and Priorities after Mass Violence*, ed. Rosalind Shaw, Lars Waldorf, and Pierre Hazan (Stanford, CA: Stanford University Press, 2010), pp. 275–284.

[6] Paul Gready and Simon Robins, "From Transitional Justice to Transformative Justice: A New Agenda in Practice," *The International Journal for Transitional Justice* 8 (2014), pp. 7–10. See also Wendy Lambourne, "Transitional Justice after Mass Violence: Reconciling Retributive and Restorative Justice," in *Julius Stone: A Study in Influence*, ed. Helen Irving, Jacqueline Mowbray, and Kevin Walton (Sydney: Federation Press, 2010), p. 34; Wendy Lambourne, "Transitional Justice and Peace-Building after Mass Violence," *International Journal of Transitional Justice* 3 (2009), p. 30. Rama Mani argues that transitional justice has prioritized "rectificatory" over distributive justice, insufficiently taking into account the needs of developing countries and the underlying structures

Although the fields of peace-building and transitional justice have made important strides in thinking critically about the longer-term drivers of reconciliation and its resonance and linkages to various forms of justice, a starting concern of this book is the emergence and dominance of a narrow and polarizing research orientation linking transitional justice and reconciliation. Within transitional justice, early literature often focused on reconciliation as a process of psychological change and social learning in which individuals and groups altered their perceptions of each other and/or the past.[7] Drawing on the South African TRC's notion of "social" or "dialogue" truth, some argued, for instance, that truth commissions could facilitate reconciliation by generating "points of conversion" through dialogue and exchange.[8] While the literature on South Africa has since become more self-critical and divided, particularly as more systematic empirical research came out,[9] empirical literature beyond South Africa has been more pragmatically inclined. A rich interpretive body of research has examined the processes through which individuals and communities negotiate the parameters of civilian life.[10] Importantly, this often ethnographic scholarship examines individuals' and communities' definitions of reconciliation in their own terms. In a range of contexts, qualitative studies have laid out ways in which communities have managed to live together and find common ground even in the face of lingering grievances and shortcomings in justice and

that perpetuate suffering and exploitation. Mani, *Beyond Retribution*, p. 18. See also Rama Mani, "Dilemmas of Expanding Transitional Justice," *International Journal for Transitional Justice* 2 (2008), pp. 253–265.

7 Priscilla B. Hayner, *Unspeakable Truths: Facing the Challenge of Truth Commissions* (New York, NY: Routledge, 2002); Martha Minow, *Between Vengeance and Forgiveness: Facing History after Genocide and Mass Violence* (Boston, MA: Beacon Press, 2000). An important question in early literature is whether truth commissions or trials could foster more nuanced and tolerant understandings: truth commissions or trials. Laurel E. Fletcher and Harvey M. Weinstein, "Violence and Social Repair: Rethinking the Contribution of Justice to Reconciliation," *Human Rights Quarterly* 24 (2002), pp. 573–639; Kirsten A. Ainley, "Responsibility for Atrocity: Individual Criminal Agency and the International Criminal Court," *Evil, Law and the State: Perspectives on State Power and Violence*, ed. John Parry (Amsterdam and New York: Rodopi, 2006), pp. 143–158.

8 Amy Gutmann and Dennis Thompson, "The Moral Foundations of Truth Commissions," in *Truth v. Justice: The Morality of Truth Commissions*, ed. Robert R. Rotberg and Dennis Thompson (Princeton, NJ: Princeton University Press, 2000), pp. 22–23.

9 James L. Gibson, *Overcoming Apartheid: Can Truth Heal a Divided Nation* (New York, NY: Russell Sage Foundation, 2004).

10 See, for instance, Erin Baines, "The Haunting of Alice: Local Approaches to Justice and Reconciliation in Northern Uganda," *International Journal of Transitional Justice* 1, no. 1 (2007), pp. 91–114; Kimberly Susan Theidon, "Justice in Transition: The Micropolitics of Reconciliation in Post-war Peru," *The Journal of Conflict Resolution* 50 (2006), pp. 433–457; Kimberly Theidon, *Intimate Enemies: Violence and Reconciliation in Peru* (Philadelphia: University of Pennsylvania Press, 2012).

reparations. In general, this literature has been critical of formal global interventions, arguing in favor of locally run and culturally rooted justice and reconciliation.[11] On the other end of the spectrum, while a large comparatively oriented literature has examined the effectiveness of transitional justice across cases, it has tended not to engage with reconciliation, which it sees as immeasurable given its arguably subjective nature. Unlike the ethnographic literature, it tends to focus on the macro level, drawing largely on quantifiable criteria, such as democratic institution-building and the implementation of human rights, to assess impact.[12]

The focus on impact assessment is important and welcome, particularly in what has long been a heavily normatively laden field. At the same time, there is room between both extremes – the large-N quantitative literature that seeks to evaluate transitional justice, irrespective of institution and context, and the ethnographic micro-level qualitative literature, which tends to use local culture and individual preferences as benchmarks for evaluation. Although in the last two decades, scholars and practitioners have argued that transitional justice should facilitate peace-building and address broader longer-term contextually specific root causes of conflict, how it should do so is less clear.[13] To date, the

[11] Rosalind Shaw and Lars Waldorf, *Localizing Transitional Justice: Interventions and Priorities after Mass Violence* (Stanford, CA: Stanford University Press, 2010).

[12] Tricia Olsen, Leigh Payne, and Andrew Reiter argue that transitional justice's normative foundations are a consequence of its commitment to preferences, and seek to provide empirically grounded and testable claims. Tricia D. Olsen, Leigh A. Payne, and Andrew G. Reiter, *Transitional Justice in Balance: Comparing Processes, Weighing Efficacy* (Washington, DC: United States Institute for Peace, 2010); Tricia D. Olsen, Leigh A. Payne, Andrew G. Reiter, and Eric Wiebelhaus-Brahm, "When Truth Commissions Improve Human Rights," *International Journal of Transitional Justice* 4 (2010), pp. 457–476; Jack Snyder and Leslie Vinjamuri, "Trials and Errors: Principle and Pragmatism in Strategies in International Justice," *International Security* 28 (2003), pp. 5–44; Hunjoon Kim and Kathryn Sikkink, "Explaining the Deterrent Effect of Human Rights Prosecutions for Transitional Countries," *International Studies Quarterly* 54 (2010), pp. 939–963. Although coming from a different starting point, a recent normative scholarship prominent among scholar–practitioners also seeks to standardize objectives and evaluation criteria, by drawing on recent practices to capture emerging consensus in the field. Pablo de Greiff, "Theorizing Transitional Justice," in *Transitional Justice*, Nomos, Volume L, ed. Melissa Williams, Rosemary Nagy, and Jon Elster (New York, NY: New York University Press, 2012), p. 18; David A. Crocker, "Reckoning with Past Wrongs: A Normative Framework" (June 2004), p. 11. Available at: http://terpconnect.umd.edu/~dcrocker/Courses/Docs/Reckoning%20with%20past%20wrongs.pdf.

[13] The United Nations and the International Center for Transitional Justice argue that transitional justice should address the root causes of violence, engage and empower citizenry, strengthen political structures, and facilitate civic participation. The International Center for Transitional Justice, "What Is Transitional Justice?" (2008) and the United Nations, "What Is Transitional Justice? A Backgrounder" (February 20, 2008). Available at: www.un.org/en/peace-building/pdf/doc_wgll/justice_times_transition/26_02_2008_background_note.pdf. See also a critical normative literature, particularly Gready and Robins, "From Transitional Justice to Transformative Justice."

literature lacks a strong understanding of societal reconciliation and its relationship to transitional justice, and the fields of peace-building and transitional justice continue to be atomized from each other.

In this book, I argue that the scholarship's limited attention to societal reconciliation and the normative and discursive substantive contributions of transitional justice has resulted in a narrow empirical research agenda. There are also discrepancies between academic theory and the policy community. While formal transitional justice mechanisms often focus their efforts on the civic sphere,[14] empirical scholarship on reconciliation has often focused on the impact of formal justice on individual healing and community reconciliation.[15] Although a rich philosophical literature has emerged on the drivers and nature of reconciliation at different levels of analysis, more needs to be done to integrate this wide-ranging conceptual work on reconciliation into a coherent empirical research program. This also requires further thinking through the nature of harm and what aspects of harm transitional justice can and should address, particularly with regard to complex and protracted internal violence. Although protracted conflicts have often been sites of multiple cycles of violence, I am concerned that transitional justice theory and practice has tended to focus on direct stakeholders and immediate experiences of harm. More work is needed to think about the relationship of transitional justice to broader collective harm and the indirect stakeholders of reconciliation.

Procedural Reconciliation: Cumulative Repair and a Dynamic Contextual Approach

In this book, I seek to broaden conceptual understandings of reconciliation to think about ways in which societies normalize – or alter and overhaul – political and social relations in the aftermath of longer-term divisive conflicts. Reconciliation, I argue, often occurs in less visible and unexpected ways. In the conceptual sections of the book, I look at what I refer to as procedural reconciliation as a future-oriented process on the

[14] Paul Gready, *The Era of Transitional Justice: The Aftermath of the Truth and Reconciliation Commission in South Africa and Beyond* (New York, NY: Routledge, 2011); Richard A. Wilson, *The Politics of Truth and Reconciliation in South Africa: Legitimizing the Post-Apartheid State* (Cambridge, UK: Cambridge University Press, 2001).

[15] This applies also to academic and policy literature on the contribution of transitional justice to peace-building. Often focusing on ex-combatants, participation in transitional justice is theorized to help reintegration by providing ex-combatants with a voice, allowing them to show contrition, and facilitating participation in rituals and cleansing, thereby building trust in affected communities. See Lars Waldorf, "Just Peace? Integrating DDR and Transitional Justice," in *Transitional Justice and Peace-building on the Ground*, ed. Chandra Lekha Sriram, Jemima García-Godos, Johanna Herman, and Olga Martin-Ortega (London: Routledge, 2013), p. 67.

societal level and outline an often tense and contentious politics of reconciliation. I conceive of procedural reconciliation as a critical and ongoing process, which is open ended and becomes contested and revisited over time.[16] Theoretically, I make the case that conceptualizing reconciliation as a more limited and abstract societal endeavor makes it possible to highlight partial instances of reconciliation even in deeply divided and hostile contexts. While transitional justice may not bring about deep-seated psychological transformation and a convergence of viewpoints, it can still facilitate a normative and discursive process through which groups and individuals pursue claims related to the past. This process does not resolve conflict, but it fosters coexistence by transferring conflict into the public sphere.

In the theoretical and empirical sections of the book, I offer a dynamic and fluid conception of transition. Transitional justice processes, I contend, are more than temporary pedagogical instruments. In charged social and political transitions, they become arenas and expressions of politics – spaces where individuals and groups pursue grievances and aspirations and stake out social standing and legitimacy.[17] Plugging into an older philosophical literature at the intersection of transitional justice, social psychology, education, and democratization, I maintain that post-war contexts offer a particular type of momentum as political entrepreneurs and civil society mobilize around future objectives and visions. While this energy can generate further conflict, it can simultaneously strengthen and bestow legitimacy on nonviolent political channels and activism. Rather than identify a defined endpoint that individuals or societies reach, procedural reconciliation is an active and often unpredictable process that operates at multiple levels and takes varying forms over time. From this perspective, transitional justice and peace-building processes are unlikely to change viewpoints, particularly where abuses are within living memory and actors' identities are embedded in their roles in conflict. They can, however, alter the parameters of normative engagement and political behavior. Existing empirical research has often underappreciated these significant, although more long-term and indirect,

[16] Claire Moon, "Prelapsarian State: Forgiveness and Reconciliation in Transitional Justice," *International Journal for Semiotics of Law* 17 (2004), pp. 185–197; Adrian Little, "Disjunctured Narratives: Rethinking Reconciliation and Conflict Transformation," *International Political Science Review* 33 (2012); Andrew Schaap, *Political Reconciliation* (Ithaca, NY: Cornell University Press, 2001).

[17] Rolando Ames Cobián and Félix Reátegui, "Toward Systemic Social Transformation: Truth Commissions and Development," in *Transitional Justice and Development: Making Connections*, ed. Pablo de Greiff and Roger Duthie (New York, NY: Social Science Research Council, 2009), p. 146.

dynamics, tending to evaluate transitional justice for its direct impact on social perceptions and political behavior.

Applied to the case studies of Sierra Leone and Peru, I am interested in the challenges and possibilities of reconciliation in protracted intrastate conflicts. Throughout the book, I emphasize the importance of context in shaping local experiences and perceptions of transitional justice. I look at post-war Sierra Leone and Peru as settings of deep-rooted societal insecurity. More so than earlier Cold War transitions, where strong authoritarian states and military governments committed abuses, I contend that transitions from protracted intrastate conflicts present intense and multifaceted challenges. They are often characterized by weak and failed states and fragile peace agreements, making them vulnerable to future violence and spoilers.[18] Where violence continues sporadically or presents a continued threat, attempts to create accountability likely augment fear and mistrust among local populations. Intrastate conflicts are also likely to present additionally complex challenges of recovery through their politicization of ethnic–sectarian or class divisions, which often further politicize injustice. In Peru, for instance, where the majority of victims represented an indigenous and largely rural population, the ethnic undertones of the conflict had a harmful double impact, reinforcing a sense of victimization among affected populations and distancing the conflict from the experiences of the country's coastal middle classes. The impoverished background of many victims of the Peruvian military, in turn, further magnified the effects of violence and suffering in heavily hit areas. Protracted conflicts also tend to be characterized by political violence at the hands of state agents and insurgency groups, as well as micro-level communal violence.[19] Manifold experiences of violence leave multiple parallel legacies. While political violence at the hands of state agents perpetuates mistrust and fear of authority, communal violence shatters social norms and communal life.[20] Where political violence degrades civic trust and institutions, leaving individuals atomized and disempowered, long-term communal violence and population displacement tear apart the social fabric, affecting everyday social interactions.[21] These

[18] Kimberly Theidon describes a general condition of simmering low-intensity intrastate conflicts. *Entre Prójimos: Violencia y La Política de la Reconciliación en el Perú* (Lima, Perú: Instituto de Estudios Peruanos, 2004).

[19] Azar, *The Management.*

[20] Fionnuala Ní Aoláin and Colm Campbell, "The Paradox of Transitions in Conflicted Democracies," *Human Rights Quarterly* 27, 1 (2005), pp. 185–197.

[21] Quinn, "What Is Reconciliation," p. 181. See also Pablo de Greiff, "Articulating the Links between Transitional Justice and Development: Justice and Social Integration," in *Transitional Justice and Development: Making Connections*, ed. Pablo de Greiff and Roger Duthie (New York, NY: Social Science Research Council, 2009), pp. 28–75.

micro- and macro-level legacies of protracted conflict are pervasive and reinforce each other with diminished trust and social capital at the micro-sphere augmenting tensions and suspicion at the macro level.

My interest in this book is in how and the extent to which transitional justice can meet these challenges. As I will detail in the empirical chapters of the book, both the Sierra Leonean TRC and the Peruvian CVR took on broad mandates to facilitate peace-building and post-conflict reconstruction. In Sierra Leone, where the marginalization of youth played an important role in the war, the TRC put emphasis on empowering youth and the reintegrating of ex-combatants, setting up separate hearings for children and rehabilitation and community service for former soldiers.[22] In Peru, following the long-term marginalization of rural and indigenous populations and a concentration of violence in remote areas, the CVR prioritized furthering cultural pluralism, promoting social justice, raising public awareness, and empowering victims and marginalized regions.[23] Both commissions sought to further national integration and generate political capital by advancing a conception of political democratic reconciliation and participatory nation-building.

Yet, as I will argue in the chapters on Sierra Leone and Peru, affected populations in both countries often faulted the commissions for their insufficient contribution to conflict transformation. Here, the empirical chapters in the book therefore will also address the social politics of transitional justice and reconciliation. In Sierra Leone and Peru, the establishment of formal justice processes generated strong discussions between domestic and international actors and between practitioners at the grassroots and national levels. In both cases, I argue that a combination of normative and strategic factors shaped the establishment and impact of transitional justice institutions. I pay attention to how international and domestic agents prioritized certain approaches and preferences over others, and how they conceived of their own work and contribution to conflict transformation.[24]

The book thus works backwards to understand transitional justice institutions at the time of their establishment and operation before turning to present-day popular experiences of peace-building and transitional

[22] See "Recommendations on Governance," in *Witness to Truth: Report of the Sierra Leone Truth and Reconciliation Commission*, Volume 2, Chapter 3 (Accra: Graphic Packaging Ltd., 2004), pp. 117–224.

[23] See the CVR Report, Volume 1, Chapters 1–3; Carlos Iván Degregori, *Qué Difícil es Ser Dios: El Partido Comunista del Perú – Sendero Luminoso y el Conflicto Armado Interno en el Perú: 1980–1999* (Lima: Institute of Peruvian Studies, 2010), and Dr. Salomón Lerner Febres; Interview by author, Lima, Peru, February 10, 2011.

[24] Séverine Autsessere, "Hobbes and the Congo: Frames, Local Violence and International Intervention," *International Organization* 63, no. 2 (2009), pp. 249–280.

justice. I argue that the two are intricately linked. Studying institutions and their objectives on their own terms is important to better understand popular experiences of justice. As I will argue in Chapters 4 and 5, transitional justice agents in both Sierra Leone and Peru invested significant energies into "sensitization" and legitimizing their work. Sometimes this was primarily at the civil society level with insufficient popular outreach. With regard to truth commissions, in particular, the basis on which commissions solicited popular participation had a strong impact on popular experiences of transitional justice, both positive and negative. Participants and affected communities often critiqued commissions on their own terms, expressing frustration that commissions had not delivered.

I also maintain that a close understanding of institutional aims and variances provides a fuller picture of the successes and failures of transitional justice processes in severely constrained environments. Throughout the book, I highlight endogeneity. I pay attention to the ways in which political and social realities both enabled and constrained the establishment, trajectories, and reception of transitional justice. In both Sierra Leone and Peru, I argue that the conditions that transitional justice institutions were set up to address also severely constrained their impact over time. In each context, the long-term marginalization of remote areas and a dirty war at the hands of state and military agents eroded political trust and faith in authority in affected communities. Communal violence and the collaboration of civilians with military agents and insurgent groups left intense resentment and suspicion at the micro level. The concentration of violence in remote parts of the country also distanced the conflict from populations less affected by violence, particularly middle classes in the capital cities. Insufficient follow-up – particularly in reparatory justice – augmented suspicion, resulting in a loss of momentum and legitimacy, as well as disappointment in formal justice, especially among victims.

Despite these shortcomings, I argue that transitional justice in Sierra Leone and Peru had dynamic, multifaceted, and often unintended consequences. I take a broader view, focusing on transitional justice processes as arenas for political agency and expression. Looking at multiple levels of analysis, I consider both macro and micro dimensions of peacebuilding and reconciliation, and take into account varying and often indirect effects over time. In each case, I detail a complex and dynamic relationship between formal mechanisms and local civil society. Formal institutions simultaneously provide a forum for advocacy and give rise to criticism and contestation. In Sierra Leone and Peru, I thus examine the interaction of formal justice, particularly TRCs, and micro-level civil society efforts, notably Fambul Tok in Sierra Leone and Asociación Nacional de Familiares de Secuestrados, Detenidos y Desaparecidos del

Perú (ANFASEP) in Peru. Although community organizations often mobilized in criticism of formal justice and presented their work as alternative pathways, they must also be understood as outcomes of formal justice. While in Peru, memory politics strengthened democratic norms and procedures, in Sierra Leone, the contestation of formal justice reinforced a turn toward localism and political decentralization. Conducted in a polarized post-conflict climate, the CVR generated vigorous debate and counter-narratives. At the same time, large sections of civil society today turn toward the capital to pursue their claims. Peru's large-scale truth-seeking process reinforced a language of rights and obligations through which actors publicly explain and rationalize their behavior. Although contentious, this process strengthened democracy by channeling conflict into the political sphere. The Sierra Leonean TRC, in contrast, generated less attention and debate. The severe post-war challenges facing the country, a youthful ex-combatant demographic, and long-standing traditions of restorative justice bolstered pragmatism and tolerance for reintegration and reconciliation. Instead, the TRC clashed with civil society where it insufficiently engaged local frameworks and authority structures. Here, as well, criticisms of the TRC led to countermovements, motivating local actors and organizations to advance alternative community peace-building and reconciliation. Yet, while local efforts, notably Fambul Tok, contributed to communal reconciliation and peace-building, grassroots processes often strengthened decentralized authority structures and frameworks, reinforcing a tendency toward localism in the post-war era. Cumulatively, I thus highlight the very different experiences and consequences of transitional justice in each country. Although a type of procedural reconciliation emerged in each case, in Peru, this was a more centralized and democratic process, while in Sierra Leone a greater focus emerged on decentralization and bolstering grassroots mechanisms of conflict resolution.

Methods and Case Selection: Legacies of Violence and Agency in Sierra Leone and Peru

In this book, I utilize a qualitative open-ended interpretive methodology. Impact assessment and legacy are currently on the forefront of transitional justice research and practice. While some favor evaluating transitional justice mechanisms according to their legal mandates,[25] it is useful

[25] Audrey R. Chapman and Patrick Ball, "The Truth of Truth Commissions: Comparative Lessons from Haiti, South Africa, and Guatemala," *Human Rights Quarterly* 23 (2001), pp. 1–43. However, Brahm cautions that assessing transitional justice institutions according to their own legal mandates can undervalue their broader impact on society.

to distinguish between success (whether an institution has finished its work on its own terms) and impact (measured by independent criteria).[26] A narrow focus on mandate can obscure how meanings and practices can change over time.[27] This is especially important for the book's qualitative analysis of societal reconciliation, which examines shared norms and discourses and the relationship between reconciliation and collective memory.

More specifically, I employ an open and flexible longitudinal approach. Although coming from different starting points, both comparatively and ethnographically oriented scholars have tended to evaluate the impact and contribution of transitional justice mechanisms according to exogenous criteria. Comparatively oriented scholars often derive these standards externally through social science indicators, while ethnographic researchers have tended to inductively identify benchmarks of legitimacy and normative objectives through the preferences and values of local stakeholders.

In this book, I am interested in the indirect, and even unexpected, cumulative qualitative effects of transitional justice and peace-building processes. I look at transitional justice and peace-building processes as endogenous to contextual constraints and opportunities, and take a big-picture interpretive view. My approach is constructivist in its treatment of transitional justice mechanisms as interventions that potentially alter and shape local norms, values, politics, and perceptions, as well as expressions of particular contexts. As such, I view the institutions under study as both actors and products of local, domestic, and global social, political, and economic environments. The analysis of procedural reconciliation as an open-ended process thus departs from some of the ethnographic literature's emphasis on local understandings and individual and community preferences as barometers for evaluation.[28] Methodologically, the analysis of procedural reconciliation necessitates an embedded analysis that captures the significance of language in terms of its relationship to societal norms and identities. At the same time, I make the case that assessing procedural reconciliation requires a detached (and sometimes

Eric Brahm, "Uncovering the Truth: Examining Truth Commissions Success and Impact," *International Studies Perspectives* 8 (2007), p. 18.

[26] Ibid., 18.

[27] See Bronwyn Leebaw, "Legitimation or Judgment? South Africa's Restorative Approach to Transitional Justice," *Polity* 36, no. 1 (2003), pp. 23–51.

[28] See for example Simon Robins for important work centered around preferences. Simon Robins, "Challenging the Therapeutic Ethic: A Victim-Centred Evaluation of Transitional Justice Process in Timor Leste," *International Journal of Transitional Justice* 6, no. 1 (2012), pp. 1–23.

uncomfortable) macro perspective that abstracts stakeholders' personal experiences and frustrations from the net effects of their behavior.[29]

I also offer a distinctive and significant cross-regional comparison. While Peru and Sierra Leone are very different cases, they share important similarities. Both countries experienced complex and protracted social conflicts in which state actors and insurgent groups committed violence against civilians. Victims predominantly came from poor and rural backgrounds. The Revolutionary United Front (RUF) in Sierra Leone and the Shining Path in Peru recruited from a youthful and marginalized demographic, establishing a presence among university students and rural youth. Importantly, both conflicts were fought largely in remote areas. Concentrated violence in marginalized regions militarized societies, resulting in the emergence of civil militias and personalized micro violence. In both contexts, these unequal experiences of violence also distanced the conflict and their legacies from the emotional identifications of coastal and middle-class populations. Additionally, Peru and Sierra Leone are sites of multifaceted transitional justice and peacebuilding experiences. While in Sierra Leone, the relationship between the TRC and the SCSL was generally tense, in Peru the CVR sought to make a contribution to criminal justice, working with the Inter-American Court to provide relevant information.

In a broader sense, the book's cross-regional research design facilitated reflection on factors that critically shaped impact in each context.[30] In Sierra Leone and Peru, transitional justice institutions took on ambitious mandates. This was particularly the case with truth commissions, which combined rigorous truth-seeking with large-scale public participation and restorative justice. In both countries, I compared formal mechanisms with civil society and community efforts to establish justice and reconciliation, notably ANFASEP and victims' organizations in Peru and Fambul Tok and peace education and reintegration efforts in Sierra Leone.

The book also benefited from a multi-stage field research framework: one with practitioners and transitional justice "communities" and

[29] For an interesting discussion of embedded research and subjectivity, see Morgan Brigg and Roland Bleiker, "Autoethnographic International Relations: Exploring the Self as a Source of Knowledge," *Review of International Studies* 36, no. 3 (2010), pp. 779–798.

[30] Some, notably South African TRC President and Anglican Archbishop Desmond Tutu, have argued that restorative justice is more authentic to African cultural worldviews and dispositions, rooted in *Ubuntu* and an ethic of forgiveness. Desmond Tutu, *No Future without Forgiveness* (Houghton, South Africa: Random House, 1999). Others have focused on the historical drivers of restorative justice. See Rosalind Shaw on the impact of the transatlantic slave trade on restorative justice in Sierra Leone. *Memories of the Slave Trade: Ritual and the Historical Imagination in Sierra Leone* (Chicago: University of Chicago Press, 2002).

the second focusing on direct stakeholders. In the first stage of the project, I worked backwards to understand the historical development of particular orientations among transitional justice institutions. Here, I targeted practitioners and experts to understand why and how actors involved in institutions chose certain pathways over time. This stage drew on elite or expert interviews with close expertise in the subject matter, generally officials involved in transitional justice processes, government officials, academics, and current civil society. I looked beyond legal mandates to incorporate institutional methodologies and self-understandings.[31] I took a dynamic historical approach, focusing on how events in one context influenced subsequent developments.[32] I was particularly interested in the effects of external factors, including domestic, regional, and global pressures, normative influences, and legacies.

The book's interpretive methodology carries over into the second stage of the research, where I focused on direct stakeholders. Here, my research targeted a broad cross-section of society, including civil society, government officials, teachers and academics, women, university students and youth, religious figures, victims, current and former military officials, and militants.[33] In each case, I asked individuals to conceptualize reconciliation and its drivers in their own words. I held open-ended and semi-structured focus groups and interviews to evaluate popular perceptions of transitional justice and reconciliation. This format also allowed participants to initially guide the conversation and ask follow-up questions, and enabled a less asymmetrical methodology.[34] I utilized a flexible research design that could adapt to the answers of participants and experiences in

[31] This objective makes the book more open to practitioners than paradigm-based academic scholarship that tends to be oriented to testing or commenting on received wisdom about the policy community. Rudra Sil and Peter J. Katzenstein, *Beyond Paradigms: Analytical Eclecticism in the Study of World Politics* (New York and London: Palgrave Macmillan, 2010).

[32] Barbara Geddes, "How the Evidence You Use Affects the Answers You Get: Rigorous Use of the Evidence Contained in Case Studies," in *Paradigms and Sand Castles: Theory Building and Research Design in Comparative Politics*, ed. Barbara Geddes (Ann Arbor, MI: University of Michigan, 2003), pp. 131–173.

[33] The chapters on Peru often use the term *afectado* (affected one) to refer to individuals who experienced violence or lost a family member in the conflict. This replaces the word "victim," which for some interviewees diminished their agency and strength as survivors. In Sierra Leone, I use "victim" as interviewees used this term. For some interviewees in both contexts, however, "survivor" did not capture indirect victims of violence: for instance, children who lost family members. These distinctions vary between individuals and are not neat categories. In Sierra Leone and Peru, individuals who experienced and survived atrocities have become leading advocates for their communities and for human rights. In Ayacucho especially, many civil society interviewees were also *afectados*, but are not identified as such.

[34] Peregrine Schwartz-Shea and Dvora Yanow, *Interpretive Research Design: Concepts and Processes* (New York and London: Routledge, 2012), p. 46. See also Gearoid Millar,

the field.[35] Rather than treat interviews as a one-off opportunity to collect information on a predetermined range of answers, I refined questions as the research advanced. I adopted a premise that I could learn from how interviewees described and understood their own roles in conflict and whether they were willing to speak candidly. How individuals presented their past behavior provided insights into the resonance of official narratives and interpretations and the extent to which a public discourse about the past had taken hold. Likewise, how individuals understood and dealt with questions of agency and responsibility during conflict shed light on the uniformity of post-conflict narratives and understandings.[36]

To engage both practitioners and stakeholders, I divided my field research between capital cities, which provided greater access to civil society and government officials, and regions that were significant in the histories of the conflicts and home to victims and many former militants. In Peru, I carried out research in Lima and in Ayacucho, in the south-central Peruvian Andes.[37] Ayacucho was the site of the first Shining Path attack and is home to a majority of victims as well as former Shining Path members. In Sierra Leone, I conducted research in Freetown, the Grafton Polio and War-Wounded Camp, and Kailahun district on the eastern border with Liberia. I carried out twelve months of field research across the two countries. I conducted all research in the native language of interviewees. In Sierra Leone, I carried out interviews in the lingua franca, English, and in several cases, with an interpreter for Krio and other languages. Many victims of the conflict and their families reside in Grafton, and the war began and ended in Kailahun and was the birthplace of many former RUF militants. In Peru, I conducted all interviews in Spanish, and on several occasions in Quechua through an interpreter in villages in Ayacucho. My research also drew upon primary sources (truth commission archives, minutes, and videos) and secondary sources,

An Ethnographic Approach to Peace-building: Understanding Local Experiences in Transitional States (Abingdon: Routledge, 2014).

35 Schartz-Shea and Yanow advocate a learning process where research design is developed and reformulated during and in response to the field research. Shea and Yanow, *Interpretive Research Design*, p. 46. This departs from more established guidelines on qualitative research, which maintain that the research design needs to be revised if the questions change. See, for instance, Robert K. Yin, *Case Study Research: Design and Methods*, 4th edition (Thousand Parks, CA: Sage, 2009).

36 For an interesting discussion on confessions, omissions, and field research, see Lee Ann Fujii, "Shades of Truth and Lies: Interpreting Testimonies of War and Violence," *Journal of Peace Research* 47 (2010), pp. 231–241.

37 In Peru, since Ayacucho is the name both of the region (*Departamento*) and the capital city of the region, I will refer to research carried out in the capital of the region as Ayacucho and will specifically identify smaller cities in the region of Ayacucho. The same applies to research carried out in the Kailahun district in Sierra Leone, as Kailahun is also the name of the capital of the district.

including academic literature and newspaper coverage. I also conducted interviews and focus groups with students and academics at universities, particularly the Pontificia Católica del Perú (PUCP) in Lima, the Universidad San Cristóbal de Huamanga (UNSCH) in Ayacucho, and Fourah Bay College in Freetown.

While I made sure to speak to individuals on various sides of each conflict, I put emphasis on engaging populations who participated in formal and informal reconciliation and justice processes. In Sierra Leone, where the TRC actively engaged ex-combatants and promoted their reintegration, I put weight on speaking to and included more ex-combatant testimonies, and studied broader processes of rehabilitation, reintegration, and reconciliation. In Peru, given the CVR's emphasis on victims and historical memory, I was particularly interested in victims' organizations and ongoing memory work. This helped me assess the normative and discursive impact of formal mechanisms on direct participants. At the same time, I critically discuss the absence of protagonists at the CVR and the current status of victims in both countries. I engage particularly with silences and engage also with stakeholders and voices, which were not heard by or marginalized from formal processes.

Ways Forward and Outline of the Book

To delve into these questions, I divide the book into eight chapters. I begin with a close assessment of transitional justice mechanisms in practice. Despite a recent emphasis on impact assessment and success in research and practice, transitional justice institutions are not homogenous.[38] In Sierra Leone and Peru, transitional justice institutions re-legitimized and redefined their objectives and methodologies as they began operating, often in reference to contextually defined causes of conflict. In Chapter 2, I provide a historical discussion of significant transitional justice experiences, laying out what I see as fundamental tensions in practice between reconciliation and truth. While institutional mandates tend to conceive of reconciliation and truth-seeking as complementary, I argue that they often prioritized one over the other. I outline challenges in implementing transitional justice in post-conflict contexts and warn against what I see as a problematic broadening of mandates and challenge of institutional overstretch.

[38] Although often categorized as formal justice, alongside criminal tribunals truth commissions are interesting for their fluid nature. Jonathan D. Tepperman, "Truth and Consequences," *Foreign Affairs* 81, no. 2 (2002), p. 129. Where truth commissions rely more directly on public participation, it is also likely that the onus on them is higher, as they must legitimize themselves to the public.

To prepare for the book's empirical chapters, the next part of the book lays out its research framework. A rigorous analysis of impact also requires a conceptual discussion of reconciliation and theoretical analysis. In Chapter 3, I distinguish between what I refer to as transformative understandings of reconciliation and my conception of procedural reconciliation. Drawing upon an older literature on social learning, social capital, democratization, and social psychology, I lay out baseline components of procedural reconciliation, including civic trust, shared norms and discourses, and solidarity. In doing so, I define procedural reconciliation as an open-ended process through which individuals and groups can make claims and voice grievances, and emphasize the normative and discursive impact of transitional justice. Procedural reconciliation, as I conceive of it, can take place with or without forgiveness and cognitive change. It is often more pragmatic in nature, yet it can generate its own momentum over time.

In the case studies, I explore the drivers and impact of transitional justice on reconciliation and peace-building across contexts. Chapters 4 and 5 provide an in-depth examination of Sierra Leone's conflict and conflict transition. In Chapter 4, I offer a historical background of the Sierra Leonean civil war and the establishment of a multipronged transitional justice approach. I consider how contextual factors, particularly underdevelopment and poverty, the youthful demographics of ex-combatants, drawn-out negotiations over a cease-fire, historical traditions of restorative justice, the regional legacy of the South African TRC, and the parallel establishment of the SCSL, pushed the TRC to take a more inclusive and even-handed stance. The TRC's methodology and aims, conception of reconciliation, historical narrative, and approach to public testimonies reflect this orientation. I argue that a combination of structure and agency shaped the Commission's work in a number of key areas. Chapter 5, in turn, examines peace-building and reconciliation in Sierra Leone. While the nature of conflict and the lack of follow-up generated widespread disillusionment, I maintain that the TRC helped disseminate a public agenda of reconciliation. Criticisms of the TRC and of international transitional justice and intervention mobilized local actors, notably Fambul Tok, to pursue alternative Sierra Leonean processes. While furthering peace-building and reconciliation at the micro level, these community efforts reflect a larger reorientation in favor of localism and decentralization among prominent sectors of civil society. Significantly in the Sierra Leonean context, while civil society activism is critical of formal justice efforts, it is also a consequence of broader justice processes, emerging out of a loss of momentum and delegitimization of formal justice. While I discuss the advantages of a community-based, organic restorative approach, I also warn that traditional practices may reinforce the social hierarchies and power structures that underpinned conflict.

As I set out in Chapters 6 and 7, in Peru, the politics and drivers of transitional justice have manifested themselves in distinct and somewhat varying manners. Chapter 6 offers a historical overview of political violence in Peru and the establishment of the CVR. As with the case of Sierra Leone, I consider how contextual factors and a combination of structure and agency entrenched a punitive human rights–based orientation in Peru. These include factors specific to the nature of conflict in the country, for example, the military's victory, unequal experiences of violence, the ethnic undertones of the conflict, and the stigmatization of insurgency groups. They also include regional traditions linking truth commissions to struggles against impunity and what officials associated with the CVR identified as a domestic and international prioritization of criminal justice and accountability at the time. The CVR's methodology and aims, conceptions of reconciliation, historical narrative, and approach to public testimonies embody this position. As in Sierra Leone, this process was in many ways ad hoc as the CVR faced its own learning curve and had to reassess and redefine its objectives along the way. The broader effects of the CVR's truth-seeking process were also distinct in Peru. As I discuss in Chapter 7, although as in Sierra Leone, the nature of political violence in Peru and a lack of follow-up also eroded popular trust, the CVR put historical memory into the public sphere and generated an intense societal interest in its work that continues into the present. While reinforcing societal cleavages and also generating a backlash against centralization, memory advocacy in this case similarly channeled conflict into the public sphere and strengthened democratic norms and practices.

Taken together, the cases provide significant implications for future theory and practice. Linking peace-building, reconciliation, and justice, in the Conclusions I emphasize the indirect normative and discursive impact of transitional justice processes in both Sierra Leone and Peru. Significantly, I also lay out the limitations of procedural reconciliation. I distinguish between violence and conflict, and caution that latent conflict may drive procedural reconciliation. I focus on the economics of transitional justice and the relationship between justice and reconciliation.

2 Contextual Variances, Transitional Justice, and Peace-Building

A Historical Overview

Questions of normative rights and obligations, procedural fairness, memory and identity, and pragmatic trade-offs in the face of competing interests and duties have a rich intellectual and historical heritage, spanning most societies around the world. Within territorially bounded collectivities, practices of restorative and retributive justice have played a central role in the regulation of societal and community interactions and in ensuring the perpetuation of a common moral fabric. At the micro and macro levels, ideas and practices related to justice and forgiveness have formed integral parts of the normative architecture underpinning group identities and have been a basis for continuing political, economic, and social collective life. Rulers and collectivities have often reworked these norms and moral frameworks after upheaval as part of a basis for a more stable or equitable postcrisis settlement.

In the twentieth century, the meaning and application of justice and redress in the aftermath of mass atrocities took on a uniquely global and institutionalized dimension. Although international humanitarian law and the laws of war have an older heritage, global involvement in ensuring accountability for their violation is unique to the twentieth century. The ad hoc military tribunals at Nuremberg and Tokyo were highly symbolic turning points in what would be a steady erosion of sovereign immunity in favor of universal jurisdiction in the next half decade. This came hand in hand with the solidification and institutionalization of global human rights and a stronger role for the individual in international relations.

The interaction of transitional justice and peace-building, however, and the domestic contribution of external transitional justice institutions, has in many ways been much more ambiguous. In this chapter, I argue that a rapid expansion of contexts in which transitional justice processes are established and a tendency to tie transitional justice mechanisms to an increasing range of ends has made these questions more pertinent. While the ideas and practices of "transitional justice" consolidated in the post–World War II era in largely domestically contained regime transitions, since the end of the Cold War, international actors have become actively involved in the dissemination and management of peace-building and justice. Partly in consequence, transitional justice mechanisms have sought to address a much wider and arguably more complex range of conflicts and circumstances, and have taken on significantly expanded mandates and objectives. This has been particularly relevant vis-à-vis protracted conflicts in the last two decades, where transitional justice institutions were explicitly mandated to facilitate peace-building and conflict transformation.

Despite a widespread conviction that transitional justice should be contextually relevant and transformative, how and whether it can do so is far less clear. While recent empirical studies have made important strides in assessing impact across cases, in important regards, interest in measurement tools and standardization has reinforced a narrow and specific empirical research agendum. Where earlier scholars displayed a strong interest in normative and discursive change and the broader identity politics surrounding transitional justice, recent impact assessment literature has tended to focus on succinct technocratic changes, including institution-building and human rights and political behavior and legislation. Although a rich interpretive and largely ethnographic literature has examined community preferences and experiences of healing and reconciliation, it has tended to focus on the micro level.

In this chapter, I offer an overview of significant domestic and global justice experiences in diverse historical circumstances. I focus, in particular, on truth and reconciliation commissions (TRCs) as important institutional attempts to facilitate conflict transformation. I examine human rights–focused transitional justice in the Southern Cone in the context of regime transitions, the South African restorative participatory approach, the UN-established didactic commissions in Central America, and recent hybrid and holistic justice in post-conflict contexts. In these cases, I detail how a combination of domestic, international, and regional challenges, legacies, politics, and norms pushed institutions to adopt certain orientations and procedures and the implications of these pathways for global learning and domestic impact. I put particular emphasis on the relatively recent establishment and experiences of transitional justice mechanisms in complex and fragile post-conflict settings. While academics and practitioners have increasingly argued that transitional justice should contribute to peace-building and conflict transformation, they have paid less attention to attempts of institutions themselves in these settings to address contextually defined root causes of conflicts. While recent TRCs, for example those in Sierra Leone, East Timor, and Peru, had mandates to respond to a range of legacies, including establishing accountability and the rule of law, and addressing strained social and economic structures and intra-communal violence, more critical analysis is important of how contextual political and social realities shape and constrain transitional justice procedures and their impact and success.

Cautious Approaches: Regime Transitions in the Southern Cone

Scattered efforts to establish accountability can be found in early records of international conflict. Jon Elster traces the origins of transitional justice to ancient Greece and the restoration of democracy after the victory over the oligarchs.[1] The two world wars, however, were fundamental turning points for the institutionalization of global ideas and practices. The memory of the Great War and a fear of unjust settlements propelled nascent thinking in the interwar period, linking post-conflict justice and the mitigation of future conflict. The Allied prosecutions at Nuremberg and Tokyo and the ratification of the Genocide Convention, in turn, were pivotal to the consolidation of international criminal law from a diverse historical tradition, including human rights law, the law of armed conflict, and just war theory. World War II and the Nazi Holocaust, more than any event, helped institutionalize a globally integrated human rights regime, also crystallizing a normative foundation that would intertwine just redress, collective memory, and atrocity prevention.

In its modern self-aware form, however, transitional justice developed as an epistemic set of practices and ideas during the Cold War in the context of regime transitions from authoritarian rule to democracy in South America. Bound up in their broader domestic political and social transformations, these early contexts gave the field a distinct legalistic orientation. The emergence of truth commissions ties intimately to this formative history. In 1974, President Idi Amin established the first truth commission in Uganda to investigate killings and disappearances at the hands of Ugandan state forces under his rule. The Commission of Inquiry into the Disappearances of People in Uganda (1974) was a response to public pressure to conduct an inquiry. However, the Commission did not publish its report, and its domestic impact was marginal at best, generating relatively little attention in either Uganda or elsewhere.[2] In 1986, the

[1] Jon Elster, *Closing the Books: Transitional Justice in Historical Perspective* (Cambridge: Cambridge University Press, 2004), p. 1.

[2] The US Institute of Peace, "Truth Commissions: Digital Collection." Available at: www.usip.org/publications/truth-commission-uganda-74. See Joanna Quinn, "Constraints: The Un-Doing of the Ugandan Truth Commission," *Human Rights Quarterly* 26 (2004).

government established a second commission, the Commission of Inquiry into Violations of Human Rights (1986–1994), which managed to hold a number of public hearings despite financial problems and lack of domestic backing.[3]

Where truth commissions appeared somewhat obscurely in the Cold War, they consolidated as a practice largely in the Southern Cone. In 1982, President Hernán Siles Zuazo established the National Commission for Investigation for Forced Disappearances in Bolivia as part of his reform agenda to investigate abuses under military rule.[4] Although the Commission documented 155 cases of disappearances, the government disbanded the Commission before it was scheduled to finish, preventing it from publishing a report and finishing its investigations. Argentina's Comisión Nacional Sobre la Desaparición de Personas, established in 1983, was the first commission to receive wide international attention and publish a report. Run by thirteen national commissioners, the Commission documented 8,960 disappearances during Argentina's seven years of military rule. Images of the Madres on the Plaza de Mayo, protesting on behalf of their missing children and grandchildren, became an important symbol, with the Commission's report, *Nunca Más!* (Never Again!), gaining wide dissemination in Argentina.[5] Also known as the Rettig Commission, the Chilean truth commission is another important reference point. President Aylwin established Chile's National Commission for Truth and Reconciliation (1991) to look into crimes committed under General Augusto Pinochet during military rule from 1973 to 1990. As the Commission did not investigate torture and nonfatal crimes, in 2003, President Ricardo Lagos set up the National Commission on Political Imprisonment and Torture, or the "Valech Commission," to look into additional abuses, including torture. President Aylwin was unable to repeal the amnesty law, Decree Law 2191, passed by the Pinochet regime without legislative authority.[6]

This history shaped early transitional justice scholarship and policy, which tended to see truth commissions as a second-best alternative to trials. Initially justified as a compromise solution in between historical amnesia

[3] Notably, a donation from the Ford Foundation to the Ugandan government.

[4] Priscilla B. Hayner, "Fifteen Truth Commissions – 1974–1994: A Comparative Study," *Human Rights Quarterly* 16 (1994), pp. 613–614.

[5] Priscilla B. Hayner, *Unspeakable Truths: Facing the Challenge of Truth Commissions* (New York, NY: Routledge, 2002), p. 100.

[6] In 1998, while in London, General Augusto Pinochet was arrested for human rights violations committed in Chile after an indictment by Spanish magistrate Baltasan Garzon. On his return to Chile, Judge Juan Guzmán Tapia indicted and charged Pinochet with a number of crimes. Pinochet died in 2006 without having been convicted of a case. By the time of his death, Pinochet had been implicated in over 300 criminal charges.

and a rigid commitment to criminal justice, early research on truth commissions was largely reflective, debating their possible contributions and relative merits vis-à-vis trials. During the Cold War, the legacy of high-profile prosecutions at Nuremberg and Tokyo reinforced a preference for trials, contributing to a view of truth commissions as an experimental innovation, unrelated to more established traditions of criminal justice. The domestic contexts of Cold War transitional justice further bolstered this cautious view. Many transitions during this period were "pacted," negotiating between incumbent and departing rulers, and military actors frequently retained a high degree of power and influence in the new regime.[7] In Chile, four of the commissioners for the Rettig Commission were supporters of Pinochet. Although in Argentina, the Comisión Nacional Sobre la Desaparición de Personas handed its findings to the prosecutor's office and contributed to the trials of several high-ranking officials, the sentences were later reversed.[8] In these tense and fragile handovers, truth commissions often appeared as a compromise where trials were impossible, rather than as instruments in their own rights.

The disciplinary background of researchers focusing on democratization further entrenched this legalistic and cautious orientation. For political scientists interested in regime change, trials were important in the establishment of rule of law and due process.[9] Focusing on "third wave" transitions, while some argued in favor of a universal obligation to prosecute,[10] others acknowledged circumstances in which trials would

[7] See, for example, Terry Lynn Karl and Philippe Schmitter, "Modes of Transition in Latin America: Southern Europe and Eastern Europe," *International Social Sciences Journal* 128 (1991), p. 275; Juan Linz and Alfred Stefan, *Problems of Democratic Transition and Consolidation* (Baltimore, MD: Johns Hopkins Press, 1996), p. 61; and Scott Mainwaring, "Transitions to Democracy and Democratic Consolidation: Theoretical and Comparative Issues," in *Issues in Democratic Consolidation; The New South American Democracies in Comparative Perspective*, ed. Scott Mainwaring, Guilermo O'Donnell, and Samuel Valenzuela (Notre Dame, IN: University of Notre Dame Press, 1992), pp. 317–326.

[8] Greg Grandin, "The Instruction of Great Catastrophe: Truth Commissions, National History, and State Formation in Argentina, Chile and Guatemala," *American Historical Review* 110 (2005), pp. 46–67.

[9] Juan Linz and Alfred Stefan list "rule of law" as their third criterion for a "consolidated democracy." *Problems of Democratic Transition and Consolidation*. While Samuel Huntington argues that criminal trials and due process play a key role in democratization, under certain conditions, regimes should not address the past: "If transformation or transplacement occurred, do not attempt to prosecute authoritarian officials for human rights violations. The political cost of such an effort will outweigh the moral gains." He warns that if leaders feel the need to prosecute, they should do so immediately and not prosecute middle- or low-ranking officials. *The Third Wave: Democratization in the Late Twentieth Century* (Norman, OK: University of Oklahoma Press, 1991), p. 231.

[10] Miriam Aukerman, "Extraordinary Evil, Ordinary Crimes: A Framework for Understanding Transitional Justice," *Harvard Human Rights Journal* 15 (2000), pp. 39–40.

undermine domestic stability.[11] Significantly, however, truth commissions were seen as a complement rather than as an alternative for trials.[12]

Global Involvement in Transitional Justice: Fact-Finding and Didactic Truth Commissions

The end of the Cold War saw the emergence of new trends in peacebuilding and transitional justice. Although the immediate post–Cold War period witnessed a rapid period of regime change as former Soviet states asserted their independence, in the 1990s, the settings of transitional justice broadened. The El Salvadorian and Guatemalan truth commissions followed conflicts with large-scale casualties, resulting in at least 75,000 and 45,000 deaths respectively. These conflicts also had a marked ethnic component in that victims predominantly represented an indigenous rural underclass. They also saw an increase in atrocities against civilians.

International agents also took an increasingly active role in transitional justice during the post–Cold War era.[13] The 1990s were a highpoint for international involvement. The UN-run and heavily foreign-staffed Comisión de la Verdad Para El Salvador (1992–1993) and the Comisión Para el Esclarecimiento Histórico (CEH) in Guatemala (1997–1999) were important truth commissions. In a similar spirit, international actors set

[11] M. Cherif Bassiouni, "Searching for Peace and Achieving Justice: The Need for Accountability," *Law and Contemporary Problems* 59 (1996), pp. 9–28; Juan E. Mendez, "Accountability for Past Abuses," *Human Rights Quarterly* 19 (1997), pp. 255–282.

[12] Although there were a few exceptions, notably, Chilean human rights lawyer José Zalaquett, who emphasized the value of truth commissions for providing information on missing family members, few considered what broader purposes truth commissions might serve in post-conflict transitions. Zalaquett argues that truth commissions are preferable to retributive justice even where criminal trials are feasible: "it [the truth] does not bring the dead back to life, but it brings them out from silence: for their families, it means the end to an agonizing, endless search." José Zalaquett, "Introduction," *Report of the Chilean Commission of National Truth and Reconciliation*, 14. Available at: www.usip.org/files/resources/collections/truth_commissions/Chile90-Report/Chile90-Report.pdf. Recent empirical literature has returned to these earlier commissions to look at their broader normative and discursive impact on memory politics and victims' movements. Elizabeth Jelin, *State Repression and the Labors of Memory* (Minneapolis, MN: University of Minnesota Press, 2003); Elizabeth Jelin, "Public Memorialization in Perspective: Truth, Justice and Memory of Past Repression in the Southern Cone of South America," *The International Journal of Transitional Justice* 1 (2007), pp. 138–156; Katherine Hite and Cath Collins, "Memorial Fragments, Monument Silences and Re-awakenings in 21st-Century Chile," *Millennium: Journal of International Studies*, Violence and Memory Forum 38 (2009), pp. 379–400; Francesca Lessa, *Memory and Transitional Justice in Argentina and Uruguay: Against Impunity* (New York, NY: Palgrave, 2013).

[13] Ruti Teitel, "Transitional Justice Genealogy," *Harvard Human Rights Journal* 16 (2003), pp. 69–94.

up and managed the the UN-established and UN-administered ad hoc criminal tribunals in Rwanda and the former Yugoslavia.

Although in many ways the Central American commissions carried forward a regional emphasis on accountability and truth-seeking, the El Salvadorian and Guatemalan commissions employed a distinctive format and methodology. Prominent external commissioners ran the commissions, which received funding from the United Nations and Western NGOs. The Commissions mainly conducted their work behind closed doors, and consciously avoided public engagement, instead emphasizing historical fact-finding and the use of rigorous social science methodology.[14]

While truth commissions have employed a range of truth-seeking methods, ranging from quantitative to forensic approaches, the Central American didactic commissions took a purposefully "scientific" approach. Scientific methods take as their starting points the possibility of finding new information and refuting widely held assumptions.[15] The Central American commissions put heavy emphasis on the assignation of guilt and victimization.[16] Both were able to generate large databases, cataloguing details of the conflict. Their final reports gave figures for the number of conflict-related deaths and disappearances, and provided details on their ethnicities and demographic distributions. The CEH report concluded that the violence systematically targeted indigenous people and that state agents were largely responsible. It was able to generate long-term interpretations of the conflicts, also blaming

[14] The Comisión Para el Esclarecimiento Histórico emphasized truth over reconciliation, asserting the importance of an objective historical record for democratization and using social scientists for data collection. CEH Report. While the prologue to the Guatemalan truth commission argues that "knowing the truth of what happened will make it easier to achieve national reconciliation," it also posits uncertainty as to whether reconciliation can be achieved, and that it is most important to "recognize the facts of history and learn from the Nation's suffering."

[15] As opposed to interpretive truths, which start with particular hypotheses and objectives and use empirical evidence as support. Audrey R. Chapman and Patrick Ball, "The Truth of Truth Commissions: Comparative Lessons from Haiti, South Africa, and Guatemala," *Human Rights Quarterly* 23 (2001), p. 22.

[16] In their view, one of the benefits of quantitative techniques when it comes to commissions is that they can generate macro truths – "specifics of particular events, cases, and people." Macro truths seek to portray a big picture of the conflict, emphasizing structural causes and broader social, political, and economic contexts. Audrey Chapman and Patrick Ball, "Levels of Truth: Macro-Truth and the Truth Commission," in *Truth and Reconciliation in South Africa: Did the Truth Commission Deliver?* ed. Audrey R. Chapman and Hugo Van Der Merwe (Philadelphia, PA: University of Pennsylvania Press, 2008), p. 144. Alex Boraine refers to "forensic truth" or "hard facts" as covering specific data on human rights abuses and details on the circumstances in which abuses were committed and accountability. *A Country Unmasked: Inside South Africa's Truth and Reconciliation Commission* (Oxford: Oxford University Press, 2000), pp. 288–291. See also the South African TRC's discussion of types of truth. *The South African TRC Report*, Volume 1, Chapter 5, "Concepts and Principles," p. 111.

international actors, in particular, the United States. The CEH used its data to provide evidence of genocide against indigenous populations[17]

While practitioners on-site justified the utilization of systematic data collection and social science methodology to minimize bias and politicization, both commissions have since generated controversy for their presentation of responsibility,[18] and their limited popular engagement. Although some argue that the global management of transitional justice provides a critical layer of impartiality and political independence,[19] both commissions generated little public involvement or domestic backing.[20] In El Salvador, although key political parties nominally supported the Commission during peace agreements, neither the government nor the military acknowledged the report nor accepted accountability. Despite considerable popular backing, the El Salvadorian Commission came out against national prosecutions for fear of future instability. Here, the government pushed through an amnesty law one week after the report was released, and not a single individual faced trial.

In many ways, however, the impact of the Central American commissions on accountability has been more dynamic and complex than their immediate lack of popular engagement suggests. This is particularly the case in Guatemala, where recent efforts to prosecute war crimes have made use of the Commission's work. Efforts to bring civilian "military commissioner" Felipe Cusanero Coj to justice began in 2003 when surviving family members from the highland community of Choatalúm publicly denounced Cusanero and took him to Court. Despite military threats and intimidation, the publication of the CEH's reports in 1998 and 1999, and the trials of former dictators Romeo Lucas García and José Efraín Ríos Montt, created momentum. The August 31, 2009 sentencing of Cusanero marks the first conviction of a military member for a crime against humanity and acknowledgment of state disappearances in

[17] The report states, "the movement of Guatemala towards polarization, militarization, and civil war was not just the result of national history," and holds colonialism and the United States responsible for creating an unjust economic structure, which perpetuated a racist social system and concentrated wealth in the hands of a small minority. CEH Report, available online at: http://shr.aaas.org/guatemala/ceh/report/english/conc3.html.

[18] While the El Salvadorian Commission found state agents responsible for 93 percent of documented violations, for instance, it structured its report into parallel categories, containing equal numbers of specific examples of violence committed by state actors and the Frente Farabundo Marti Para la Liberacion Nacional.

[19] Jeremy Sarkin, "The Necessity and Challenges of Establishing a Truth and Reconciliation Commission in Rwanda," *Human Rights Quarterly* 21 (1999), pp. 808–809.

[20] Margaret Popkin, "The Salvadoran Truth Commission and the Search for Justice," in *Truth Commissions and Courts: The Tensions between Criminal Justice and the Search for Truth*, ed. William Schabas and Shane Darcy (Dortrecht, Netherlands: Kluwer Academic Publishers, 2004), p. 8. For Hayner, closed truth commissions put less pressure on perpetrators to acknowledge wrongdoing. Hayner, *Unspeakable Truths*.

a Guatemalan court. This process was not linear, yet attempts to censor and delay accountability often inadvertently gave momentum to victims' families and activists. In 2003, Montt's bids for presidency further mobilized victims' families, leading to his eventual prosecution.

The South African Participatory TRC

The establishment of the South African TRC was a turning point in theory and practice, linking transitional justice to an unprecedented extent to healing and reconciliation. Established by South Africa's post-apartheid parliament in 1995, the TRC's widespread outreach and popular methodology created a distinct participatory model of truth commissions, based on large-scale popular engagement, hearings and testimonies, and transparent and open proceedings. In contrast to earlier regime transitions, investigating political violence, the TRC also considered nonpolitical crimes committed by civilians. While it looked at apartheid as criminal, it moved beyond a political focus on rights and obligations to elevate horizontal relationships between individuals within society. The African National Congress (ANC) leadership's linking of the Commission to restorative justice and Christian themes of contrition and forgiveness also helped generate a victim-centered and rehabilitative conception of truth commissions in this context, tying testimony to personal healing and reintegration of perpetrators.[21] Interest in the TRC also coincided with an expanding global focus on broader issues affecting civilians in warfare, particularly human security and gendered violence.[22]

The development of a restorative participatory process, however, was gradual and somewhat ad hoc in South Africa. As was the case among the South American commissions, many of the African National Council's (ANC) original justifications for the TRC were pragmatic. Early on, key members of the ANC noted the challenges and dilemmas of prosecuting apartheid crimes, citing the weak judicial system after years of apartheid, the obstacle of finding evidence given the secretive nature of apartheid crimes, the refusal of many whites to see apartheid as criminal, and the disruption and added trauma that trials might cause victims and disenfranchised black South Africans. For many ANC officials, the challenge

[21] For Robert Rotberg, public engagement was the primary accomplishment of the South African TRC, which he argues should be a model for future TRCs. Robert I. Rotberg, "Truth Commissions and the Provision of Truth, Justice and Reconciliation," in *Truth v. Justice: the Morality of Truth Commissions*, ed. Robert I. Rotberg and Dennis Thompson (Princeton, NJ: Princeton University Press, 2000), pp. 3–21.

[22] See, for example, Neil J. Kritz, *Transitional Justice*.

of future coexistence called for prudence, rather than punishment.[23] The systematic nature of apartheid crimes, the debilitating legacy of apartheid on everyday life, and the marginalization of black communities led an increasing number of ANC members to promote a victim-centered approach, which would simultaneously create accountability for violations. As South African minister of justice Dullah Omar remembers:

> The idea of a Truth Commission goes back to ANC decisions. When the national Executive Committee of the ANC discussed what had happened in the country, and in particular what happened in ANC training camps like Quatro, there was a strong feeling that some mechanisms must be found to deal with all violations in a way which would ensure that we put our country on a sound moral basis. And so a view developed that what South Africa needs is a mechanism, which would open up the truth for public scrutiny. But to humanize our society we had to put across the idea of moral responsibility – that is why I suggested a combination of the amnesty process with the process of victims' stories.[24]

As plans to establish a TRC advanced, key members of the ANC and civil society began to redefine the TRC's purpose. Anglican Archbishop and TRC president, Desmond Tutu, played an important role in setting out the moral basis of the Commission, embedding and legitimizing the TRC within traditions of restorative justice, communitarian values, and religious faith. Referring to the TRC as a "third way" between doing nothing or "forgetting" and the retributive justice practiced at Nuremberg and Tokyo, Tutu criticized retributive justice as impersonal, not victim-centered, and Western in origin and orientation. Presenting restorative justice as a humane and morally superior form of justice and indigenous to South Africa,[25] calls for a TRC grew stronger in the 1980s within the framework of social and political resistance against apartheid. As theological movements called upon South African churches to challenge the apartheid regime, TRC proponents drew on township restorative justice to develop the concept of *Ubuntu* as the moral basis of the TRC, defining it as the "healing of breaches" and the "restoration of imbalances."[26] During this period, ANC leaders urged South Africans to make the townships "ungovernable," while developing their own political structures for later democratic rule.[27] The association of restorative justice with African and Christian values and communal justice allowed activists to link formal justice with perpetuating the status quo and informal justice

[23] Desmond Tutu, *No Future without Forgiveness* (Houghton, South Africa: Random House, 1999), p. 30.
[24] In Antjie Krog, *Country of My Skull* (London: Vintage Books, 1999), p. 8.
[25] Tutu, *No Future without Forgiveness*, pp. 34–35 and pp. 51–52. [26] Ibid.
[27] Bronwyn Leebaw, "Legitimation or Judgment? South Africa's Restorative Approach to Transitional Justice," *Polity* 36 (2003), pp. 23–51.

with political change. In this context, activists presented forgiveness and reconciliation as virtues in the postapartheid era.[28]

The South African TRC had several unique features. One was public participation and engagement. Early on, the TRC identified popular participation as a key method and objective. First, the TRC called for open and transparent proceedings and an inclusive process, which included hearings in different parts of the country with a range of stakeholders, including victims and perpetrators. Second, the TRC offered a space for subjective narrative truths. Unique among truth commissions, the TRC's fourfold categorization of truth includes an "objective factual truth," a "personal or narrative truth," "social or dialogue truth," and "healing or restorative truth."[29] The Commission's conception of "social" or "dialogue" truth particularly stands out. South African Constitutional Court Judge Albie Sachs argues that the main strength of the TRC was its "hearing all different viewpoints ... receiving inputs from all sides."[30]

While the Commission's objective to generate social truth frequently fell short in practice – victims and perpetrators often did not attend the same hearings or participated only indirectly in the case of amnesty hearings – the TRC's emphasis on public participation and its interpretive and inclusive understanding of truth had important consequences for its broader methodology and epistemology. The TRC's goal of generating widespread and inclusive participation, particularly from perpetrators and those more antagonistic to its work, led it to reach out extensively to the white community and offer provisions, most controversially amnesty to elicit disclosure of crimes.

In many ways, the TRC's truth-seeking efforts highlight dilemmas between the restorative and victim-centered objectives of its mandate. On the one hand, the TRC identified representing the victims of apartheid and documenting their experiences as its primary task.[31] The Commission

[28] Tutu praised Nelson Mandela's path of forgiveness and tolerance as coming from a position of strength and dignity and taking the moral high ground. Tutu, *No Future without Forgiveness*, pp. 39–40.

[29] The South African TRC Report.

[30] The purpose of social truth is transcending "divisions of the past by listening carefully to the complex motives and perspectives of all those involved," providing a conducive environment, where all possible views could be considered and weighed, and subjecting the TRC to "public scrutiny and critique" through open hearings and the media, and inviting "people from all walks of life" to participate. South African TRC Final Report, 1, no. 5 (1998), pp. 29–45.

[31] The Truth and Reconciliation Act stated that the truth commission would help victims heal by giving them a platform to tell their stories and by serving as a public form of acknowledgment. As stated by the South African truth commission, "Acknowledgement is an affirmation that a person's pain is real and worthy of attention. It is thus central to the restoration of the dignity of victims." The South African TRC Report, Volume 1, Chapter 5, p. 114.

recommended reparations and sought to dignify and acknowledge victims through its hearings and narration. The TRC's report reflects its "narrative truth." While it acknowledges that all groups committed violations, the Commission calls the struggle against apartheid "just," although sometimes misguided, and identifies the state as the perpetrator. It further identifies apartheid as a crime against humanity and states that the regime was involved in an "evil undertaking." The symbolic nature of its earliest hearings, which were deliberately held in the Eastern Cape, also reflects this narrative stance. As Tutu points out in his recollections, the Eastern Cape was the birthplace of the black resistance movement. It was also the site of the first higher education institutes for blacks; the birthplace of many black leaders, including Nelson Mandela, Thabo Mbeki, and Steve Biko; and the setting of the worst apartheid crimes.[32]

On the other hand, the TRC strove to produce a "restorative truth" by producing a historical memory that would unite South Africans and encourage individuals from all racial backgrounds to testify. In his introduction to the TRC, Tutu states, "South Africa is soaked in the blood of her children of all races," taking a stance that individuals, not groups, were victims of apartheid. The TRC portrays both the crimes of members of the ANC and of white South Africans as acts of specific individuals running astray, rather than as the result of a concerted or collectively sanctioned policy. The TRC's hearings included only about 8.5 percent (1,818) of the more than 21,000 people who produced statements.[33]

Foreshadowing the diverging trajectories of the Sierra Leone an and Peruvian truth and reconciliation commissions, the TRC's simultaneous attempt to take a moral stance against apartheid and provide a unifying platform isolated both blacks and whites.[34] While the TRC presented truth and reconciliation as complementary, its simultaneous objective to offer an inclusive forum and represent and honor the systematic oppression and brutalization of apartheid victims became particularly contentious. Although relatively few whites came forward, the TRC's efforts to reach out to white South Africans – its special appeals for whites to participate and hearings on issues specifically relevant to white South

[32] Tutu, *No Future without Forgiveness*, pp. 87–88.

[33] Chapman and Ball, "The Truth of Truth Commissions," p. 29. According to the TRC report, the statements it chose for public hearings depended on three factors: the nature of the abuse, an effort to represent "all sides of the conflicts of the past" from as many perspectives as possible, and a representation of various genders, ages, and racial groups in the areas where the hearings were held. The South African TRC Report, p. 148.

[34] Brandon Hamber and Gunnar Theissen, "A State of Denial: White South Africa's Attitudes to the Truth and Reconciliation Commission," *Indicator South Africa* 15 (1998), pp. 8–12.

Africans – did not go unnoticed.[35] Concerns emerged particularly among black South Africans over the TRC's emphasis on inclusivity. For some, the Commission's attempt to represent victims of all sides of the conflict sent a signal that the TRC had elevated interracial national reconciliation over critically condemning apartheid and the suffering of its victims.[36] Many whites, on the other hand, criticized the TRC as one-sided, citing its failure to implicate ANC members. Although it initially set up the TRC, the ANC criticized the Commission's "even-handed" approach and its sustained efforts to solicit white participation.[37] Tensions became particularly heated over the TRC's extensive focus on violence committed by black youth on behalf of Nelson Mandela's wife, Winnie Madikizela-Mandela.[38] After the testimony of former ANC member Bantubonke Harrington Holomisa, the ANC expelled Holomisa from the party, demanding that high-profile ANC members, while free to approach the TRC in confidence, maintain loyalty in public. Both members of the ANC and former president F.W. de Klerk eventually tried to prevent the TRC from publishing its report.[39] The South African TRC was the first commission to have a court of law confront its findings as some victims and their families sought to overrule the TRC, particularly its amnesty provision, as unconstitutional.[40]

The TRC's impact and legacy have been mixed. While some see the TRC as a blueprint for other societies,[41] the TRC has also generated intense criticism, particularly with the passage of time. One concern is that most of the statements before the Commission were not sworn in nor tested by cross-examination.[42] The socially contingent nature of

[35] As noted by Chapman and Ball, the TRC created an unequal opportunity for whites to appear in hearings. Of the 21,000 people who gave statements to the truth commission, 1,800 were chosen to testify at hearings. Chapman and Ball, "The Truth of Truth Commissions," p. 39. See also Bronwyn Leebaw, *Judging State Sponsored Violence: Imagining Political Change* (Cambridge: Cambridge University Press, 2011), pp. 81–82.

[36] Leebaw, "Legitimation or Judgment?" p. 45.

[37] TRC officials responded that the ANC had put "unity above truth." See Krog, *Country of My Skull.*

[38] Boraine, *A Country Unmasked*, pp. 221–257.

[39] Tutu describes the loss of ANC support as a significant personal disappointment. Tutu, *No Future without Forgiveness.* For Krog, however, from an institutional standpoint, it illustrates the extent to which the TRC took on a "moral life of its own and is willing to oppose the party that gave it birth." Krog, *Country of My Skull*, pp. 174–175.

[40] Aletta J. Norval, "Memory, Identity, and the (Im) possibility of Reconciliation: the Work of the Truth and Reconciliation Commission in South Africa," *Constellations* 5 (1998). The TRC's omission of the military or cross-border raids (the boycott) is also a weakness on the participatory model.

[41] Rotberg, "Truth Commissions and the Provision of Truth, Justice and Reconciliation."

[42] Mark Freeman, *Truth Commissions and Procedural Fairness* (Cambridge: Cambridge University Press, 2006), p. 72. This shortcoming may be more of a logistical consequence than an epistemological choice – in participatory commissions, officials invest significant

storytelling is another challenge. Rather than produce a national history that encompasses the diversity of individual experiences and perspectives, ethnographic work has found that individual testimonies in front of the TRC responded to and incorporated themes and language of the TRC's larger social narratives.[43] Some have questioned whether public acknowledgment is helpful without an apology,[44] and the extent to which the TRC indeed shaped longer-term perceptions.[45] According to James Gibson's 2004 representative sampling of 3,700 of South Africa's major racial, ethnic, and linguistic groups, most South Africans feel ambivalent about the TRC. Sixty percent of blacks and 75 percent of other races believe examining the past will reopen old wounds. Groups are evenly divided over whether their children should learn about past atrocities.[46] In addition, Gibson finds that whites and Asians feel the most reconciled, while blacks feel the least.[47] Perhaps most concerning has been a hardening of viewpoints over time given the persistence of deep-seated structural injustices and socioeconomic inequality since the cessation of the TRC. According to the South African Barometer Report, in 2003, respondents generally separated economic opportunity from reconciliation, looking at reconciliation as a process of "forgiveness" and positive interracial relations. By 2010, however, respondents identified socioeconomic inequality as the largest fault line preventing interracial reconciliation in South Africa.[48] As I will examine in detail in relation to Sierra Leone and Peru, these responses

effort and time into gathering testimonies, leaving little space for analysis – the subjective nature of memory creates additional challenges, especially for victims, who may suffer from posttraumatic stress and have trouble recollecting the past. Martha Minow, *Between Vengeance and Forgiveness: Facing History after Genocide and Mass Violence* (Boston, MA: Beacon Press, 2000).

43 Wilson claims that individuals who supported the South African TRC had been persuaded by the TRC's discourse. Richard A. Wilson, *The Politics of Truth and Reconciliation in South Africa: Legitimizing the Post-Apartheid State* (Cambridge, UK: Cambridge University Press, 2001). Minow, *Between Vengeance and Forgiveness*; Hayner, *Unspeakable Truths*, pp. 141–145.

44 Charles S. Maier, "Overcoming the Past? Narrative and Negotiation, Remembering and Reparation: Issues at the Interface of History and the Law," in *Politics and the Past: On Repairing Historical Injustices*, ed. John Torpey (Lanham, MD: Rowman & Littlefield Publishers, 2003), pp. 295–304.

45 David Mendeloff, "Truth-seeking, Truth-telling and Postconflict Peace-building: Curb the Enthusiasm," *International Studies Review* 6 (2004); Eric Brahm, "Uncovering the Truth: Examining Truth Commissions Success and Impact," *International Studies Perspectives* 8 (2007), pp. 255–282.

46 James L. Gibson, *Overcoming Apartheid: Can Truth Heal a Divided Nation* (New York, NY: Russell Sage Foundation, 2004).

47 Ibid.

48 Institute for Justice and Reconciliation, "The South African Reconciliation Barometer Dialogue Report," p. 10.

indicate reconciliation's contingent nature. As the South African experience indicates, environmental changes can lead to cognitive dissonance and disenchantment over time as communities reevaluate their earlier more positive experiences.

Intrastate Conflicts and Conflict Transformation: Mixed-Method TRCs

The 1990s saw a marked increase in the severity and intensity of intrastate conflicts. In East Timor, Sierra Leone, Peru, the Democratic Republic of Congo, Chad, the Central African Republic, Uganda, and Liberia, transitional justice processes were established in complex post-conflict settings. These intrastate conflicts featured systematic atrocities against civilians and violence at the hands of multiple parties. They also often contained multiple levels of violence, including political violence, from state actors, and intimate communal violence, often at the hands of people who know each other.

Global transitional justice has only partially taken into account the immense and multifaceted challenges of post-conflict recovery. On the one hand, transitional justice at the turn of the century saw an intensification of post–Cold War trends. Transitional justice in the early 2000s consolidated as a field, reflected in the establishment of centers to study transitional justice and an emphasis on best practices.[49] In recent decades, international policymakers and academics have also endorsed a more multifaceted or "holistic" orientation. Holistic justice, as the International Center for Transitional Justice and the United Nations put it, builds on the strengths of multiple mechanisms to optimize results.[50] Just as criminal sanctions require a high burden of proof to identify perpetrators and determine their guilt, reparations require accurate information to identify victims and harm.[51] A second cornerstone of holistic justice is a participatory and culturally sensitive orientation. As the United Nations notes, holistic justice should integrate local ownership and practices with global expertise.[52] Recent UN-established

[49] This process reached its apex with the signing of the Rome Statute in 1998 and the establishment of the International Criminal Court and the gradual erosion of sovereign immunity through a number of high-profile prosecutions of leaders.

[50] Ruti Teitel, "Transitional Justice Genealogy," *Harvard Human Rights Journal* 16 (2003), pp. 69–94.

[51] David A. Crocker, "Reckoning with Past Wrongs," p. 9.

[52] United Nations, "What is Transitional Justice? A Backgrounder," (February 20, 2008). Available at: www.un.org/en/peace-building/pdf/doc_wgll/justice_times_transition/26_02_2008_background_note.pdf. See also UN Secretary General, "The Rule of Law and Transitional Justice in Conflict and Post-Conflict Societies – Report of the Secretary General," UN Security Council (2011).

hybrid courts in Sierra Leone and East Timor are prominent examples, established on-site, in parallel to truth commissions and local restorative processes, and employing a mix of international and domestic personnel.[53] Both also put increased emphasis on "sensitization," outreach, and legacy.[54] Finally, holistic justice seeks to promote civic participation and democratization, and to transform the root causes of the conflict, thereby contributing to peace-building and conflict prevention.

At the same time, and mirroring trends in peace-building, the simultaneously varied and complex nature of transitional justice settings and transitional justice's expanding normative agenda raises important questions as to the normative underpinnings, methods, and impact of transitional justice. More ethnographically oriented scholars have critiqued the global emphasis on formal justice and its prescriptive orientation. This literature calls for an emancipatory approach that advances communal agency and transforms unjust structural frameworks and oppression.[55]

Despite a growing interest in long-term conflict transformation, more research and reflection are needed on the challenges facing transitional justice in fragile and complex post-conflict settings. While recent transitional justice theory and practice have sought to overcome earlier dichotomies – between peace and justice, and between retributive and restorative mandates and procedures[56] – this reorientation has been primarily

[53] Although both courts later engendered criticism for insufficiently engaging domestic populaces and fostering local ownership. These hybrid tribunals were established on sites where violence took place, as opposed to the International Criminal Tribunal for Rwanda and the International Criminal Tribunal for the former Yugoslavia, established in Tanzania and The Hague, respectively.

[54] See, for instance, Roger Mac Ginty, "Gilding the Lily? International Support for Indigenous and Traditional," *Palgrave Advances in Peace-building*, ed. Oliver Richmond (Basingstoke, UK: Palgrave, 2010), pp. 347–366; and "Hybrid Peace: The Interaction between Top-down and Bottom-up Peace," *Security Dialogue* 4 (2010), pp. 391–412; Rami Mani, *Beyond Retribution: Seeking Justice in the Shadows of War* (Cambridge and Maldon, MA: Polity Press, 2007); Harvey M. Weinstein, Laurel E. Fletcher, and Patrick Vinck, "Stay the Hand of Justice," in *Localizing Transitional Justice: Interventions and Priorities after Mass Violence*, ed. Rosalind Shaw, Lars Waldorf, and Pierre Hazan (Stanford, CA: Stanford University Press, 2010), pp. 27–48; Moses Chrispus Okello, "Afterword: Elevating Transitional Local Justice or Crystallizing Global Governance," in *Localizing Transitional Justice: Interventions and Priorities after Mass Violence*, ed. Rosalind Shaw, Lars Waldorf, and Pierre Hazan (Stanford, CA: Stanford University Press, 2010), pp. 275–284.

[55] See Paul Gready and Simon Robins, "From Transitional Justice to Transformative Justice: A New Agenda in Practice," *The International Journal for Transitional Justice* 8 (2014), pp. 339–361. Mac Ginty, "Gilding the Lily."

[56] Rachel Kerr and Erin Mobekk, *Peace and Justice: Seeking Accountability after War* (Cambridge: Polity Press, 2007).

normative in nature, lacking empirical substantiation.[57] As the Sierra Leonean and Peruvian cases highlight in the empirical chapters that follow, the global application of transitional justice to conflict settings both intensifies earlier dilemmas and challenges and raises new questions. Two of these challenges have emerged in recent qualitative research. A first issue is ownership – who sets up and conducts transitional justice and peace-building and with what consequences? Despite a recent emphasis on hybridity and local participation and outreach, formal transitional justice has had a particularly poor track record in these areas. This applies particularly to globalized processes of transitional justice. While the Sierra Leonean and East Timorese hybrid tribunals set up headquarters and conducted their work largely in the capital cities of Freetown and Dili, victims and insurgents predominantly came from rural and remote areas.[58] Concerns about ownership and partnership also apply to cases of domestic transitional justice, such as Peru. As Chapters 6 and 7 will detail, affected communities in Ayacucho have raised concerns over the rural and poor, the rural and poor demographic of the majority of victims and the concentration of formal mechanisms in the capital.

A second fundamental challenge concerns preferences, particularly with regard to the needs of survivors of violence. As I will elaborate in Chapters 6 and 7, in Peru, socioeconomic class correlates strongly with victimization, and played a significant role in shaping local preferences and perceptions of justice. As Lisa Laplante and Kimberly Theidon note, compared to Argentina, where mothers of the disappeared sometimes criticized reparations as a state tactic to evade criminal responsibility, poor populations in Peru have had to prioritize practical considerations

[57] See Rebekka Friedman and Andrew Jillions, "The Pitfalls and Politics of Holistic Justice," *Global Policy* 6, no. 2 (2015), pp. 141–150.

[58] Tim Kelsall faults globalized transitional justice for insufficiently engaging and understanding Sierra Leonean culture and excluding victims and war-affected communities. Tim Kelsall, "Truth, Lies, Ritual" and *Culture under Cross-Examination.* Similarly, Gearoid Millar maintains that testimony and Western conceptions of agency do not resonate in Sierra Leone, finding more favorable views of the TRC among local elites than ordinary people, who considered it to be a disturbance. Gearoid Millar, " 'Ah Lef Ma Case Fo God': Faith and Agency in Sierra Leone's Post-war Reconciliation," *Peace and Conflict: Journal of Peace Psychology* 18, no. 2 (2012), pp. 135 and 139. See also Gearoid Millar, "Assessing Local Experiences of Truth-telling in Sierra Leone: Getting to 'Why' Through a Qualitative Case Study Analysis," *The International Journal of Transitional Justice* 4 (2010), pp. 477–496. Taking a gendered lens, Chris Coulter similarly finds that at the local level, talking about war experiences was shameful for women and a source of stigmatization. She warns that formal mechanisms have undermined women's reintegration to civilian life and the restoration of normalcy. Chris Coulter, *Bush Wives and Girl Soldiers: Women's Lives through War and Peace in Sierra Leone* (Ithaca: Cornell University Press, 2009), p. 180.

and basic needs, notably, housing and education for their children, over retributive justice.[59] Theidon also focuses on class in her broader work, comparing elite hostility to national reconciliation in Lima to more pragmatic community reconciliation in villages in the Andes. While middle-class Peruvians in the capital cities were more concerned about corruption charges than with abuses and disappearances, communal reconciliation in affected villages was often pragmatic and functional – a way to rebuild communal life and labor.[60] In both Sierra Leone and Peru, I will argue that variances in preferences related both to victims' experiences in the conflict and their present concerns and situations.[61]

A third, albeit less researched concern, in recent conflict to peace transitions is the extent to which institutions have and can successfully incorporate conflict transformation into their mandates and procedures. As I will detail in the following chapters, the Sierra Leonean TRC (2003) and the Peruvian CVR (2003) sought to contribute to peace-building and address root causes in their respective societies.[62] These "mixed methods" commissions took on broader mandates and drew on previous practices. Both the Peruvian and Sierra Leonean commissions produced extensive historical reports, identifying systematic patterns of victimization and responsibility. At the same time, the Sierra Leonean and Peruvian commissions took influence from the South African restorative model in giving a voice to direct victims of conflict and marginalized communities. Both incorporated public hearings and sought to provide an inclusive platform, although as I will argue in the book's subsequent empirical chapters, in each case, their relationship with protagonists was complex and often strained.

At the same time, both commissions were tasked with contributing directly to peace-building and conflict transformation in their respective contexts. In the process, they distanced themselves from previous truth commissions. Identifying the marginalization of indigenous populations and political neglect as root causes of the conflict, the CVR presented criminal justice as a component of reconciliation, using the information it gathered to contribute to the prosecutions of military members

[59] Lisa J. Laplante and Kimberly Susan Theidon, "Truth with Consequences: Justice and Reparations in Post-Truth Commission Peru," *Human Rights Quarterly* 29 (2007), p. 243. See also Maria Elena García, *Making Indigenous Citizens: Identity, Development and Multicultural Activism in Peru* (Stanford, CA: Stanford University Press, 2005).

[60] Kimberly Susan Theidon, "Justice in Transition: The Micropolitics of Reconciliation in Post-war Peru," *The Journal of Conflict Resolution* 50 (2006), p. 454.

[61] Simon Robins offers a thoughtful discussion of preferences in Timor Leste. Robins, "Challenging the Therapeutic Ethic," p. 15.

[62] The Commission for Reception, Truth and Reconciliation in East Timor (2005) another important example.

domestically and at the Inter-American Court. Additionally, the CVR sought to generate political and social capital and government accountability by holding hearings in marginalized regions, raising awareness, and strengthening cultural pluralism. Where the Sierra Leonean TRC identified the marginalization of youth as an underlying driver of conflict, it put emphasis on youth integration and empowerment. Both commissions emphasized the rectification of structural injustice and made recommendations for sociopolitical reforms and reparations.[63]

Rigorous examination of how and whether transitional justice can address the root causes of conflict is vital for informed contextual reflection on the promises and challenges facing transitional justice in complex conflict transitions. Closer attention to practices is also important to draw out relevant lessons and standards of evaluation that reflect stakeholders' experiences and expectations. Recent research on Sierra Leone and Peru has yielded interesting insights into communal understandings of healing and reconciliation. Yet scholarly focus on the commissions' limited impact on interpersonal reconciliation and healing stands in contrast to both commissions' procedures and methodologies.[64] As I argue in the following empirical chapters, both the Sierra Leone and Peruvian commissions consciously distanced themselves from the therapeutic model of restorative justice, associated with literature on the South African TRC. Instead, both promoted a democratic understanding of reconciliation as civic nation-building and rights-based citizenship and solidarity. I maintain that a close understanding of practices is significant for the analysis of impact over time. As I will detail in Chapters 5 and 7, stakeholders' evaluations and experiences of truth commissions in both Sierra Leone and Peru reflected how institutions had legitimized and promoted their work. In each case, the lack of follow-up to the commissions' recommendations and insufficient progress in reparatory justice were especially acute grievances, resulting in a severe loss of legitimacy and momentum, frustrated expectations, and a sense of abandonment, particularly among those most severely affected by conflict.

Conclusions

In the last two decades, transitional justice mechanisms have emerged in a range of challenging conflict transitions, often with varying levels of global

[63] The Sierra Leonean TRC Report, Volume 2, Chapter 3, "Recommendations."

[64] Rebekka Friedman, "Restorative Justice: Promises and Limitations," in *Evaluating Transitional Justice: Accountability and Peace-building in Post-Conflict Sierra Leone*, ed. Kirsten Ainley, Rebekka Friedman, and Christopher Mahony (Basingstoke: Palgrave Macmillan, 2015), pp. 55–76.

support. In this chapter, I detailed how transitional justice institutions in various settings oriented themselves in response to a combination of domestic, regional, and international challenges and objectives, legacies, and normative influences and pressures. Although often legitimized through local and global norms and practices, I made the case that the historical trajectories of transitional justice mechanisms frequently involved trial and error and pragmatism. Decisions to pursue certain pathways over others, however, have had lasting consequences both within individual contexts and for broader global learning and policy. The varying orientations of transitional justice institutions, in turn, have shaped their domestic reception and impact and stakeholders' experiences and expectations.

Setting the stage for the book's subsequent empirical chapters, tensions within and between transitional justice institutions require careful critical reflection. While academic literature and transitional justice mandates, for instance, have tended to look at truth and reconciliation as complementary goals, in practice, I have made the case that they are often in conflict. When conceptualized as inclusive mechanisms, truth commissions face thorny questions of whose experience they should represent and whom they should target as their audience. Should they focus on validating those who suffered the most and should their report be primarily a history of the oppressed? Or if truth commissions are to facilitate social repair and communal healing, should they target those who are the most suspicious and antagonistic toward coexistence? In practice, the historical experience of truth commissions indicates that they have often had to prioritize reconciliation or truth, facing difficult choices and trade-offs.

Similarly, discords between institutions merit further scrutiny. While recent theory and practice have sought to move past prior impasses by advocating hybridity and methodological pluralism, I have raised the concern that this broadening has been primarily normative in nature. Setting the stage for the rest of the book, notions of holistic justice and positive complementarity are embodied in the expanded mandates of recent truth commissions and their efforts to pursue multiple goals and target various stakeholders at once. As I will detail in the subsequent empirical chapters on Sierra Leone and Peru, where both truth commissions operated alongside trials, each struggled with their varied mandates and their relationships to protagonists. While the TRC actively promoted ex-combatant participation by taking a more neutral and conciliatory stance, the CVR limited its engagement with protagonists. In an already strained sociopolitical context, it weighed its potential engagement of ex-combatants against its primary commitment to accountability and victims' justice, eventually focusing its work and resources on the latter.

3 Procedural Reconciliation

Reconciliation is paramount to conflict transformation. As the majority of conflicts today are intrastate, some level of reconciliation – or at least coexistence – is vital to future peace and stability. Scholars and practitioners have increasingly recognized that reconciliation should be transformative in aim and scope, and that it should address the needs and experiences of those most directly affected by violence: victims, former combatants, and their descendants. These populations tend to bear the primary daily legacies of violence both psychologically and in their relations with others and their abilities to make ends meet.

In practice, reconciliation is immensely difficult to conceptualize. For victims, as the empirical chapters of this book will make clear, reconciliation holds positive and negative connotations. On one level, reconciliation invokes a stigma of sacrifice and letting go; it places a disproportionate burden on victims for the sake of broader societal goals of peace or development.[1] On another level, affected populations often conceive of reconciliation in aspirational terms. As many of my interviewees put it, reconciliation is a deep-rooted desire for internal peace and an unburdening of the past, a yearning to define one's own identity and destiny, undetermined by past experiences and the actions of others.

Reconciliation is also dynamic and occurs at multiple levels: at the communal, societal, and political levels, and at the internal level, within individuals themselves. Reconciliation advances in everyday interactions and nonactions, as well as in individual and collective memories and relationships. These realms are interconnected and reinforce each other, yet they are also often in tension. I argue that experiences of reconciliation are inherently fluid, varying between political and social contexts and from one individual to the next.

Although reconciliation has historically featured less prominently in political theory and philosophy, concerns about healing and justice in the

[1] Richard A. Wilson, *The Politics of Truth and Reconciliation in South Africa: Legitimizing the Post-Apartheid State* (Cambridge: Cambridge University Press, 2001).

face of mass atrocities are longer-standing lines of inquiry. Following the Nazi Holocaust, German-born Jewish American political theorist Hannah Arendt and her mentor, German-Swiss psychiatrist and philosopher Karl Jaspers, debated whether forgiveness and contrition belonged in the public sphere and to what extent outsiders should encourage these processes. As I will detail in this chapter, their respective work and correspondence foreshadow significant concerns for the study of reconciliation today, particularly the liberating potential of forgiveness and the potential for social learning and moral introspection. Scholars of political philosophy, International Relations, peace-building, social psychology, and restorative justice have displayed an interest in forgiveness, historical rights, and obligations. Engagement with reconciliation, as I will also set out, has been intricately bound to the study of memory, rooted especially in the European experiences of World Wars I and II and the outbreak of ethnic violence in the former Yugoslavia in the 1990s. The increased prominence of restorative justice in socio-legal studies, as well as the writings of critical pragmatists and civic humanists, offer other inroads to the study of reconciliation.

In this chapter, I offer a conception of what I call "procedural reconciliation," which I distinguish from what I identify as more linear and transformative understandings. Transformative reconciliation focuses on the direct impact of transitional justice on perceptions and viewpoints, and is pronounced in the literature on truth commissions. On the one hand, proponents herald truth commissions as a victim-centered and restorative form of justice, which provide a framework for individual and community healing by allowing victims to air viewpoints and changing social perceptions.[2] On the other side of the spectrum are those who argue that formal mechanisms should not intrude upon the personal and subjective spheres of reconciliation and forgiveness, and that reconciliation is more relevant at the community level, where it could benefit from local culture and authority structures.[3]

I caution that transformative understandings of reconciliation have also reinforced a narrow and empirical research agenda tied to psychological change and social learning. Early empirical research on reconciliation within transitional justice frequently drew upon the South African experience. As I detailed in Chapter 2, the South African TRC generated a distinct therapeutic conception of truth commissions linked to trauma

[2] See *Truth v. Justice: The Morality of Truth Commissions*, ed. Robert R. Rotberg and Dennis Thompson (Princeton, NJ: Princeton University Press, 2000).

[3] Roger Mac Ginty, "Gilding the Lily? International Support for Indigenous and Traditional Peace-building," *Palgrave Advances in Peace-building* (Basingstoke, UK: Palgrave, 2010), pp. 347–366.

relief and restorative justice, and an understanding of reconciliation rooted in social psychology and theology. It gave rise to a conception of reconciliation on the micro level connected to forgiveness, individual healing, and interpersonal and communal repair.

Building on the previous chapter, while I argue that formal transitional justice and official truth-seeking processes have a potentially important role to play in post-war societies, I suggest a recalibration of what formal mechanisms are able to offer and a broadening of theoretical conceptions of reconciliation and its drivers. I advocate for a more indirect and critical understanding of impact in which transitional justice mechanisms give rise to broader normative and discursive effects.[4] More specifically, I offer a more fluid and long-term conception of reconciliation. I highlight what I see as varying degrees of reconciliation, contrasting transformative reconciliation – which requires cognitive reassessment – with procedural reconciliation as an ongoing and flexible process of generating shared norms and procedures. Procedural reconciliation does not work toward a predetermined vision of a post-conflict society. Rather, it broadens normative and discursive societal engagement. As the empirical chapters will demonstrate in more concrete terms, while procedural reconciliation may be driven by, and can reinforce, conflict, it is nevertheless an important and perhaps more realistic development in deeply divided societies.

Conceptualizing Reconciliation

Reconciliation has only recently become a more prominent area of academic inquiry in the social sciences. Much of the older literature on reconciliation focused on the micro level of personal healing and interpersonal repair. Some of the earliest studies of reconciliation arose in the 1970s from older strands of peace-building (a largely practitioner-driven scholarship). While a niche area in peace-building, many of these scholars were drawn to reconciliation for its religious resonance. Early conceptions of reconciliation were often rooted in theology, tying reconciliation to Christian themes of forgiveness and healing and confessional processes of contrition and repentance.[5]

[4] Even in the South African case, the TRC ended up focusing much of its work on the civic sphere. Recent mixed-method TRCs in Sierra Leone and Peru have taken this orientation further by explicitly distancing themselves from the goals of personal healing and interpersonal reconciliation. Instead, both commissions promoted a democratic understanding of national reconciliation between society and state.

[5] See Howard Zehr, "A Restorative Framework for Community Justice Practice," in *Criminology, Conflict Resolution and Restorative Justice*, ed. Kieran McEvoy and Tim Newburn (New York, NY: Palgrave Macmillan, (2003), pp. 135–152; and "Restoring Justice in God and the Victim: Theological Reflections on Evil, Victimization, Justice, and

Scholars and practitioners have widely recognized that there are varying levels and degrees of reconciliation. Charles Villa-Vicencio conceives of gradients of reconciliation as a spectrum with coexistence at the one end and forgiveness on the other.[6] Reconciliation, which involves the practical creation of working relationships and institutions and the cultivation of trust and respect, falls in the middle. Forgiveness, if it happens at all, emerges in the long run, as a result of reconciliation and the normalization of societal relations. Importantly, reconciliation is a more gradual process of accommodation and relationship-building, in which parties internalize more tolerant outlooks.[7] Reconciliation requires a minimum agreement on the past and future, at least some level of recognition of each other's suffering, and the anticipation of mutual security and well-being.[8] As I will set out in the empirical chapters, reconciliation also occurs at various levels. These broadly include micro-reconciliation, at the personal level in terms of individuals coming to terms and making peace with their own pasts, at the interpersonal level as a restored relationship between aggrieved parties, and at the communal level, as repair of the social fabric and social capital. They also include macro-reconciliation at the societal and political levels, in terms of a new relationship between groups in society, and between society and state, respectively.

Academic literature has said less about the drivers and aims of reconciliation. In the rest of the chapter, I will distinguish between two main orientations – what I refer to as transformative and procedural reconciliation. I will argue that transformative reconciliation is linear in orientation. It tends to focus on the cognitive sphere on perceptions. Those engaged

Forgiveness," in *Neighbors Who Care*, ed. Lisa Barnes Lampman and Michelle D. Shattuck (Washington, DC: William B. Eerdmans Publishing Company, 1999), pp. 131–159. See also John Paul Lederach, "Civil Society and Reconciliation," in *Turbulent Peace: The Challenges of Managing International Conflict*, ed. Chester A. Crocker, Fen Osler Hampson, and Pamela Aall (Washington, DC: US Institute of Peace, 2001), pp. 841–854; and *The Moral Imagination* (Oxford: Oxford University Press, 2005).

6 Charles Villa Vicencio, "Reconciliation," in *Pieces of the 2004: Keywords on Reconciliation and Transitional Justice*, ed. Charles Villa-Vicencio and Erik Doxtader (Cape Town, South Africa: Institute for Justice and Reconciliation, 2004), p. 8.

7 Brandon Hamber and Grainne Kelly, "A Working Definition of Reconciliation," in *Reconciliation(s): Transitional Justice in Postconflict Societies*, ed. Joanna Quinn (Montreal and Kingston: McGill-Queen's University Press, 2009); Louis Kriesberg, "Changing Forms of Coexistence," in *Reconciliation, Justice and Coexistence: Theory and Practice*, ed. Mohammed Abu-Nimer (Lanham, MD: Lexington Books, 2001), p. 48.

8 Louis Kriesberg, "Coexistence and the Reconciliation of Communal Conflicts," in *The Handbook of Interethnic Coexistence*, ed. Eugene Weiner (New York: Continuum, 2000), pp. 47–64. Daniel Bar-Tal and Gemma H. Bennink argue that reconciliation is a process in which cognitive disconnects are brought into equilibrium. Daniel Bar-Tal and Gemma H. Bennink, "The Nature of Reconciliation as an Outcome and as a Process," in *From Conflict Resolution to Reconciliation*, ed. Yaakov Bar-Siman-Tov (Oxford: Oxford University Press, 2004), pp. 11–38.

in its assessment also tend to be more uniform in their research methodology – focusing on developing external benchmarks with which to identify and assess levels of reconciliation. Procedural reconciliation, as I will set out in this chapter and the case studies in the book, is more open-ended. It occurs when a shared process is in place to address conflict. Where transformative reconciliation seeks to move away from conflict toward convergence, procedural reconciliation can be driven by conflict and can reinforce and generate conflict. That said, procedural reconciliation is nonviolent and does require certain prerequisites in order to take place. Although also generating broader cumulative effects over time, procedural reconciliation advances indirectly through spillover and the cultivation of trust and solidarity than through direct transformation. Procedural reconciliation is therefore a more agency-based understanding of reconciliation, and, I will argue, conducive to interpretive and open-ended methodological approaches.

Transformative Reconciliation

Transformative reconciliation looks at reconciliation as a definitive end point and process whereby individuals or collectivities change their viewpoints and behavior in congruence with each other. It is ambitious in scope and has permeated a lot of the literature on transitional justice, especially on truth commissions, given its focus on perceptions.

Like procedural reconciliation, transformative reconciliation comes in different guises. A first is the social contact hypothesis. In brief, according to the social contact hypothesis, direct interaction and constructive engagement help individuals overcome stereotypes and facilitate new relationships. This scholarship looks at reconciliation as a process of accommodation and relationship-building, in which parties internalize more tolerant outlooks and/or change their views over time.[9] Sociologist Louis Kriesberg argues that reconciliation requires a minimum agreement on the past and future, e.g., some level of recognition of each other's suffering, and the anticipation of mutual security and well-being.[10] Daniel Bartal and Gemma Benink look at reconciliation as a process whereby cognitive disconnects are brought into equilibrium.[11]

Transitional justice scholarship and practice often implicitly invoke the social contact hypothesis by linking reconciliation to collective memory.

[9] Hamber and Kelly, "A Working Definition of Reconciliation"; Kriesberg, "Changing Forms of Coexistence," p. 48.

[10] Kriesberg, "Coexistence and the Reconciliation of Communal Conflicts," pp. 47–64.

[11] Bar-Tal and Bennink, "The Nature of Reconciliation as an Outcome and as a Process," pp. 11–38.

Since World War II, efforts to establish historical accountability and truth-seeking have become important centerpieces in the theory and practice of reconciliation. Scholars have increasingly treated memory as a variable in conflict – both as a driver of violence and as a form of conflict resolution through which grievances are honored and addressed and groups find common ground. Interest in the linkages between reconciliation and memory grew out in part of fears of repressed memories. The outbreak of violence in the former Yugoslavia in the 1990s, during which nationalist leaders exhumed mass graves of ethnic partisans killed during World War II, has served as an emblematic example for scholars and practitioners of the incendiary potential of unaddressed violence.[12] In this case, Marshall Tito's suppression of past grievances was a temporary solution, setting the groundwork for a situation in which ethnic entrepreneurs could later politicize not only past injustices but also their hidden and unaccounted for nature.[13] Repressed memory was seen as the inverse of the social contact hypothesis – where a lack of contact and suppressed grievances incited fears and froze antagonisms.

The emergence of truth and reconciliation commissions, in turn, reinforced an interest in historical memory and investigation to counter negative stereotypes and grievances. On both the macro[14] and the micro levels, scholars have posited that reconciliation requires a demystification of evil and of violence – a normalization of atrocities as human. For Andrew Schaap, reconciliation (what he calls "political forgiveness") is a response to "frailty." It involves a view of evil as "banal" and "mundane in the sense that it is of the world."[15] Bert van Roermund argues that atrocities need to become more comprehensible for societies to move forward. Reconciliation requires a recognition that "what the oppressors

[12] Kritz, *How Emerging Democracies Deal with Former Regimes*. For example, Elizabeth Kiss, "Moral Ambition with and beyond Political Constraints," in *Truth v. Justice: The Morality of Truth Commissions*, ed. Robert R. Rotberg and Dennis Thompson (Princeton, NJ: Princeton University Press, 2000), p. 72.

[13] A "Balkan paradigm" has entrenched a fear of antagonistic memories, and has put memory work on the forefront of conflict resolution and prevention efforts. See Robert M. Hayden on the politicization of ethnic massacres for nationalist purposes, "Imagined Communities and Real Victims: Self-Determination and Ethnic Cleansing in Yugoslavia," *American Ethnologist* (1996), pp. 783–801; Bette Denich, "Unbury the Victims: Rival Exhumations and Nationalist Revivals in Yugoslavia," American Anthropological Association Annual Meeting (Chicago, 1991), pp. 1–14.

[14] Susan Dwyer maintains that, just as individual well-being requires making sense of and incorporating severe disruptions into personal narratives, the survival of a community or nation "depends upon how it manages to incorporate and accommodate these disturbances and challenges to its prevailing narrative of self-understanding." "Reconciliation for Realists."

[15] Andrew Schaap, *Political Reconciliation* (Ithaca, NY: Cornell University Press, 2001), p. 111.

did to the oppressed belongs to the evil humans do to each other, and not to a mythic evil that intrudes on the world of humans from outside."[16] This demystification both allows for the cultivation of stronger intergroup bonds as they shift their viewpoints of each other but also helps individuals heal internally as they acquire stronger and more positive views of the world.

Building on this, early transitional justice scholarship took a strong interest in the sociopsychological processes through which antagonistic and closed narratives transformed into more inclusive and nuanced understandings.[17] At the intersection of social psychology and transitional justice, much of this literature posits that truth commissions, in comparison with trials, offer a greater pedagogical contribution to social learning.[18] Due to scarce resources and the difficulty of bringing individuals to trial, war crimes tribunals arguably had a more limited didactic scope. Additionally, given their emphasis on free will, trials less easily accounted for individual moral choice during war and the complex social contexts and psychological pressures that characterize mass violence.[19] In contrast, truth commissions, which operate directly on the site of violence, may better shed light on long-term structural causes and systematic patterns. They can also reveal institutional responsibility, illuminating causes and patterns of victimization and direct and indirect beneficiaries and bystanders.[20] Susan Dwyer thus recommends an open

[16] Bert van Roermund, "Rubbing Off and Rubbing On: The Grammar of Reconciliation," in *Lethe's Law: Justice, Law, and Ethics in Reconciliation*, ed. Emilios Christodoulidis and Scott Veitch (Oxford: Hart Publishing, 2001), p. 183.

[17] David A. Crocker, "Reckoning with Past Wrongs: A Normative Framework," (June 2004), p. 9. Available at http://terpconnect.umd.edu/~dcrocker/Courses/Docs/Reckoning%20with%20past%20wrongs.pdf; Priscilla B. Hayner, *Unspeakable Truths: Facing the Challenge of Truth Commissions* (New York, NY: Routledge, 2002), p. 161; Donna Pankhurst, "Issues of Justice and Reconciliation in Complex Political Emergencies: Conceptualising Reconciliation, Justice and Peace," *Third World Quarterly* 20 (1999), p. 224.

[18] Laurel E. Fletcher and Harvey M. Weinstein, "Violence and Social Repair: Rethinking the Contribution of Justice to Reconciliation," *Human Rights Quarterly* 24 (2002), pp. 573–639; Kirsten A. Ainley, "Responsibility for Atrocity: Individual Criminal Agency and the International Criminal Court," *Evil, Law and the State: Perspectives on State Power and Violence*, ed. John Parry (Amsterdam and New York: Rodopi, 2006), pp. 143–158.

[19] This is an old argument made by Hannah Arendt in her coverage of the trial of Adolph Eichmann. *Eichmann in Jerusalem: A Report on the Banality of Evil* (London: Faber & Faber, 1963). Similarly, Judith Shklar argues that the legalistic paradigm is ill suited to explaining the social forces and psychological dimensions that characterize mass violence. Judith Shklar, *Legalism: Law, Morals, and Political Trials* (Cambridge, MA: Harvard University Press, 1986).

[20] Martha Minow contends that the biggest setback for truth-seeking is that trials focus on a few individuals and do not account for the "complex connections among people that make massacres and genocides possible." Martha Minow, *Between Vengeance and*

process through which political representatives accommodate past events into new, mutually acceptable narratives.[21] Narratives do not need to be in full alignment, but they should establish parameters which can incorporate all narratives. Carlos Sluzki argues that reconciliation requires a shift of narratives from victimization to progress and empowerment.[22]

Recent empirical literature has produced some evidence to link collective memory and reconciliation. In South Africa, James L. Gibson finds that the TRC countered collective narratives of blame and victimization.[23] He argues that the TRC's detailed historical account – particularly its assignation of individual guilt – helped expose more nuanced understandings of the past, and so some of the TRC's most controversial findings were also its most important. For example, it showed that black-on-black violence was vicious and widespread during apartheid, and that whites were also victims. The airing of the TRC's findings shifted attitudes and created tolerance: "As facts are assembled, juxtaposed, and sifted, perceptions lose their black-and-white character, taking on more subtle and nuanced shades."[24] Recognition of common humanity acknowledges that not all members of another group committed injustices, and refrains from assigning collective guilt to subsequent generations.[25] This recognition can potentially generate remorse from offending parties, and thereby deescalate fear and hostility.

A second variant of transformative reconciliation looks at transitional justice mechanisms, especially truth commissions, as providing a forum for dialogue. Amy Gutmann and Dennis Thompson criticize the understanding of reconciliation as shared truth, maintaining that it negates the values of pluralism and dissent.[26] Deliberative democracy is based on principles of recognition and respect, as well as communication through reason: "In a democracy, leaders should give reasons for their decisions, and respond to the reasons that citizens give in return."[27] Reasons appeal to principles, which other individuals, based on principles of fairness and

Forgiveness: Facing History after Genocide and Mass Violence (Boston, MA: Beacon Press, 2000), p. 47.

21 Ibid., p. 96.

22 Carlos Sluzki, "The Process towards Reconciliation," in *Imagine Coexistence: Restoring Humanity after Violent Ethnic Conflict*, ed. Antonia Chayes and Martha Minow (Cambridge, MA: Jossey-Bass, 2003).

23 James L. Gibson, *Overcoming Apartheid: Can Truth Heal a Divided Nation* (New York, NY: Russell Sage Foundation, 2004).

24 Ibid, p. 76.

25 Louis Kriesberg, "Reconciliation: Aspects, Growth, Sequences," *International Journal of Peace Studies* 12 (2007), p. 5.

26 Ibid.

27 Amy Gutmann and Dennis Thompson, *Why Deliberative Democracy?* (Princeton, NJ: Princeton University Press, 2004), p. 3.

rationality, will not reasonably reject, and which are acceptable to all citizens. Participants do not argue for "argument's sake" or "truth's own sake" but to influence government decisions or affect future decision-making.[28] Truth commissions serve as microcosms of democratic deliberation, contributing to democracy as a pathway to politics, and normatively through "example" by incorporating pluralistic and representative staffing and procedures and principles of mutual respect.[29] Dialogue leads to "points of conversion" and compromise, and fosters tolerance and cultivated reciprocity.[30] Following this logic, while the South African TRC did not lead to a common narrative of the past, dialogue through truth-seeking can bring certain baseline values to the surface – in this case, that apartheid and the institutions that perpetuated it were wrong.

Deliberative democracy is closer to procedural reconciliation in that it allows for disagreement and rejects the necessity of a shared understanding of truth. Yet, like other variants of transformative reconciliation, it seeks to alter viewpoints and relationships through the *direct* engagement of stakeholders.[31] In transformative reconciliation, truth-seeking leads to reconciliation to the extent that it fosters dialogue and leads to a convergence of viewpoints and transitional justice mechanisms directly engage affected populations.

Shortcomings of Transformative Reconciliation

Given its wide-reaching objectives, in practice, transformative reconciliation has been problematic, particularly when tied to formal justice. One significant challenge is the emphasis of transformative reconciliation on cognitive change. This applies particularly to more ambitious realms of psychological transformation, such as contrition and forgiveness. Transformative reconciliation frequently conceives of forgiveness as both a driver and a positive outcome of reconciliation.

[28] Ibid., p. 5.

[29] Amy Gutmann and Dennis Thompson, "The Moral Foundations of Truth Commissions," in *Truth v. Justice: The Morality of Truth Commissions*, ed. Robert R. Rotberg and Dennis Thompson (Princeton, NJ: Princeton University Press, 2000), pp. 22–23.

[30] Ibid., p. 38.

[31] While Gutmann and Thompson argue that reconciliation should not demand individual psychological transformation, they also cede that victim participation will require significant preexisting public commitment (p. 35). For a discussion of democratic deliberation and truth commissions, see Rosemary Nagy, "Reconciliation in Post-Commission South Africa: Thick and Thin Accounts of Solidarity," *Canadian Journal of Political Science* 35, no. 2 (2002), pp. 323–346.

The relationship between forgiveness and reconciliation is a thorny subject. On the one hand, both on the individual and societal levels, forgiveness appeals as a force for healing and liberation. For Hannah Arendt, forgiveness represents the highest form of human freedom and agency.[32] It stands in contrast to revenge – the "natural, automatic reaction to transgression and which because of the irreversibility of the action process can be expected and even calculated." Forgiveness can never be predicted; "It is the only reaction that acts in an unexpected way and thus retains, though being a reaction, something of the original character of action."[33] Forgiveness is the opposite of vengeance, transmitting power to act "anew and unexpectedly, unconditioned by the act which provoked it."[34] When freely chosen, forgiveness becomes a form of autonomy – a sense of self not defined by victimization or the actions of others. Arendt identifies punishment as the alternative, but not the opposite, of forgiveness: "Both have in common that they attempt to put an end to something that without interference could go on endlessly."[35] The choice to forgive allows victims to take a moral high ground and distance themselves from perpetrators of violence, which links forgiveness to autonomy – a sense of self not defined by victimization or the actions of others.[36]

From a restorative justice perspective, as well, forgiveness is important for its emancipatory potential, with an impulse toward reconciliation already internal to individuals. From a communitarian standpoint, Desmond Tutu maintains that forgiveness is how a person becomes "whole" again. Membership in a community defines individuals; a fragmented society of atomized hurting individuals "dehumanizes" all and leaves each individual worse off.[37] Jeffrie Murphy and Jean Hampton argue that forgiveness already resonates as a norm for many people. For them, it reflects an "innate desire" to live in a "world where forgiveness is regarded as a healing and restoring value."[38] The ability to forgive

[32] Hannah Arendt, *The Human Condition* (Chicago: Chicago University Press, 1998); see also Rosemary Lerner Rizo Patron, "Between Conflict and Reconciliation: The Hard Truth," *Human Studies* (2007). Although forgiveness is closely tied to reconciliation, national reconciliation as conceived in this chapter is distinct from forgiveness.

[33] Arendt, *The Human Condition*, pp. 240–241. See also Jean Bethke Elshtain, "Politics and Forgiveness," in *Burying the Past: Making Peace and Doing Justice after Civil War*, ed. Nigal Biggar (Washington, DC: Georgetown University Press, 2001), pp. 45–64; Schaap, *Political Reconciliation*; Lederach and Appleby, "An Ethic of Reconciliation"; and Patron, "Between Conflict and Reconciliation."

[34] Arendt, *The Human Condition*, p. 241. [35] Ibid.

[36] Elshtain, *Politics and Forgiveness*; Schaap, *Political Reconciliation*; Lederach and Appleby, "An Ethic of Reconciliation," p. 24.

[37] Desmond Tutu, *No Future without Forgiveness* (Houghton, South Africa: Random House, 1999), p. 35.

[38] Jeffrie G. Murphy and Jean Hampton, *Forgiveness and Mercy* (Cambridge: Cambridge University Press, 1988).

changes the individual's relations to her surroundings, reinforcing an outlook characterized by agency and strength, rather than despair.

On the other hand, there are serious concerns with regard to institutionalizing an ethic of forgiveness. Many have noted the theological roots underpinning the theory and practice of reconciliation and forgiveness, particularly in Christianity, where it ties into wider themes of redemption and contrition.[39] The specific religious foundations of ideas of reconciliation thus raise immediate concerns about their export and application elsewhere. Yet even where reconciliation and forgiveness do resonate, institutionalizing a process to encourage forgiveness or officially sanctioning forgiveness risks undermining its value to the individual. In *The Sunflower*, Simon Wiesenthal reminisces about his experience with a dying Nazi soldier, Karl Seidl.[40] Wiesenthal refuses Seidl's request for forgiveness for a crime he committed a year earlier – his participation in the burning of a house containing Jewish families. However, he later grapples with the decision with a range of academics, theologians, activists, and survivors. While some argued in favor of forgiveness, most were adamant that Wiesenthal should not offer forgiveness on behalf of victims who never had a chance to speak, since Seidl did not directly harm his confidant.

The granting of or even encouraging of forgiveness on behalf of others continues to be a thorny issue for transformative reconciliation. Andrew Schaap warns that leaders should neither encourage nor officially condone a process of political forgiveness that officially forgives perpetrators of violence.[41] Political forgiveness "bargains away" victims' freedom and takes away their dignity and choice in how to respond to the violation.[42]

In this vein, a shortcoming of the South African TRC is that the Commission – while not obliging victims to forgive – actively promoted a discourse of forgiveness, embedding forgiveness in communitarian and moral–religious frameworks.[43] Jacques Derrida takes up this criticism in his discussion of forgiveness and cosmopolitanism: "Forgiveness must engage two singularities ... the guilty and the victim. As soon as a third

[39] For a discussion on Judeo-Christian roots of reconciliation, see Gearoid Millar, "Between Western Theory and Local Practice: Cultural Impediments to Truth-Telling in Sierra Leone," *Conflict Resolution Quarterly* 29, no. 2 (2011), p. 183.

[40] Simon Wiesenthal, *The Sunflower: On the Possibility and Limits of Forgiveness* (New York, NY: Schocken Books, 1998).

[41] Schaap, *Political Reconciliation*. [42] Ibid., p. 187.

[43] For example, Wilson, *The Politics of Truth and Reconciliation in South Africa*, pp. 119–121. Paul E. Digeser argues that an ethic of forgiveness is illiberal in the public sphere, where individuals do not share the emotional bond to others. In addition, a liberal society learns to accommodate unresolved conflicts into the social framework.

party intervenes, one can speak of amnesty, reconciliation, reparation, but certainly not of forgiveness in the strict sense."[44]

A second problem is that transformative reconciliation necessitates direct interaction and engagement. Along this vein, truth commissions, for instance, are effective to the extent that they alter the perceptions of direct participants or of the broader audiences following their work. These assumptions have been particularly hard to bear out in practice. Even in the South African setting, which actively promoted "social" or "dialogue truth,"[45] victims and perpetrators often did not show up at the same hearings or participated only indirectly (as in the case of amnesty hearings).[46] How truth commissions should bring about deliberation and a convergence of viewpoints is also unclear. Empirical studies of South Africa frequently note the defensive reactions of South Africans of different backgrounds to the TRC,[47] the tendency of hearings to attract a small, self-selective audience (usually black South Africans), and the indifference and/or defensive reactions of large segments of the population. In a rich personal account, South African journalist Antjie Krog describes the barriers of communicating meaningful testimony across racial groups, finding that black victims often misinterpreted testimony of perpetrators at hearings. She cites her own struggles as a white Afrikaner to sometimes understand the cultural codes and expressions of blacks.[48]

In the rest of the chapter, I will now elaborate a conception of procedural reconciliation. While components of procedural reconciliation have appeared in scattered empirical and normative scholarship and the mandates of transitional justice institutions, empirical research on reconciliation has less systematically sought to examine procedural

[44] Jacques Derrida, *On Cosmopolitanism and Forgiveness: Thinking in Action* (London: Routledge, 2001), p. 42.

[45] The TRC entrenched this understanding into its conception of "social" or "dialogue" truth. According to Constitutional Court Judge Albie Sachs, who is credited with adding social truth to the TRC's mandate, the main strength of the TRC is that it was based "on hearing all different viewpoints, on receiving inputs from all sides." The purpose of social truth was to transcend "divisions of the past by listening carefully to the complex motives and perspectives of all those involved," providing a facilitative environment where all possible views could be "considered and weighed," subjecting the TRC to "public scrutiny and critique" through open hearings and the media, and inviting "people from all walks of life" to participate. The South African TRC Report. See also Sachs' own account in *Healing of a Nation*, ed. Alex Boraine and Janet Levy (Cape Town: Justice in Transition, 1995).

[46] Wilson, *The Politics of Truth and Reconciliation*, p. 154; Claire Moon, *Narrating Political Reconciliation: South Africa's Truth and Reconciliation Commission* (Lanham, MD: Lexington Books, 2008).

[47] Brandon Hamber and G. Thiessen, "A State of Denial: White South Africa's Attitudes to the Truth and Reconciliation Commission," *Indicator South Africa* 15 (1998), pp. 8–12.

[48] Antjie Krog, *Country of My Skull* (London: Vintage Books, 1999), pp. 354–355. See also Nagy, "Thick and Thin."

reconciliation. Although procedural reconciliation resonates with broader practical and philosophical traditions in transitional justice, particularly restorative justice, transitional justice scholars have often focused narrowly on particular aspects of these schools.

Procedural Reconciliation

Procedural reconciliation is a consequence to a commitment to and acceptance of a common process and procedure, whose form and nature may vary across time and place. Its defining features include its emphasis on agency and pragmatism, its generalized societal focus, and its open-ended nature.

Procedural Reconciliation as Agency-Based and Pragmatic

First, procedural reconciliation is pragmatic in orientation and agency-based. While the theological and psychological roots of the reconciliation literature have generated criticism,[49] there are valuable – and often overlooked – reflections in early accounts, particularly with regard to the drivers of reconciliation. Mennonite scholar-practitioner John Paul Lederach argues that reconciliation provides a place for "truth and mercy to meet, where concerns for exposing what has happened and for letting go in favor of renewed relationship are validated and embraced."[50] Drawing on political theory and theology, Daniel Philpott associates reconciliation with an ethic of "mercy."[51] Reconciliation is the willingness to see an individual as more than or separate from his/her actions: a rehumanizing process. It does not mean that the victim forgets the harm done, but that he or she accepts the perpetrator as a citizen in good standing and "wills new relationships" for the sake of a common future.[52] Philpott continues this theme in his subsequent work, identifying mercy as the central ethic driving political reconciliation.[53]

Agency is an important theme in procedural reconciliation. However, procedural reconciliation is distinct from and independent of forgiveness. Unlike forgiveness and contrition, which require internal psychological transformation and are oriented toward the past, procedural reconciliation

[49] See, in particular, Millar, "Between Western Theory and Local Practice" and "Ah Lef Ma Case fo God."

[50] John Paul Lederach, *Building Peace: Sustainable Reconciliation in Divided Societies* (Washington, DC: US Institute of Peace, 1997).

[51] Daniel Philpott, "Reconciliation: An Ethic for Peace-building," in *Strategies of Peace*, ed. Daniel Philpott and Gerard Powers (Oxford: Oxford University Press, 2010), p. 9.

[52] Ibid., p. 24.

[53] Daniel Philpott, *Just and Unjust Wars: An Ethic of Political Reconciliation* (Oxford: Oxford University Press, 2012).

is future-oriented. As I set out in the empirical chapters, procedural reconciliation can occur with or without forgiveness, making it psychologically possible even where forgiveness is not.[54] Belfast-based conflict practitioner David Bloomfield cites his interview with a British activist working at an NGO dedicated to British–Irish reconciliation whose eleven-year-old son was killed by an IRA bomb: "I will never forgive the people who killed my son, but I am completely committed to the process of reconciliation."[55] Individuals have agency – they can choose to commit themselves to reconciliation as a valuable individual or societal end, irrespective of forgiveness.

Procedural Reconciliation as a Generalized Societal Process

A second characteristic of procedural reconciliation is its societal focus. Much of the theory and practice of transitional justice – as well as (critical variants of) peace-building – have focused on the micro level. This is particularly manifest in empirical research on reconciliation, which has tended to engage less with the political dimensions of protracted violence. This is especially pronounced among critically oriented scholars, who have often taken issue with the top-down institution-building approach advocated by liberal peace-building.[56] This generally ethnographic literature has offered a valuable critique of liberal peace-building for its prioritization of finite objectives, such as security and state-building, over longer-term economic redistribution and community emancipation and empowerment. It has also advanced an important normative orientation in favor of "everyday" grassroots and victim-centered processes.

My concern is that there is a risk of depoliticizing the broader political effects of violence. The tendency to view state- and nation-building processes with suspicion as instruments of political legitimization has

[54] Susan Dwyer, "Reconciliation for Realists," *Ethics and International Affairs* 13, no. 1 (1999) p. 106. Villa-Vicencio, "Reconciliation," p. 8; Joanna Quinn, "What is Reconciliation?" in *Reconciliation(s): Transitional Justice in Postconflict Societies*, ed. Joanna Quinn (Montreal and Kingston: McGill-Queen's University Press, 2009), pp. 182–183; David Bloomfield, "On Good Terms," *Berghof Report* 14 (Berlin: Berghof Research Center for Constructive Conflict Management, October 2006), p. 24; Dwyer, "Reconciliation for Realists"; Kriesberg, "Coexistence and the Reconciliation of Communal Conflicts"; Kriesberg, "Reconciliation," p. 5.

[55] Bloomfield, "On Good Terms," p. 25.

[56] There has been a tendency for more critically oriented peace-building scholars to dichotomize approaches to transitional justice and peace-building, contrasting between international versus local, formal versus informal, and political versus social/communal. Oliver P. Richmond, "A Post-Liberal Peace: Eirenism and the Everyday," *Review of International Studies* 35 (2009). See also Mac Ginty, "Gilding the Lily?" and "Hybrid Peace: The Interaction between Top-down and Bottom-up Peace," *Security Dialogue* 4 (2010). See also Wendy Lambourne's conception of transformative justice. "Transitional Justice and Peace-building."

further augmented wariness among critical scholars of the political components of peace-building. In practice, the political and social imperatives of peace-building and transitional justice are both crucial and reinforce one another. Peace entails the repair of ruptured social fabric and relationships, as much as political and economic infrastructure and frameworks.[57] In protracted conflicts, violence at the hands of state actors erodes personal security and trust in political institutions and undermines personal dignity and civic recognition.[58] Although less visible, the legacies of political violence leave deep and ongoing social and political damage on political participation and social structures. Prolonged violence erodes the foundations of collective life, resulting in "diminished agency" – a mistrust and suspicion of authority and fatalism about collective action.[59] Trust at the micro and macro levels are linked and feed off each other. Whereas state violence erodes trust in institutions and generates conditions of insecurity, as Joanna Quinn argues, interpersonal trust sets "the foundations of democratic participation, the strengthening of civic institutions, and the reestablishment of social relations."[60]

Significantly, procedural reconciliation addresses broader understanding of indirect and long-term harm. Where much of the theory and practice of restorative justice seeks to repair interpersonal relationships and community bonds at the micro level, procedural reconciliation, as I define it, focuses on generalized social and political repair. In addition to the wounds inflicted upon direct victims, it recognizes the harm to victims' family members and wider community caused by prolonged violence. Daniel Philpott distinguishes between primary and ongoing secondary wounds: "Primary wounds are unprompted by prior injustices and the memories that they leave. Primary wounds, in contrast, cause secondary wounds, through a chain of events involving memories, emotions, and judgments, culminating in further acts of injustice."[61] While

[57] As Daniel Philpott notes, normative understandings of conflict transformation are already implicit objectives in transitional justice procedures and mandates. *Just and Unjust Wars*, pp. 23–24.

[58] Rami Mani, *Beyond Retribution: Seeking Justice in the Shadows of War* (Cambridge and Maldon, MA: Polity Press, 2007), p. 5.

[59] Pablo de Greiff, "Articulating the Links between Transitional Justice and Development: Justice and Social Integration," in *Transitional Justice and Development: Making Connections*, ed. Pablo de Greiff and Roger Duthie (New York, NY: Social Science Research Council, 2009), pp. 28–75.

[60] Quinn, "What is Reconciliation?" p. 181.

[61] Primary wounds include violation of victims' human rights, harms to the victim's person, victim's ignorance of the source and circumstances of political injustices, lack of acknowledgment of the victim's suffering, the standing victory of the wrongdoers' political injustice, and harm to the person of the wrongdoer. Daniel Philpott, *Just and Unjust Peace: An Ethic of Political Reconciliation* (Oxford: Oxford University Press, 2012), pp. 33–41.

both diminish human flourishing, primary wounds perpetuate secondary wounds.[62] The less visible and more indirect effects of chronic violence on individual and communal political agency and social relations are particularly pervasive legacies of protracted violence.[63] How grievances and memories are exacerbated and passed down in securitized contexts with little public space for grieving and memorialization is particularly important.[64]

While ethnographically oriented scholars have emphasized the pragmatic drivers of reconciliation, much of this empirical research has taken a micro-level focus. A rich ethnographic literature has examined processes through which individuals and communities negotiate the parameters of civilian life.[65] Importantly, this scholarship has examined individuals' and communities' definitions in their own terms – for example, communities' nuanced differentiation between forgiveness and coexistence in Ayacucho,[66] and ex-combatants' integration as a "cooling of hearts" in Sierra Leone.[67]

[62] Ibid.

[63] Daya Somasundaram offers an excellent psychosocial account of collective trauma. *Scarred Communities. Psychosocial Impact of Man-Made and Natural Disasters on Sri Lanka Society* (New Delhi: Sage, 2014).

[64] Maja Zehfus, *Wounds of Memory: The Politics of War in Germany* (Cambridge: Cambridge University Press, 2011). While less prevalent in scholarship on reconciliation, a wide interdisciplinary literature has examined the relationship of public and private memory and trauma. See Paul Fussell, *The Great War and Modern Memory* (Oxford: Oxford University Press, 2000); Jay Winter, *Sites of Memory, Sites of Mourning: The Great War in European Cultural History* (Cambridge: Cambridge University Press, 1998); Paul Connerton, *How Societies Remember* (Cambridge: Cambridge University Press, 1989); Marianne Hirsch, "The Generation of Postmemory," *Poetics Today* 29, no. 1 (2008), pp. 29–54; and Harald Welzer, "Collateral Damage of History Education: National Socialism and the Holocaust in German Family Memory," *Social Research* 75, no. 1 (Spring 2008), pp. 287–314.

[65] Erin Baines, "The Haunting of Alice: Local Approaches to Justice and Reconciliation in Northern Uganda," *International Journal of Transitional Justice* 1, no. 1 (2007), pp. 91–114; Shaw, 2005 and 2010; Kimberly Susan Theidon, "Justice in Transition: The Micropolitics of Reconciliation in Post-war Peru," *The Journal of Conflict Resolution* 50 (2006), pp. 433–457; Kimberly Theidon, *Intimate Enemies: Violence and Reconciliation in Peru* (Philadelphia: University of Pennsylvania Press, 2012); Rosalind Shaw, "Linking Justice with Reintegration? Excombatants and the Sierra Leone Experiment," in *Localizing Transitional Justice: Interventions and Priorities after Mass Violence*, ed. Rosalind Shaw and Lars Waldorf (Stanford, CA: Stanford University Press, 2010). My interviewees frequently distinguished "genuine reconciliation" from "forced coexistence."

[66] Theidon, *Intimate Enemies*, pp. 362–365; see also Theidon, "Justice in Transition"; Renzo Salvador Aroni Sulca, "Aprendimos a convivir con los senderistas y militares: violencia política y respuesta campesina en Huamanquiquia, 1980–1993" (We Learned to Live with the Shining Path and Soldiers: Political Violence and the Peasant Response in Huamanquiquia, 1980–1993), *Investigaciones Sociales* 10, no. 17 (2006): pp. 261–284.

[67] Rosalind Shaw, "Rethinking TRCs: Lessons from Sierra Leone," *Special Report* (USIP Press, 2005); Kieran Mitton, "A Pragmatic Pact: Reconciliation and Reintegration in Sierra Leone," in *Evaluating Transitional Justice: Accountability and Peace-building in*

While the qualitative literature's micro-level focus may reflect the disciplinary and ethnographic orientation of scholars researching reconciliation (particularly those carrying out anthropological work), scholars from other disciplines have also looked at individual viewpoints in relation to reconciliation. Phil Clark distinguishes "broader, systemic, society-wide peace-building aims of ending violence and safeguarding against future conflict" from reconciliation's "deeper, inter-personal relationship-focused processes," cautioning that reconciliation requires peace, which is both positive and negative.[68] Similarly, for Leigh Payne, reconciliation, or recognition of common "humanity" between perpetrators and victims, is a deeper transformative experience and distinct from more pragmatic democratic coexistence.[69]

Although individuals are ultimately the stakeholders of reconciliation, procedural reconciliation focuses explicitly on the societal level.[70] Procedural reconciliation also is distinct from coexistence in that coexistence, as defined here, is an outcome (a minimal state of relations between antagonistic parties) while reconciliation is a process to facilitate coexistence.[71] Reconciliation is an active process of engagement, which requires agency. Even if tense and limited, procedural reconciliation is a type of reconciliation in so far as parties implicitly or explicitly channel disagreements through nonviolent processes. In contrast to intimate micro-reconciliation, described above, which requires internal healing and the active restoration of bonds between aggrieved parties, procedural reconciliation is often pragmatic and generalized. Procedural reconciliation takes place between individuals who do not know each other, and at the political/institutional level through the construction of new relationships between society and state.

Post-Conflict Sierra Leone, ed. Kirsten Ainley, Rebekka Friedman, and Christopher Mahony (Basingstoke: Palgrave Macmillan, 2015), pp. 217–240.

68 Phil Clark, *The Gacaca Courts and Post-Genocide Justice and Reconciliation in Rwanda: Justice without Lawyers* (Cambridge: Cambridge University Press, 2010), p. 45.

69 Leigh Payne, *Unsettling Accounts: Neither Truth Nor Reconciliation in Confessions of State Violence* (Durham and London: Duke University Press, 2008), p. 138.

70 As I argued in Chapter 2, to some extent my focus on the macro level also reflects recent transitional justice practices, particularly truth commissions, which in some cases have moved from emphasizing micro-reconciliation – the theological, psychological, and spiritual processes, through which individuals deal with their pasts and/or each other – toward political reconciliation based on constitutional democracy, human rights, the rule of law, and justice. Paul Gready, *The Era of Transitional Justice: The Aftermath of the Truth and Reconciliation Commission in South Africa and Beyond* (New York, NY: Routledge, 2011).

71 My interviewees in Peru and Sierra Leone also often raised the distinction between coexistence as an end state ("cool relations") versus reconciliation as an active process.

Procedural Reconciliation as Open Ended

Third, procedural reconciliation is possible amid conflict and contestation and does not direct contact and deliberation or even shared agreement on the past. It embraces varying interpretations and identifications. Individuals and groups may have multiple and even competing narratives. Instead, procedural reconciliation seeks a generalized baseline commitment to discursive pluralism – a tolerance for diverse and often antagonistic narratives. Procedural reconciliation is an ongoing process. Transitional justice mechanisms may not generate moral introspection or agreement over the past, but they can increase solidarity and awareness by encouraging civic participation and putting historical memory into the public sphere. Rather, a reconciled society provides space for competing and often tense and irreconcilable narratives and identities.[72] Claire Moon argues that reconciliation includes narratives that are not reconciled, not forgiving, and that often call for punishment.[73] These narratives should generate critiques, including critiques of reconciliation processes.[74]

Normative Foundations of Procedural Reconciliation

While these characteristics distinguish procedural from transformative reconciliation, it is important to survey some of the normative underpinnings of procedural reconciliation. Long-standing traditions in criminology, such as restorative justice, embody rationales from both transformative and procedural reconciliation. I argue that more attention to normative underpinnings of procedural reconciliation is important to recognize the wider potential impact and functions of transitional justice practices. The mandates of transitional justice institutions and normative theory often implicitly contain elements of procedural reconciliation, yet they have less rigorously and explicitly theorized these. In the rest of this chapter, I outline a conception of procedural reconciliation that advances streams of restorative justice and normative and discursive spillover.

Restorative Justice

Restorative justice is a normative theory of social repair that seeks to directly involve stakeholders and affected communities within justice proceedings. Tony Marshall defines restorative justice as "a process

[72] Schaap, *Political Reconciliation*, pp. 9–25.

[73] Claire Moon, "Prelapsarian State: Forgiveness and Reconciliation in Transitional Justice," *International Journal for Semiotics of Law*, 17 (2004), pp. 184–197.

[74] Adrian Little, "Disjunctured Narratives: Rethinking Reconciliation and Conflict Transformation," *International Political Science Review* 33 (2012), p. 86.

whereby all the parties with a stake in a particular offense come together to resolve collectively how to deal with the aftermath of the offense and its implications for the future."[75] While restorative justice is rooted in the historical practices of many societies, contemporary restorative justice emerged within a specific historical context. In the 1990s, restorative justice movements appeared in North America and Europe as a result of a growing dissatisfaction with rehabilitation and punishment programs. For an increasing number of criminologists, mainstream justice mechanisms were offender-centric and insufficiently involved victims.[76] Feminists, focusing often on sexual violence, argued that justice mechanisms should shift focus away from perpetrators and toward victims and an understanding of harm. After a series of initiatives to study restorative justice in indigenous communities, over the last three decades restorative approaches began to appear in many Western countries. In North America, restorative approaches were frequently applied to juvenile crimes. For Philpott, restorative justice, despite its long pedigree in numerous world cultures, is a recognizable school – a "global network of people who hold common ideas about justice and who carry on disputes about these ideas."[77] Inspirations for the contemporary restorative justice movement include *Ubuntu* in sub-Saharan Africa, practices of North American tribes, the Maori in New Zealand, and Christian theology, especially the Mennonite tradition.[78]

Restorative justice has only recently been applied to nation-states, through the development of the South African TRC. In traditional settings, restorative justice was commonly practiced at the community level as a form of conflict resolution, usually for lesser offenses such as adultery or theft, and especially for youth transgressors. Since the 1970s, in Western societies, victim–offender reconciliation processes have brought together victims and offenders with a mediator to find a restitution agreement as an alternative to sentencing after the offender's conviction.[79] Criminal courts have also started to acknowledge and offer restorative procedures as alternatives to prosecutions.[80]

[75] Tony F. Marshall, "The Evolution of Restorative Justice in Britain," *European Journal of Criminal Policy and Research* 4 (1996), p. 37, cited in John Braithwaite, "Restorative Justice: Assessing Optimistic and Pessimistic Accounts," *Crime and Justice* 25 (1999), p. 5. Restorative justice practices have been found in many cultures in world history. John Braithwaite includes ancient Arab, Greek, Roman, Indian Hindu, Buddhist, Taoist, and Confucian cultures. Braithwaite, "Restorative Justice," p. 3.

[76] Ibid. [77] Philpott, *Just and Unjust Peace*, pp. 64–65. [78] Ibid.

[79] As Philpott notes, expanded practices of restorative justice conferences, including family and friends of the victim and offender, have also begun to appear in Western contexts. Philpott, *Just and Unjust Peace*, p. 65.

[80] Ibid.

In the broader study of criminology, its community-building and participatory character distinguishes restorative justice. While theorists and practitioners often present restorative justice as an alternative to – or reform of – retributive justice, theorists of restorative justice tend to conceive of it as a "hybrid" of retributive and rehabilitative justice.[81] Like rehabilitative justice, restorative justice seeks to reintegrate perpetrators and deter future crimes. Like retributive justice, it sanctions individual behavior and establishes appropriate punishment. Instead, restorative justice is distinguished by its goal to democratize punishment by making it more consensual and participatory.[82]

Although varied and flexible, restorative practices commonly emphasize repair. More specifically, they seek to advance two types of restoration: restoring victims and their communities to their position before the harm and restoring the perpetrator to society as a rights-abiding citizen. In this vein, some argue that restorative justice is more victim-centered than retributive justice. In mainstream criminal justice, victims only serve as witnesses in proceedings. They have no chance to speak with offenders and develop a deeper understanding of their motivations.[83] Martha Minow maintains that trials give victims a chance to speak only to determine the defendant's guilt: "Trials interrupt and truncate victim testimony with direct and cross-examination and conceptions of relevance framed by the elements of the charges. Judges and juries listen to victims with skepticism tied to the presumption of the defendants' innocence."[84] In restorative proceedings, in contrast, victims can face the perpetrator and voice their position. They may also question the perpetrator's motivations and rationales.

Second, restorative justice seeks communal repair by reintegrating and rehabilitating the perpetrator. Proponents argue that restorative justice is more future-oriented, because it gives perpetrators a chance to acknowledge their guilt.[85] While retributive justice does not require perpetrators to admit wrongdoing, restorative justice aims to publicly shame the perpetrator into recognizing the wrongfulness of his or her acts. John

[81] Albert Dzur, "Restorative Justice and Civic Accountability for Punishment," *Polity* 36 (2003), p. 6.
[82] Ibid. [83] Ibid., p. 14. [84] Minow, *Between Vengeance and Forgiveness*, p. 238.
[85] Since theories of both restorative justice and retributive justice often claim to seek reconciliation as an end goal, Miriam Aukerman provides the following distinction: "While retributive accountability involves proportional punishment, restorative accountability demands an acknowledgement by offenders of their culpability and willingness to make good. While retributive justice allows society to punish an offender as a means of achieving reconciliation, restorative justice requires society to include the offender in the process of reconciliation." Miriam Aukerman, "Extraordinary Evil, Ordinary Crimes: A Framework for Understanding Transitional Justice," *Harvard Human Rights Journal* 15 (2000), p. 20.

Braithwaite argues that communities need to shame individuals in reintegrative ways, demonstrating respect and a willingness to listen to their testimony while simultaneously condemning their deeds.[86]

Restorative justice embodies both transformative and procedural dimensions of reconciliation. Restorative justice seeks to facilitate internal processes of contrition and forgiveness and to repair broken relationships. Yet, it also goes beyond the aggrieved parties, aiming to generate communal solidarity and cohesion. Although restorative justice has traditionally focused on more intimate micro-relations between individuals who know each other, the latter process-oriented components of restorative justice become relevant to procedural reconciliation.

Integration and Spillover

Integration and spillover theory is another inroad to procedural reconciliation. Integration theory provides an important angle for transitional justice, particularly in light of recent critiques from critical peace-building. Critical scholars on truth commissions and formal justice have often focused on the normative roots of truth-telling in modern European civic nation-building processes. Tim Kelsall argues that truth commissions' main roots lie in Western modernity: "The practice of confession, it should be remembered, has been an outstanding cultural node in the historical experience of the West ... The drama of healing through public confession and grief ... enlists a number of tropes in the Christian imaginary, such as suffering, martyrdom, and resurrection ... explains in part the widespread fascination with truth commissions."[87] Rosalind Shaw links truth-telling to broader North American and European nation-building practices: the "product of a culture of memory that arose from specific historical processes in North America and Europe."[88] In her view, the concept of healing a "wounded or traumatized" nation rests on a "nation-building rhetoric that anthropomorphizes the nation as a feeling, suffering entity," derived from Durkheimean "nineteenth century models of society as akin to an organism that can be healthy or sick."[89]

[86] John Braithwaite argues that over-punishment can actually hinder the goal of developing a just society, as it undermines the social cohesion on which legal institutions depend. *Crime, Shame, and Reintegration* (Cambridge, UK: Cambridge University Press, 1989).

[87] Kelsall, "Truth, Lies, Ritual," p. 383. Citing Foucault's *The History of Sexuality*, he further flags the influences of Catholicism, psychotherapy and psychoanalysis, and even mass appeal TV talk shows, in which "ordinary people confess extraordinary intimate details of their lives to public audiences."

[88] Shaw, "Rethinking Truth and Reconciliation Commissions," p. 7.

[89] Ibid. Similarly, Millar locates TRCs in a broader Western reconciliation literature rooted in trauma psychotherapy, where talking is meant to bring about healing, and in Christian theology. Chris Coulter locates truth-telling in a belief "within that diffuse entity we call

These criticisms raise important concerns about the global export of transitional justice. Yet while the resonance of truth commissions to Western nationalist narratives and practices may explain international interest in truth-seeking processes, it is also important to recognize truth commissions in their novelty and as a departure from Western experiences. Here, it is equally plausible that Western interest in transitional justice, and truth commissions in particular, reflects a lack of comparable historical experience. The novelty of truth commissions arises precisely out of a tendency for what scholars of nationalism have long identified as historical amnesia in Western nation-building trajectories.[90]

If anything, I would venture that fear of historical amnesia and unaddressed legacies holds significant weight in explaining the ideological appeal of truth commissions and historical commemoration. Following the trauma of two world wars in Europe, practice-oriented political philosophers, many of whom were activists in their own societies, became vocal critics of the lack of critical and open interrogation of the past.

The conscientious use of historical study and debate to promote change is less conventional in political philosophy and is found in scattered and teleological political thought. Some of this literature arose in Germany after World War II. Responding to the Allied "You Are Guilty" placards placed around occupied Germany, Karl Jaspers objects to the external collective assignation of guilt.[91] At the same time, he warns that criminal prosecutions and reparations do not exonerate the German population at large. Individuals still maintain their status as autonomous agents. They are connected in ways that are not immediately apparent and bear moral responsibility even for their inactions.[92] While only individuals themselves can determine their own moral guilt, national dialogue can facilitate introspection and show the indirect ways in which individuals are connected and responsible. According to Jaspers, personal and public moralities become linked through critical reflection. Sympathetic

the international humanitarian community that testifying about violence and humiliation, talking about what happened to them during the war, would be cathartic and healing for people." Coulter, *Bush Wives and Girl Soldiers*, p. 179.

[90] Ernest Renan, "What is a Nation?" (1882) in *Becoming National: A Reader*, ed. Geoff Eley and Ronald Grigor Suny (New York and Oxford: Oxford University Press, 1996), pp. 41–55. See also Benedict Anderson, who argues that "all profound changes in consciousness, by their very nature, bring with them characteristic amnesias. Out of such oblivions, in specific historical circumstances, spring narratives." *Imagined Communities: Reflections on the Origin and Spread of Nationalism* (London: Verso, 1977), p. 204.

[91] Karl Jaspers, *The Question of German Guilt* (New York, NY: Dial Press, 1948), pp. 40–42.

[92] Ibid., pp. 63–64.

identification and communication enable the assumption of deeper responsibility and transform the collective consciousness.[93]

Particular understandings of harm implicitly accompany and underpin normative understandings of reconciliation and historical rectification. The emphasis on social learning underpins an understanding of conflict and mass violence in which individuals are able to commit atrocities through the abdication of personal responsibility and agency during times of social breakdown. Gesine Schwan attributes German participation in the Holocaust to "the readiness with which so many people gave up their moral responsibilities in favor of simply obeying orders, or conforming with everyone else."[94] She stresses the loss of previously held political values and of social solidarity, calling for a process of truth-telling and public dialogue that will lead to acknowledgment of responsibility and the reconstruction of shared democratic values.[95]

Purposeful attempts at integration are also found within functionalist and neofunctionalist traditions in International Relations on regional European integration. For neofunctionalists, states would initially integrate in limited economic or functional areas.[96] Over time, they hoped that this limited cooperation would spill over into other spheres and deepen ties between partnering states. Political spillover, in turn, would lead to the creation of supra-governance institutions, ranging from the European Union to voluntary organizations, such as the United Nations.

What emerges in these purposeful accounts is a deep-rooted desire to collectively address the past in order to foster new social and political frameworks and identifications. In the North American context, as well, interest in empiricism and critical public engagement arose in strands of critical civic humanism and gained strength in the second half of the twentieth century. Also more teleological, civic humanists stressed critical empirical historical study as a vehicle for social emancipation and a deterrent against future injustices.[97]

The emphasis on collective introspection and social learning as tools for social progress embodies an inherently constructivist understanding of society. Important early manifestations appear in the writings of critical pragmatists, calling for public dialogue and critical education as catalysts

[93] Ibid., p. 79.

[94] Gesine Schwan, "The 'Healing' Values of Truth-Telling: Chances and Social Conditions in a Secularized World," *Social Research* 65 (1998), p. 730.

[95] Ibid., 737.

[96] David Mitrany, *A Working Peace System* (Chicago: Quadrangle Books, 1966).

[97] "Sympathy," as defined by John Dewey, is both a literal concern for the direct suffering of others and a "cultivated imagination for what men have in common and a rebellion at whatever unnecessarily divides them." *How We Think* (New York and London: D.C. Heath and Company, 1933).

for change. Writing during periods of political transition and social upheaval, pragmatists were concerned with how to create tolerance and inclusion.[98] For John Dewey, neither bloodline nor nationality define a society; rather, society emerges through learned experience.[99] Pragmatists put emphasis on education and critical historical study as vehicles for social progress and solidarity: "Intelligent understanding of past history is to some extent a lever for moving the present into a certain kind of future."[100] Critical reflection and cultivated empathy help nurture new collective identifications.

Components of Procedural Reconciliation

Procedural reconciliation resonates with broad principles of restorative justice and normative and discursive spillover. Much like community-level restorative justice, it shifts justice to stakeholders by encouraging the participation of affected communities. However, at the macro level the affected community is society at large and the ruptured relationship is between society and the state. The norms that restorative justice seeks to repair (or newly foster) are political participation, a sense of collective responsibility, respect for human rights, and accountability. Procedural reconciliation is generalized, taking place between individuals who do not know each other. Although it also requires a normative reorientation, it sets out fewer demands for psychological transformation and moral introspection. Instead, it entails a gradual political and social empowerment and normative and discursive spillover. Although procedural reconciliation is open-ended, it seeks (and can be assessed according to its contribution to) two core areas: shared norms and discourses and pluralism and inclusivity.

Shared Norms and Discourses

First, procedural reconciliation is a process of generating *shared* practices and forms of engagement. It requires – and facilitates – channels, mechanisms, and processes through which groups and individuals can

[98] Ibid.

[99] John Dewey, *Democracy and Education: An Introduction to the Philosophy of Education* (New York, NY: Macmillan, 1916), pp. 5–6.

[100] John Dewey, *Experience and Education* (New York, NY: Macmillan Company, 1938), p. 12. While Richard Rorty maintains that there is no universal "human nature," he argues that "sentimental education" can enable individuals to view each other as human beings deserving of equal human rights. "Human Rights, Rationality and Sentimentality," in *On Human Rights*, ed. S. Shute and S. Hurley (New York, NY: Basic Books, 1993), pp. 112–134.

make demands and pursue politics. As a baseline, procedural reconciliation necessitates a shared commitment to common political procedures and shared values, and also requires norms against violence and impunity and a commitment to pluralism. This, of course, can take different forms. Charles refers to reconciliation as the "ability to talk."[101]

While the normative and discursive potential of transitional justice has deep roots in philosophical literature and criminology, empirical research has paid less attention to its contribution in this regard.[102] Transitional justice processes are, however, in many ways, uniquely suited to normative and discursive change. They operate during what Peruvian social scientists Rolando Ames Cobián and Félix Reátegui refer to as highly charged Weberian charismatic moments.[103] Following prolonged violence or authoritarian rule, political transitions offer particular momentum as political entrepreneurs and civil society mobilize around future objectives and visions and seek to redefine the political landscape. Transitional justice mechanisms solicit participation through the mobilization of political agency. They appeal to and promote values and reforms, and articulate political rights and duties.

As I will illustrate in this book's empirical chapters, truth-seeking and memory work can also generate significant, although underemphasized, normative and discursive effects. Although less integrated into current empirical research, early scholarship in social legal studies also expressed interest in the broader substantive impact of trials. Building on Argentine lawyer Carlos Nino, Mark Osiel argues that criminal trials have long had underappreciated yet important substantive effects.[104] Even where divisive, during transitions to democratic rule, prosecutions play a critical signaling role, reaffirming respect for the rule of law and due process. For Osiel, the ability of political actors to carry out mass atrocities depends upon "embedded common social practices and networks," for example, command-and-obey structures. Transitional justice processes offer alternative normative parameters. Reliance upon common legal procedures

[101] Charles Villa-Vicencio, *Walk with Us and Listen: Political Reconciliation in Africa* (Washington, DC: Georgetown University Press, 2009).

[102] As Eric Wiebelhaus-Brahm has remarked, to date the literature lacks societal understanding of restorative justice. "Uncovering the Truth." An exception is Philpott's conception of political reconciliation, which builds on restorative justice and various strands of theology. Philpott, *Just and Unjust Peace*.

[103] Rolando Ames Cobián and Félix Reátegui, "Toward Systemic Social Transformation: Truth Commissions and Development," in *Transitional Justice and Development: Making Connections*, ed. Pablo de Greiff and Roger Duthie (New York, NY: Social Science Research Council, 2009), p. 146.

[104] Mark Osiel, *Mass Atrocity, Collective Memory, and the Law* (New Brunswick, NJ: Transaction, 1997), pp. 2–3. See also Carlos Santiago Nino, *Radical Evil on Trial* (New Haven and London: Yale University Press, 1996).

ensures "moral disagreement among antagonists remains mutually respectful, within the courtroom and beyond."[105] As criminal trials restore a sense of equality in front of the law and provide a frame of reference, these common procedures create a "safe environment," signaling a return to order and fostering shared norms and trust.

While truth commissions often set out a pedagogical agenda – to promote more accommodating and nuanced views – in practice, their effects may be more long term and indirect. This may be through generating a more victim-centered culture by embedding norms of listening and empathy into their procedures.[106] They can also help generate norms of accountability, playing a shaming function and bringing social stigma to perpetrators.

Most significantly, however, official investigations can play a role in the civic sphere as forums for mobilization. Truth-seeking processes can open new channels of political participation. In South America, Elizabeth Jelin maintains that historical investigations provided political currency to activists. Mobilizing around official truth-seeking processes, so-called memory entrepreneurs channel memory into the public sphere through the physical inscription of memory on territorial markers and by raising questions of obligation and representation.[107] Public memory serves as a resource for affected groups to mobilize and pursue their claims.[108] While memory activism can undermine its aims by leading to censorship and creating new conflicts, struggles for truth can gradually shift power toward victims' groups.[109] The recent trial of General Augusto Pinochet is a high-profile example of a more indirect cumulative process in which official memories generated counter-discussions and public campaigns. In this context, the passage of time, a changing domestic political opportunity structure, judicial change, and political fallout resulting from Pinochet's arrest in the United Kingdom revitalized campaigns for criminal justice.[110] In this longer-term analysis, contestation and conflict are vital for democratization. Focusing on perpetrator confessions in charged contexts, Payne argues that airing of controversial testimonies erodes power from authoritarian regimes and reinforces campaigns for human

[105] Ibid. [106] Kiss, "Moral Ambition."

[107] Elizabeth Jelin, "Public Memorialization in Perspective: Truth, Justice and Memory of Past Repression in the Southern Cone of South America," *The International Journal of Transitional Justice* 1 (2007), p. 142.

[108] Elizabeth Jelin, *State Repression and the Labors of Memory* (Minneapolis, MN: University of Minnesota Press, 2003), p. 6.

[109] Ibid., pp. 148–149.

[110] See Cath Collins, "Human Rights Trials in Chile: During and after the 'Pinochet Years'," *The International Journal of Transitional Justice* 4 (2009), pp. 10–17.

rights and accountability.[111] As perpetrators and political agents publicly justify their actions, activists mobilize their own constituents around "performance acts," thereby challenging official representations.[112] Memory politics creates a language of human rights and accountability that actors may draw on to justify and legitimize their claims.[113]

Building on this, and linking to procedural reconciliation, truth commissions are unlikely to lead to agreement – or even direct engagement – and will expose friction and provoke disagreement and debate. However, they can reinforce a process of making claims and addressing the past. Individuals and communities may disagree over the nature of truth or each other's narratives while still respecting a truth-seeking process. They can appreciate and respect the importance of memory and transparency and of having a voice and testimony.

Comparative impact studies have tended to underappreciate these indirect and dynamic effects of accountability. Often focusing on formal quantitative measurement indicators,[114] the long-term and broader substantive impacts of transitional justice require further scrutiny. Transitional justice processes mobilize political agency – they create a significant, albeit fraught, public discourse about memory, rights, and entitlements. They can also generate intense frustration and disappointment where follow-up bodies, governments, and society fail to meet expectations later on. In Guatemala, for instance, the Comisión para el Esclarecimiento Histórico (CEH) generated criticism for its lack of popular engagement and impact.[115] Popular dissatisfaction over the CEH mobilized civil society and religious leaders. Under the leadership of Bishop Juan Gerardi, the Catholic Church played a strong role in producing a separate commission, the Recovery of Historical Memory Project (REMHI), which sent 700 "agents of recovery" to villages to collect testimonies and provide psycho-spiritual support.[116] Shortly after REMHI presented its final report, which implicated some powerful military actors, individuals operating under military orders murdered Gerardi in his home.[117] While the assassination was a tragic testament to a divisive and contentious past, it also revealed a more complex process whereby

[111] Payne, *Unsettling Accounts*, p. 38. [112] Ibid.

[113] See Katherine Hite and Cath Collins, "Memorial Fragments, Monument Silences and Re-awakenings in 21st-Century Chile," *Millennium: Journal of International Studies, Violence and Memory Forum* 38 (2009), pp. 379–400.

[114] See Tricia D. Olsen, Leigh A. Payne, and Andrew G. Reiter, *Transitional Justice in Balance: Comparing Processes, Weighing Efficacy* (Washington, DC: USIP Press, 2010).

[115] Although a number of NGOs distributed popular summaries in Spanish, the report was not accessible to the majority of El Salvador's population. Mani, *Beyond Retribution*, pp. 104–105.

[116] Philpott, *Just and Unjust Wars*, p. 100. [117] Ibid.

civil society filled a void left by official efforts, even under significant opposition and risk.

These normative and discursive effects of transitional justice are difficult to predict and may counter institutions' own formal objectives. While the South African TRC, for instance, attempted to eliminate race from its mandate, inviting testimony from a wide social and political demographic, race still featured in many victims' testimonies.[118] The South African TRC provided a rallying point and political forum to work out new civic identities for later discussion and campaigns, even for those critical of its aims and work.

What is important for procedural reconciliation is the extent to which transitional justice mechanisms disseminate generalized solidarity and what happens over time after transitional justice processes have ceased operation. Of interest is whether there is spillover into the policies and practices of civil society and whether integration into transitional justice practices and forums create new organizations. Spillover is particularly important in the normative and discursive realm. For instance, procedural reconciliation becomes relevant to the extent that organizations and individuals make greater use of human rights language or integrate more fully into political processes. What is fundamental is that there is a more widespread commitment to change through agreed-upon processes and procedures.

Inclusivity and Pluralism

Although, as I discussed earlier, procedural reconciliation is open ended in its form and character, in order to work, it rests on inclusivity and value pluralism as core values. At a minimum, procedural reconciliation requires individuals to adhere to the possibility of nonviolent change. This entails a level of civic trust, a belief that broadly representative political channels are in place, and that political participation will pay off and will not put individuals and their constituencies at risk. Procedural reconciliation rests on a generalized understanding of citizenship – a sense that the state and its institutions are legitimate and an understanding of the self as a rights-bearer before the state. Civic trust is also important as an element of life that is particularly damaged by violence. Generalized societal insecurity and mistrust are self-generating conditions.[119] For economist Albert Hirschman,

[118] Madeleine Fullard and Nicky Rousseau, "Truth-Telling, Identities and Power in South Africa and Guatemala," Research Brief, International Center for Transitional Justice (June 2009), pp. 54–86.

[119] Diego Gambetta, "Can We Trust Trust?" in *Trust: Making and Breaking Cooperative Relations*, ed. Diego Gambetta (Oxford: Oxford University Press, 2000), pp. 213–237.

trust is a "moral resource," a resource whose "supply increases rather than decreases through use and which become depleted if not used."[120]

Transitional justice offers a potential important contribution to procedural reconciliation in at least two ways. First, transitional justice mechanisms can serve as forums to offer acknowledgment. Although less prevalent in empirical research, the generation of civic trust has played a central role in the normative agenda of scholar-practitioners and transitional justice mandates.[121] The fostering of civic trust requires credible acknowledgment and respect – at the least, the recognition of another's humanity.[122] In South Africa, Alex Boraine and Dumisa Ntsebeza maintain that victims perceived the TRC's recognition of abuses and the shaming of offenders to be a form of justice and accountability.[123] Official acknowledgment is especially important where victims belonged to marginalized communities and after experiences of political violence. For the late Peruvian commissioner and anthropologist, Carlos Iván Degregori, testimony in front of the CVR, especially where individuals testified in languages other than Spanish, offered a "double reparation," simultaneously acknowledging the victim as a rights-bearing citizen and recognizing cultural pluralism as a value in democracy.[124]

[120] Albert Hirschman, "Against Parsimony: Three Easy Ways of Complicating Some Categories of Economic Discourse," *American Economic Review* 1 (1984), pp. 11–28.

[121] While academic literature on truth commissions often focuses on the potential therapeutic benefits of testimony, transitional justice institutions often concentrate on the use of testimony as a form of voice and acknowledgment. As Priscilla Hayner puts it, truth commissions are less useful for revealing new information than for providing individuals with a forum and opportunity to speak about their experiences and receive recognition. Hayner, *Unspeakable Truths*, p. 25. TRC officials often refer to this objective as "dignification," the formal political acknowledgment and honoring of individuals as worthy of equal respect and status as citizens. Aryeh Neier, "What Should be Done about the Guilty?" *NY Review of Books* 1 (1990), p. 32; Crocker "Reckoning with Past Wrongs"; Pablo de Greiff, "Theorizing Transitional Justice," in *Transitional Justice*, Nomos, Volume L, ed. Melissa Williams, Rosemary Nagy, and Jon Elster (New York, NY: New York University Press, 2012), p. 11.

[122] However, he focuses on the micro level on intergroup conflicts. Kriesberg, "Reconciliation," p. 6.

[123] Dumisa B. Ntsebeza, "The Uses of Truth Commissions: Lessons for the World," in *Truth v. Justice: The Morality of Truth Commissions* (Princeton, NJ: Princeton University Press, 2000), pp. 158–169; Alex Boraine "Truth and Reconciliation in South Africa: The Third Way," in *Truth v. Justice: The Morality of Truth Commissions*, ed. Robert I. Rotberg and Dennis Thompson (Princeton, NJ: Princeton University Press, 2000), pp. 141–157. Similarly, André Du Toit argues that acknowledgment was the primary contribution of the South African TRC. "The Moral Foundations of the South African TRC: Truth as Acknowledgement and Justice as Recognition," in *Truth v. Justice: The Morality of Truth Commissions*, ed. Robert R. Rotberg and Dennis Thompson (Princeton, NJ: Princeton University Press, 2000), pp. 122–140.

[124] Carlos Iván Degregori, *Qué Difícil es Ser Dios: El Partido Comunista del Perú – Sendero Luminoso y el Conflicto Armado Interno en el Perú: 1980–1999* (Lima: Institute of Peruvian Studies, 2010).

While hearings offer a direct form of acknowledgment, truth-seeking processes may also play more indirect signaling functions. Following prolonged uncertainty and political violence, official acknowledgment takes a symbolic stance against future atrocities. The generation of civic trust serves as part of a broader process of de-securitization. Matthew Hoddie and Caroline Hartzell maintain that reconciliation requires costs on all sides.[125] The willingness to bear costs and take risks itself signals "conciliatory intent" and builds confidence and trust. Official acknowledgment takes a stance against the former regime and the perpetrators, and legitimates the new regime and respect for human rights.[126]

Second, transitional justice is important for civic trust to the extent that it fosters knowledge and transparency. Bridging the micro and macro levels, truth commissions play a potentially significant role by generating information. By providing information on missing persons, truth-seeking processes provide a resource for victims and their families, allowing survivors to better pursue their claims through democratic channels. On the micro level, knowledge can also help enhance a sense of personal security by contextualizing atrocity and countering atomization of suffering. Drawing on his work with victims at the South African TRC, psychologist, Brandon Hamber, argues that victims of torture often suffer a perception of vulnerability and maintain a traumatized understanding of society and others. Violence undermines victims' personal autonomy and faith in society and institutions. In his view, the TRC helped victims come to terms with past atrocities by creating a more accurate understanding of the past.[127] Truth-telling creates a common framework for expression by showing victims that torture and abuses were indicative of a "social cataclysm," rather than individually held experiences.[128]

[125] Matthew Hoddie and Caroline Hartzell, "Signals of Reconciliation: Institution-building and the Resolution of Civil Wars," *International Studies Review* 7 (2005), pp. 21–40.

[126] Mike Kaye, "The Role of Truth Commissions in the Search for Justice, Reconciliation and Democratisation: The Salvadorian and Honduran Cases," *Journal of Latin American Studies* 29 (1997), pp. 693–716. See also De Grieff, "Theorizing Transitional Justice."

[127] Brandon Hamber, "Dealing with the Past and the Psychology of Reconciliation," Public Address at International Symposium on the Contribution of Psychology to Peace (Cape Town, 1995) in Nagy, "Reconciliation in Post-Commission South Africa," p. 337. See also Howard Zehr, *Changing Lenses: A New Focus for Crime and Justice* (Scottsdale, PA: Herald Press, 1990). For some, truth itself is valuable in setting the grounds for healing and forgiveness. In South Africa, Steve Biko's mother stated shortly before her death: "Yes, I would forgive my son's killers ... But first I must know what to forgive, which means I must be told fully what happened and why." In Aletta J. Norval, "Memory, Identity, and the (Im)possibility of Reconciliation: The Work of the Truth and Reconciliation Commission in South Africa," *Constellations* 5 (1998), p. 258.

[128] Minow, *Between Vengeance and Forgiveness*; Rosemary Nagy, "Reconciliation in Post-Commission South Africa: Thick and Thin Accounts of Solidarity," *Canadian Journal of Political Science* 35 (2002), pp. 323–346; Kiss, "Moral Ambition."

Reconciliation requires a re-humanization of the other and recognition that "what the oppressors did to the oppressed belongs to the evil humans do to each other, and not to a mythic evil that intrudes on the world of humans from outside."[129]

In addition to the vertical components noted above (acknowledgment and the fostering of transparency and knowledge), procedural reconciliation requires a horizontal component – a level of solidarity. Like civic trust, at the national level, this solidarity is generalized. It entails "norms of reciprocity"[130] and "generalized trust" – the "standing decision to give individuals, even those whom one does not know through direct personal contact, the benefit of doubt."[131] Solidarity requires tolerance and respect for difference and mutual recognition of other individuals and groups as citizens.[132] This recognition can be thin – a commitment to nonviolence and shared procedures (negative peace).[133] Thicker solidarity, in turn, entails social capital and cohesion: strong social networks and intergroup identifications.[134] The recent UNHCR "Imagine Coexistence Project" in post-war Rwanda and the former Yugoslavia conceives of reconciliation as stages of transformation, identifying an initial goal of coexistence that can lead to more ambitious integration and relationship-building over time.[135] While solidarity can be thin or thick, as a baseline,

[129] van Roermund, "Rubbing Off and Rubbing On," p. 183.

[130] Quinn, "What is Reconciliation?" pp. 182–183.

[131] Wendy M. Rahn and John E. Transue, "Social Trust and Value Change: The Decline of Social Capital in American Youth, 1976–1995," *Political Psychology* 19 (1998), p. 545.

[132] Hoddie and Hartzell, "Signals of Reconciliation"; Timothy D. Sisk, *Democratization in South Africa: The Elusive Social Contract* (Princeton, NJ: Princeton University Press, 1995), pp. 21–40.

[133] The scholarship frequently cites the lack of social justice and continued economic structural inequality as significant barriers to reconciliation. See Gready, *The Era of Transitional Justice*, pp. 210–223; Nagy, "Reconciliation in Post-Commission South Africa"; and Daniel Bar-Tal and Gemma H. Bennink, "The Nature of Reconciliation as an Outcome and a Process," in *From Conflict Resolution to Reconciliation*, ed. Yaacov Bar-Simon-Tov (Oxford: Oxford University Press, 2004), p. 27.

[134] Rosemary Nagy distinguishes thin solidarity, based on procedures and pluralism, from thick solidarity, based on strong emotive bonds. Nagy, "Reconciliation in Post-Commission South Africa," p. 327. See also Hamber and Kelly, "A Working Definition of Reconciliation."

[135] Antonia Chayes and Martha Minow, eds. *Imagine Coexistence: Restoring Humanity after Violent Ethnic Conflict* (Cambridge, MA: Jossey-Bass, 2003). See also Yehudith Auerbach, "The Role of Forgiveness in Reconciliation," in *From Conflict Resolution to Reconciliation*, ed. Yaacov Bar-Siman-Tov (Oxford: Oxford University Press, 2004), pp. 149–176; Donald W. Shriver, Jr., *An Ethic for Enemies: Forgiveness in Politics* (Oxford: Oxford University Press, 1998). David Mendeloff distinguishes between negative reconciliation as "non-lethal coexistence" and positive reconciliation as "intergroup harmony and cooperation." "Truth-seeking, Truth-telling and Post Conflict Peace-building: Curb the Enthusiasm," *International Studies Review* 6 (2004), pp. 365–366. For F. Van Zyl Slabber, reconciliation is a "relationship that is restored (or created anew) to the extent that the parties can move on in peace while accepting each

it requires mutual recognition of other individuals as citizens deserving of respect and protection, and a willingness to live together in the future. In this realm, as well, solidarity entails a commitment to nonviolence and a reliance on common procedures to resolve disputes.

In terms of procedural reconciliation, here, of primary interest is how affected populations and those working with them (activists and civil society) evaluate transitional justice. Vertically, procedural reconciliation would mean that stakeholders would feel more empowered as citizens and would perceive a sense of justice and accountability. Horizontally, affected populations would believe that others participated in good faith, and that they feel included as part of society. Procedural reconciliation would also require tolerance of others as deserving standing as citizens notwithstanding severe disagreements over the justness and validity of past and present positions and actions.

Conclusions

Reconciliation is an active and burgeoning academic and policy arena. Much of the theory and practice of reconciliation, however, speaks past each other, in part due to the lack of agreement on what reconciliation means and its drivers. I argued in this chapter that academic theory has often focused on a transformative understanding of reconciliation tied to cognitive change and social learning. Transformative reconciliation is ambitious and linear and requires fundamental psychological change.

In contrast, procedural reconciliation, as I defined it, provides a framework that channels conflict into the public sphere and reinforces common norms and procedures for dealing with conflict and addressing its legacies. I drew on a diverse normative literature and practices to offer an agency-based and constructivist understanding of reconciliation. As an active and contentious process that takes place primarily in the civic sphere, I argued that procedural reconciliation is particularly relevant to recent practices of transitional justice. This applies especially to recent truth commissions, which, as I argued in Chapter 2, have increasingly concentrated their efforts on the civic sphere and democratization. I highlighted important indirect effects of transitional justice, particularly its potential to mobilize civil society and serve as a catalyst for alternative memories.

other's integrity." "Truth without Reconciliation, Reconciliation without Truth," in *After the TRC: Reflections on Truth and Reconciliation in South Africa*, ed. W. James and L. van de Vijver (Cape Town: David Philip, 2000), p. 70.

The relevance of procedural reconciliation to recent practices makes it an important framework. At the same time, in contexts of prolonged political violence, procedural reconciliation holds additional significance: it strengthens political access for marginalized populations and provides a framework of activism. Even where it is contentious, transitional justice can transfer conflict into nonviolent channels and legitimize a discourse of rights and obligations. Over time, this framework can generate solidarity, shared norms and discourses, and civic trust. Particularly significant, as I will highlight in the subsequent chapters, are the often unexpected normative and discursive effects of transitional justice, which can vary in form and content, and can take on their own momentum.

4 Underdevelopment, Peace-Building, and Marginalization

The Establishment of a Restorative Agenda in Sierra Leone

Bad bush nɔ dE fɔ trowe bad pikin.

–Krio proverb, "You can't disown your own child."[1]

Sierra Leone's eleven-year civil war caused 70,000 casualties and left over 2.6 million people displaced. The war involved widespread atrocities and systematic violence against civilians, including forced recruitment of child soldiers, rape and sexual slavery, and amputations of limbs. The conflict took an immense toll on civilian life, causing large-scale social upheaval and damage to political and economic infrastructure, and straining social norms and the societal fabric, particularly intergenerational relations. As the site of a large-scale high-profile international transitional justice effort, the end of the war has again brought the country to international attention. For a number of external observers, Sierra Leone presents a successful case study of a "two-track approach," offering a "living laboratory" for future international interventions on how truth commissions and criminal courts can work in parallel.[2] Critical observers have since interrogated this positive narrative, questioning the resonance of the liberal origins and political and normative objectives of global justice in the Sierra Leonean context and raising concerns about ownership and the sidelining of local culture and traditions.

The origins of transitional justice in Sierra Leone are more than an academic interest. As I will argue in this chapter and the next, mounting concerns within Sierra Leone that global justice is undermining domestic restorative justice and excluded local actors have generated intense internal debates over what transitional justice should entail and tie into a politics of legitimacy between the international and national, and the macro and micro levels. As I will detail in the subsequent chapter, these concerns, coupled

[1] A Krio proverb frequently shared in interviews. The literal translation is "you can't throw a bad child in the bush."

[2] William Schabas. *The UN International Criminal Tribunals: The Former Yugoslavia, Rwanda, and Sierra Leone* (Cambridge; New York: Cambridge University Press, 2006) p. 76.

with the ongoing challenges facing the country, have mobilized local actors to search for and revitalize local conflict resolution and peace-building mechanisms, reinforcing a turn toward localism in the post-TRC period.

In this chapter, I will provide an analysis of the establishment and framework of the multiple transitional justice mechanisms within Sierra Leone. Given the abundant literature on the various aspects of the Sierra Leonean civil war, its drivers, actors, and their motivations, this chapter will offer only a short history and focus on aspects of the war that become important for transitional justice and reconciliation.[3] Specifically, I argue that factors having to do with the Sierra Leonean civil war and post-war context reinforced a restorative orientation among important actors involved in Sierra Leone's justice process. While international intervention and a drawn-out cease-fire encouraged a certain pragmatism toward the Revolutionary United Front (RUF), the persistence of the conflict's root causes and the legacies of the war reinforced the urgency of reconciliation, linking reconciliation to conflict prevention and development. At the same time, the complex nature of post-war guilt, particularly in light of the youthful demographics of many ex-combatants, further bolstered the normative value of restorative justice.[4] As the peace process advanced, advocates embedded their justifications for the Commission within a history of restorative justice among Sierra Leone's ethnic communities and drew normative ground from a regional, and what some identified as an "African," legacy of restorative justice, associating truth commissions with reconciliation and peace-building.

[3] Excellent sources on the war include Ibrahim Abdullah, *Between Democracy and Terror: The Sierra Leone Civil War* (Dakar: Council for the Development of Social Science Research in Africa, 2004); Daniel Bergner, *Soldiers of Light* (London: Penguin, 2005); Douglas Farah, *Blood from Stones: The Secret Financial Network of Terror* (Broadway Books, 2004); Lansana Gberie, *A Dirty War in West Africa* (Bloomington, IN: Indiana University Press, 2005); David Keen, *Conflict and Collusion in Sierra Leone* (Oxford: James Currey Ltd, 2005); Krijn Peters, *War and the Crisis of Youth in Sierra Leone* (Cambridge: Cambridge University Press, 2011); Funmi Olonisakin, *Peacekeeping in Sierra Leone: The Story of UNAMSIL* (London: Lynne Rienner Publishers, 2008); John-Peter Pham, *Child Soldiers, Adult Interests: The Global Dimensions of the Sierra Leone Tragedy* (New York, NY: Nova Science Publishers, 2005); William Reno, *Corruption and State Politics in Sierra Leone* (New York, NY: Cambridge University Press, 1995); Paul Richards, *Fighting for the Rainforest* (The International African Institute in association with James Currey/ Heinemann, 1996). On the RUF, see Kieran Mitton, *Rebels in a Rotten State: Understanding Atrocity in the Sierra Leone Civil War* (Oxford: Oxford University Press, 2015) and Zoe Marks, *The Internal Dynamics of Rebel Groups in War: The Politics of Material Visibility and the Organizational Capacity in the Revolutionary United Front* (PhD Thesis, Oxford University, 2014).

[4] Not all members of Sierra Leonean civil society or society at large agreed with a restorative approach. As Rosalind Shaw notes, many also advocated a criminal justice approach and support for the TRC tended to be concentrated among a group of NGOs in Freetown. Rosalind Shaw, "Rethinking TRCs: Lessons from Sierra Leone," *Special Report, United States Institute of Peace* (2005).

I will discuss how these pragmatic and normative orientations among sectors of Sierra Leonean civil society collided with very different international objectives and ideas. Although external agents were also actively involved in setting up and running the TRC, geopolitics and conflicting interests related to the end of the war influenced the funding available for the Commission and the personnel assigned to its management. This context politicized the TRC's work while the later establishment of the SCSL had a strong influence on the TRC's work and domestic reception. Ongoing tensions between the TRC and the SCSL and insufficient local understanding of the differences between both institutions led the TRC to distance itself from the Court and to take a stronger restorative orientation. Somewhat ironically, given both institutions' efforts to stress their jurisdictional independence, the TRC's increasingly rigid restorative stance also led it to adopt a more hierarchical and stratified characterization of guilt within which the role of the tribunal was to focus on the highest perpetrators, while the TRC would engage society as a whole, including victims, ex-combatants, and witnesses. As I will elaborate more fully in Chapter 5, strong international influence and involvement in the country's peace and transitional justice processes eventually led to a normative and pragmatic reassessment among members of civil society in favor of localism and a community-focused orientation.

The Sierra Leonean Armed Conflict: 1991–2002

Since 1462, when Portuguese explorer Pedro da Cintra named the country Serra de Leao, "Lion Mountains," Sierra Leonean history has been marked by a succession of external intrusion and exploitation. The transatlantic slave trade, British colonialism, and the establishment of a neocolonial system of patronage and economic extraction after independence created the seeds of a deeply divided society. In the late 1400s, the Portuguese consolidated a presence in the country, exploiting the Sierra Leonean economy for trading purposes and slaves, which they used for their plantations in the Caribbean and Americas. As the Portuguese foothold decreased in the seventeenth century, the British took their place. In the 1700s, the British interest in Sierra Leone as a port city coincided with an active British and American abolitionist movement. Increasing British opposition to the slave trade led to the founding of Freetown in 1792 as a city for ex-slaves.[5] As the French consolidated

[5] Earl Conteh-Morgan and Mac Dixon-Fyle, *Sierra Leone at the End of the Twentieth Century* (New York: Peter Lang Publishing, 1999), p. 26. Many in these early migrations perished, due to tensions with the Temne, the harsh climate, disease, and financial weakness. These ex-slaves from the United States traced their ancestry to different parts of Africa.

a presence in neighboring countries of Guinea and Cote D'Ivoire, British interests turned toward Sierra Leone. In 1808, the British government assumed control of Sierra Leone as a full crown colony. By the 1890s, British influence gradually extended beyond Freetown into Sierra Leone's interior. Under British influence, Sierra Leone became one of the world's leading centers for the transatlantic slave trade until the nineteenth century.[6] In 1896, Britain declared a protectorate over the country's present-day borders, putting in place a society of wide-ranging linguistic, ethnic, and religious diversity and uneasy loyalties.[7] The two largest ethnic groups today are the Mende in the southeast and the Temne in the north, each of which comprise 30 percent of the population. The Krio, descendants of freed slaves from the West Indies and African-American slaves from the United States, constitute 5 percent of the population and are based largely in Freetown.

Colonial rule entrenched a two-tier system that continued after independence.[8] Centuries of indirect British rule consolidated a pattern of economic development, based on the extraction of raw materials, especially iron and diamonds, turning urban areas into centers of trade and administration, while industry and government development in rural areas remained scarce. The political effects of Sierra Leone's extractive economy and a corrupt and autocratic political system were mutually reinforcing.[9] The Sierra Leonean state lacked the resources to develop an efficient political system and bureaucracy, which inhibited it from acquiring resources.[10] While Sierra Leone's independence on April 27, 1961, saw the emergence of an active political press and political party competition, the postcolonial period increasingly witnessed social problems, particularly the growing role of ethnicity in politics. Krio former slaves in British-controlled Freetown feared political marginalization since Britain expanded its rule over the Sierra Leonean interior,[11] and subsequent settlements of ex-slaves led to the beginnings of a divide within Sierra Leonean society between the Krio and indigenous groups.[12] Tensions also existed between the North and the South. Prior to independence, the

[6] For an analysis of the slave trade and abolitionist movements, see Rosalind Shaw, *Memories of the Slave Trade: Ritual and the Historical Imagination in Sierra Leone* (Chicago: University of Chicago Press, 2002) and Nathan Nunn and Leonard Wantchekun, "The Slave Trade and the Origins of Mistrust in Africa," *American Economic Review* 101 (2011), pp. 3221–3253.

[7] Sierra Leone has sixteen official ethnic groups, some of whom share co-ethnic loyalties across borders with Liberia in the Southeast and Guinea in the North.

[8] For an extensive history, see David Harris, *Sierra Leone: A Political History* (Oxford: Oxford University Press, 2013).

[9] Keen, *Conflict and Collusion*, p. 9. [10] Ibid. [11] Ibid., p. 14.

[12] Conteh-Morgan and Dixon-Fyle, *Sierra Leone*, p. 28.

Mende and Temne subordinated their rivalries to their common opposition to the Krio, whom they resented as favorites of the British. After independence, appeals to ethnicity became a fast way to recruit support. In post-independence party politics, the Mende generally supported the Sierra Leone People's Party (SLPP), while the Temne supported the All People's Congress (APC).

By appointing Temne and other Northern leaders to ministerial positions, Sierra Leone's first government under prime minister and SLPP representative Sir Milton Margai attempted to build bridges with other ethnic groups. Like the British, Margai provided patronage to Northern chiefs and aimed to strengthen their allegiances by turning a blind eye to their abuses against their own people.[13] Yet while patronage strengthened ties between elites, it also contributed to popular unrest, feeding resentment against chiefs and causing rifts between the SLPP and the North.[14] Northerners widely perceived the British to have channeled resources and missionary activities into the resource-rich South, while neglecting their infrastructure and education. Similarly, in the North, the APC's populist and "anti-chief" platform ceded to an ethnic mandate, appealing to constituents frustrated with the Mende-dominated SLPP.[15] In 1967 election of Siaka Stevens brought the APC opposition to power. Fearful of a military coup, Stevens dismantled all opposition, maintaining an eighteen-year rule through a combination of patronage and terror. Under Stevens, the APC cabinets as well as the army gave disproportionate representation to Temnes, purging almost all Mende officers.[16] By 1992, nearly the entire army was from the North.

As social tensions mounted, interethnic marriage and the widespread use of the lingua franca, Krio, stalled the eruption of ethnic violence. A system of patronage, especially in rural areas, also mitigated tensions, particularly under the Stevens' government, which relied on a combination of patronage and intimidation to maintain loyalty.[17] Alfred Zack-Williams describes Stevens' patronage system as a network of informal markets, producing a "shadow state."[18] These factors of stability, however, also contained the seeds of unrest. In the 1980s, the government's expenditure exceeded its revenues, making Stevens unable to uphold the patronage system,[19] and Sierra Leone underwent a series of International Monetary Fund and World Bank structural adjustment policies.

[13] Keen, *Conflict and Collusion*, p. 14. [14] Ibid., p. 15.
[15] Gberie, *A Dirty War in West Africa*. [16] Keen, *Conflict and Collusion*, p. 15.
[17] Ibid., p. 19.
[18] A. B. Zack-Williams, "Sierra Leone: The Political Economy of Civil War, 1991–1998," *Third World Quarterly* 20 (1999), p. 145.
[19] Ibid.

The privatization of public services contributed to the emergence of a parallel shadow economy, revolving largely around the diamond sector, making Stevens' government less relevant to rural and urban citizens.[20]

In 1985, Stevens retired and nominated his protégé, the head of the army, Joseph Momoh, to replace him. As corruption and economic problems worsened, social unrest increased throughout the country. In 1992, six young military captains toppled Momoh in a coup d'état. At the age of twenty-five, the coup's leader, Valentine Strasser, became the world's youngest head of state. Under Strasser, the group formed the National Provisional Ruling Council (NPRC). Initially, Strasser's anticorruption platform and hopeful promises were popular both in Sierra Leone and abroad.[21] However, Strasser's appeal dimmed with charges of corruption and a deteriorating economic situation. His summary execution of opposition members a few months after his seizure of power drew sharp condemnation both at home and abroad. Increasingly, civic organizations within the country, such as Women for a Morally Engaged Nation, and donor organizations, pressed for the restoration of civilian rule.[22]

As Freetown fell into increasing political and economic unrest, a rebellion was forming in the Southeast. The RUF began as a small group of insurgents, who had trained in Liberia in the late 1980s. In Muammar Gaddafi's guerrilla camps in Libya, RUF leader, Foday Sankoh, met warlord and later Liberian president Charles Taylor, who became his source of financial support. With Taylor's encouragement, Sankoh and his two Sierra Leonean allies, Abu Kanu and Rashid Mansaray, went from Libya to Liberia, where they helped bring Taylor to power. Soon after, the three returned to Sierra Leone, where they formed the RUF.

Sierra Leone's civil war began on March 23, 1991, when the RUF invaded the village of Bomaru, approximately half a mile from Sierra Leone's Liberian border. The war lasted eleven years and was fought between the Sierra Leone Army (SLA), the RUF, and civil defense committees set up in different parts of the country. The RUF formed in the 1980s as a group of Sierra Leoneans in neighboring Liberia with support of the National Patriotic Front Liberia under Taylor. The RUF succeeded in taking control of large territories in eastern and southern Sierra Leone, rich in alluvial diamonds. Civil defense committees, which arose to protect villages from widespread abuses and looting by the army and the RUF, eventually grew more powerful than the national army and

[20] Ibid.

[21] The image of "Strasser the redeemer" ingratiated him with external dignitaries, notably Bill Clinton and Nelson Mandela.

[22] Zack-Williams, "Sierra Leone," pp. 149–150.

also committed human rights abuses.[23] The eleven-year civil war killed over 50,000 people and displaced over 500,000.[24] While the RUF became well known for amputations and its targeting of village elders and chiefs, all sides committed abuses of civilians, including sexual violence and slavery, looting and raiding villages, and recruiting and forcibly abducting child soldiers. An estimated 5,000–7,000 children fought in the war, many of whom came from refugee populations displaced by the fighting.[25] While some joined voluntarily, many were abducted. The RUF often ordered children to commit brutalities as part of their initiation, sometimes against family members.[26] Tens of thousands of civilians suffered the amputation of limbs, which was a devastating sentence in a primarily rural economy. Sexual slavery of women and girls was also widespread.

Initially, the RUF attracted considerable domestic support. Under the slogan "No More Slaves, No More Masters. Power and Wealth to the People," the RUF's promise of free education and health care and an equitable redistribution of diamond revenues resonated, particularly among the young, who resented the corruption and incompetence of Sierra Leone's ruling classes.[27] Sankoh took a particularly strong stance in criticism of the Freetown elite:

> The pattern of raping the countryside to feed the greed and caprice of the Freetown elite and their masters abroad. In our simple and humble ways we say, "No more slave and no more master." It is these very exploitative measures instituted by so-called central governments that create the conditions for resistance and civil uprising.[28]

In contrast to the tribe-based patronage system in Freetown, the RUF was a nonethnic movement, recruiting from a range of ethnic groups, religions, and social classes.[29] Some allege early RUF involvement in the establishment of "people's courts" and adult literacy classes, as well as hospitals in rural areas.[30] The RUF also drew on a largely rural and youthful support base. In the years leading up to the conflict, Sierra Leone experienced a rapid population bulge. By the beginning of the twenty-first century,

[23] As in the trial of Sam Hinga Norman at the Special Court for Sierra Leone.

[24] Gberie, *A Dirty War in West Africa*, p. 6.

[25] A. B. Zack-Williams, "Child Soldiers in the Civil War in Sierra Leone," *Review of African Political Economy* 87 (2001), p. 73.

[26] Ibid, p. 80.

[27] See Krijn Peters, *War and Crisis of Youth in Sierra Leone*. Cambridge: Cambridge University Press (2011), p. 127.
See also the RUF's original source, available at: www.sierra-leone.org/AFRC-RUF/footpaths.html.

[28] In Zack-Williams, "Sierra Leone," p. 148. [29] Ibid., p. 149.

[30] Information attributed to Philippa Atkinson in Keen, *Conflict and Collusion*, p. 40.

half of the population was under the age of twenty.[31] Paul Richards notes that the majority of combatants were made up of young males with incomplete secondary education.[32] This group was "modernized yet frustrated" – embittered by the shortage of jobs in the urban formal sectors. The shrinking resources for education and lack of jobs for those with an education encouraged middle-class youth to identify with poorer disenchanted urban youth. University students were especially critical of government corruption and nepotism.[33] Many of the early RUF rallies occurred at Fourah Bay College in Freetown. At the same time, the state's withdrawal from remote regions in the 1970s and 1980s magnified disenfranchisement, leaving these areas to patrimonial chiefs.[34] The RUF was able to recruit widely among rural disenfranchised youth, where the forced division of labor and lack of agricultural rights were the subject of significant contention. Paul Richards notes the persistence of a slave-like society across classes where rural "foster children" worked in the capital for upper classes.[35]

The demographics of RUF combatants and the influence of micro-level factors on the RUF's commission of violence have inspired a rich psychosocial literature. Kieran Mitton examines the influence of shame on RUF members' carrying out of atrocities.[36] In practice, the RUF's actions quickly departed from its ideological rhetoric. Its raiding of villages and looting and its cruel and violent acts against the people it claimed to protect isolated it from the civilian population, as did its targeting of traditional authorities and elders.[37] Although students were influential within the RUF's traditional support base, the RUF later targeted university students and intellectuals.[38] RUF violence became more indiscriminate, accusing civilians of ingratitude and of selling out the rebels, frequently rounding up and executing unaffiliated battle-age boys and men in a wave of paranoia. Over time, the RUF's profiteering further undermined its image. While Taylor used Sierra Leone's economic resources to fund the Liberian military effort, both government

[31] Ibid., p. 20. [32] Richards, *Fighting for the Rainforest.*
[33] Keen, *Conflict and Collusion*, p. 29.
[34] Paul Richards, "To Fight or to Farm? Agrarian Dimensions of the Mano River Conflicts (Liberia and Sierra Leone)," *African Affairs* 104 (2005), p. 585.
[35] Ibid. [36] Mitton, *Rebels.*
[37] Father John Emmanuel Garrick, a priest from Bundt Island, who is credited to have saved a number of civilians during the war. Garrick testified at the TRC and the Special Court for Sierra Leone. Interview by author, Freetown, Sierra Leone, August 14, 2012.
[38] Keen argues that Sankoh, likely because of his own lack of education and rural background, felt insecure around intellectuals, calling them "bookworms, pen-pushers." *Conflict and Collusion*, p. 47.

forces and the RUF used diamonds to finance the war.[39] As David Keen remarks, while the RUF eventually became a powerful force, the government could have defeated the movement in the early stages. In light of collision between government and rebel groups, especially in the arms and diamond trade, the threat of the RUF gave the government a *carte blanche* and helped it justify increasingly costly measures in defense of the country.[40]

The rise of the RUF caused social upheaval throughout Sierra Leone, contributing to the militarization of society. In early 1995, the government elicited help from the British army's Gurkhas. After the death of Canadian commander, Robert MacKenzie, the Gurkhas left the country and were replaced for a period of time by the South African mercenary group Executive Outcomes until they proved too expensive. The void left by the departure of Executive Outcomes resulted in the rise of civilian defense forces in different parts of the country, who mobilized to protect their villages. Although they emerged on a small scale, civil militias came to play an important role in the war. As the government increasingly called upon the civil defense forces, particularly the Mende-based Kamajors to drive out the RUF, civil militias developed a tense relationship with the army, who felt that the militias were challenging its role as a security provider.[41] The role of civil defense forces became more complex in other parts of the country.[42] Deputy minister of defense and leader of the Kamajors, Samuel Hinga Norman, provided an important link between the army and Kamajors, encouraging Kamajors to fight other civic associations, especially in the North. Upon Corporal Gborie's military takeover in 1997, Gborie accused the Kabbah administration of tribalism, quickly outlawing the Kamajors and pitting the two forces against each other.[43] Gborie's military coup sent Kabbah into exile in Guinea and installed President Johnny Paul Koroma, who banned civil liberties and invited the RUF to join the government, from prison. Loyal to Kabbah and Norman, the Kamajors continued to defend the South.

In January 1999, a series of international military and diplomatic interventions to promote negotiations between the government and the RUF eventually ended the war. The government and RUF signed the

[39] The RUF was responsible for the mass expulsion of civilians from the main diamond areas, and many fighters became involved in mining. Keen, *Conflict and Collusion*, p. 51.

[40] Pham, *Child Soldiers*, p. 94; Reno, *Corruption*; Arthur Abraham, "War and Transition to Peace: A Study of State Conspiracy in Perpetuating Armed Conflict," *Africa Development* (Dakar, Senegal: Codeseria, 1997), pp. 101–116.

[41] Zack-Williams, "Sierra Leone," p. 152.

[42] Danny Hoffman, "The Meaning of a Militia: Understanding the Civil Defense Forces in Sierra Leone," *African Affairs* 106, no. 425 (2007), pp. 639–662.

[43] Zack-Williams, "Sierra Leone," p. 152.

Lomé Peace Accord on July 7 1999, giving Sankoh the vice presidency and control of Sierra Leone's diamond mines in return for an end to the fighting and deployment of a UN peacekeeping force to monitor disarmament. The RUF's compliance was inconsistent and slow. After its May 2000 advance on Freetown, the British intervened to save the UN mission and the Kabbah government.[44] President Kabbah declared the war to be officially over on January 18, 2002, after a renewed UN mandate and Guinean air support led to the RUF's defeat. Since the end of the war, Sierra Leone has seen considerable political liberalization. On September 17, 2007, APC candidate Ernest Bai Koroma won after a tense competition against SLPP candidate Solomon Berewa. International and national monitors concluded that the election was fair. Although the November 2012 elections also passed without incident, initiating Koroma's second term, as I will elaborate in the next chapter, democratization and liberal peace-building have also strengthened the authority of paramount chiefs and ethnic politics, reinforcing in some cases the social hierarchies and patronage structures that underpinned the war.[45] As I will discuss in greater detail in Chapter 5, particularly important in this context is how victims became perpetrators, and vice versa, the Civil Defence Force being a prominent example. This would have a significant impact on the multiple understandings of victimhood in the war and fed into justifications and receptions of reconciliation processes at the macro and micro levels

The Establishment of a Multipronged Transitional Justice Approach

In the post-war period, Sierra Leone became the site of a high-profile multipronged international transitional justice effort. The Lomé Peace Accord, signed on July 7, 1999, called for a TRC in exchange for a general amnesty promised during the cease-fire. The process of establishing the Commission was slow and a mixed domestic–international effort. The UN High Commissioner for Human Rights, Mary Robinson, and Sierra Leonean civil society organizations, especially the Interreligious Council, carried out much of the planning. Where the Lomé agreement included few details or provisions for the Commission's mandate and methodology,[46] in the lead up to the TRC, officials engaged in planning

44 Abdullah, *Between Democracy*.
45 Peters, *War and Crisis of Youth*, p. 200. See also Richard Fanthorpe, "On the Limits of Liberal Peace: Chiefs and Democratic Decentralization in Post-War Sierra Leone," *African Affairs* 105, no. 418 (2005), pp. 27–49.
46 Humper, interview.

sessions with commissioners from other contexts, notably South Africa, and the United Nations and International Center for Transitional Justice.

Early on, nearly all aspects of the TRC's set up and management came under dispute. These include the process of appointing commissioners, where the president was to select the Commission's four Sierra Leonean commissioners from a list drafted by a panel including the president, AFRC and RUF representatives, civil society, and other interested parties.[47] While the UN High Commissioner for Human Rights was meant to select the three international commissioners, international involvement decreased after the United States took a more oppositional stance against the RUF and in support of a criminal tribunal.[48] As a result, the TRC received funding of between $6 million and $8 million, in contrast to around $250 million for the Special Court.[49] While the TRC was meant to start operations within two weeks of the signing of the Lomé agreement, it did not appoint its commissioners until July 2001. The office of the United Nations High Commission for Human Rights recommended that Bishop George Biguzzi chair the TRC. Yet, the shifting Sierra Leonean political context after the delegitimization of the RUF in May/June 2000 gave the Kabbah government almost complete autonomy to choose internal commissioners. While the TRC's enabling statute guaranteed RUF and civil society input into the selection of commissioners, by the end of the conflict, the two parties were located along ethno-regional political lines. Head of the Interreligious Council, Reverend Dr. Joseph Humper, a bishop of the United Methodist Church was elected TRC chairman instead of northern-based Biguzzi. In response to political obstacles to the Commission's establishment, the TRC did not become operational until November 15, 2001.[50] Controversies surrounding the Kabbah government's links to suspected SLPP appointees led the Kabbah government to further disengage from the TRC, making the OHCHR and Sierra Leonean civil society its main sources of support. In this polarized context, commissioners hired an external director of investigations, Howard Varney, and other external investigations personnel, to collaborate with local staff.

[47] TRC Act, 2000. Memorandum of Objects and Reasons appended to the Act: Procedure for the Selection of Nominees for Appointment to the Commission.

[48] Mahony and Sooka trace this to the UNPK crisis. Yasmine Sooka and Chris Mahony, "The Truth about the Truth: Insider Reflections on the Sierra Leonean Truth and Reconciliation Commission," in *Evaluating Transitional Justice: Accountability and Peace-building in Post-Conflict Sierra Leone*, ed. Kirsten Ainley, Rebekka Friedman, and Chis Mahony. (London: Palgrave, 2015), pp. 241–264.

[49] Ibid.

[50] The Commission mistakenly cites 1999 instead of 2001: SL-TRC Report Vol 3A, p. 346.

Eventually, the TRC employed a hybrid staff. Humper chaired the Commission. The TRC appointed four national and three international commissioners, including four men and three women, and a mixture of domestic and international staff to conduct research and take statements. The deputy chair was Justice Laura Marcus-Jones, a retired judge of the High Court. The other national commissioners were Professor John Kamara, former principal of Njala University College, and Sylvanus Torto of the Institute of Public Administration and Management, University of Sierra Leone. The internationals were Yasmin Sooka, a human rights lawyer and former commissioner of South Africa's TRC, now director of the Foundation for Human Rights in South Africa; Ajaaratou Satang Jow, former minister of education in Gambia; and Professor William Schabas, director of the Irish Center for Human Rights at the National University of Ireland. Funding for the TRC came mainly from international sources through the United Nations Development Programme, including the United States, the United Kingdom, the European Union, Germany, Denmark, Norway, and Sweden.[51] International actors also took responsibility for some follow-up projects, notably the Norwegian government, in financing the initial resettlement of amputees to disability camps, and the UN-run Disarmament, Demobilization, and Reintegration (DDR) and skills training programs for ex-combatants. The TRC presented its final report to the president of Sierra Leone on October 5, 2004, and to the United Nations Security Council on October 27, 2004. Chief Investigator for the TRC, Howard Varney, produced an overview, findings, and recommendations on November 12, 2005. The report is over 5,000 pages long and includes the names of perpetrators.

External commentators have widely covered the SCSL, Sierra Leone's UN-administered tribunal. On July 12, 2000, then president Kabbah wrote to the United Nations Security Council, requesting an ad hoc tribunal to be set up in Sierra Leone. The Security Council passed Resolution 1315, stipulating that the secretary general should negotiate an agreement with the Kabbah administration for an "independent special court." The SCSL was established in January 2002 after the Kabbah government and the Security Council agreed to the Secretary General's proposal. As the first UN-established hybrid tribunal, the decision to have a court on site, employing a mixture of domestic and international staff, reflected a conscious effort to engage the public and

[51] Priscilla B. Hayner, "The Sierra Leone Truth and Reconciliation Commission: Reviewing the First Year," *The International Center for Transitional Justice* (2004), p. 3.

bring over personnel and know-how from the ad hoc international tribunals in Rwanda and the former Yugoslavia.[52] The SCSL has detained eleven individuals in total, two of whom have died. Eight have received sentences and are serving their terms. Former Liberian president Charles Taylor's June 2012 sentencing in The Hague marked an important moment for international criminal law as the first sentencing of a former African head of state.[53]

While academic research on Sierra Leone has largely focused on formal transitional justice processes, at the community level, parallel grassroots processes have furthered reconciliation and (grassroots) reintegration in different parts of the country. Although restorative practices are widespread among West African ethnic groups, restorative justice also has a distinct national dimension in Sierra Leone. As Rosalind Shaw details, centuries of raiding and internal violence, brought about by protracted experiences of British colonialism and Sierra Leone's central role in the transatlantic slave trade, resulted in the development of complex and innovative communal conflict resolution mechanisms.[54] Following the end of the war, rural communities in different parts of the country drew upon some of these traditions to reintegrate combatants, particularly children. In the Northern town of Makeni, Shaw describes post-war ritual purification practices through which children are remade into "new social persons":

> When Caritas Makeni reunified child ex-combatants with their families, the latter sought to "change the hearts" of their children through a combination of care, support and ritual action. Usually, the eldest member of the family prayed over a cup of water and rubbed it over the child's body (especially the head, feet, and chest), asking God and the ancestors to give the child a "cool heart," a state of reconciliation and stability in which the child is settled in the home, has a proper relationship with family and community and is not troubled by nightmares and bad memories ... Some parents then drank the consecrated water that had washed their child. The consecrated water now becomes the new physical bond between parent and child.[55]

Child protection organizations, including international organizations, notably UNICEF, have also used traditional mechanisms in Mende communities. As Sierra Leonean historian Joe A.D. Alie recalls: "In parts of Kpaa Mende territory, the parents of former child combatants

[52] In particular, the Court integrated lessons learned from Rwanda and the former Yugoslavia in the areas of witness protection and sexual violence.

[53] Charles Taylor's trial took place in The Hague due to concern that the trial would cause instability, although SCSL legal officials are still responsible for running the trial.

[54] Shaw, *Memories of the Slave Trade*, pp. 11 and 15–17.

[55] Ibid., pp. 6–7.

dressed in rags and took to the streets as community members followed, singing and dancing."[56]

As I will detail in the next chapter, the TRC – and Sierra Leone's high-profile international transitional justice experience in general – also helped open a space for Sierra Leonean actors to mobilize in the post-war period. In 2007, Sierra Leonean human rights activist John Caulker founded the communal reconciliation project Fambul Tok, through his organization Forum of Conscience, after serving on the TRC Working Group, based on his view that the TRC was too internationally driven and had insufficiently engaged people in the countryside. Although Fambul Tok benefits almost wholly from external financial and research support from the American organization Catalyst for Peace, it is strongly critical of the international management of transitional justice within Sierra Leone and has positioned itself as a local and grassroots alternative.[57]

Alongside these more systematic efforts, concerned civil society organizations and individuals throughout Sierra Leone have sought to address the legacies of war within their communities, carrying out informal peace-building and reintegration.

Context and Aims: Legitimizing a Restorative Agenda

At the TRC, there's no finger-pointing. It is not about more guilty or less guilty; it's not about scapegoating.

–*Bishop Joseph Humper, Chairman of the TRC.*[58]

From its inception, the TRC framed itself as a mechanism of restorative justice, tied to democratization, peace-building, and the reintegration of ex-combatants. Negotiations to set up a TRC preceded the end of the war as part of a sustained effort to bring about a cease-fire.[59] While the end of the war had become increasingly imminent, especially after the capture of Foday Sankoh and RUF leadership in 2000, the RUF's surrender – and their conditions to turn themselves over – was far from certain. The RUF was still in operation under interim leader, Issa Sesay, and the decision to

[56] Joe A. D. Alie, "Reconciliation and Traditional Justice: Tradition-based Practices of the Kpaa Mende in Sierra Leone," *Traditional Justice and Reconciliation after Violent Conflict: Learning from African Experiences*, ed. Luc Huyse and Mark Salter. (Stockholm, Sweden: International Institute for Democracy and Electoral Assistance, 2008), p. 142.

[57] The Center for Justice and Peace-building at Eastern Mennonite University also supports the organization.

[58] Bishop Joseph Humper, interview by author, Freetown, Sierra Leone, July 28, 2009.

[59] The Sierra Leonean TRC Report; Paul James-Allen, SheKu B. S. Lahai and Jamie O'Connell, "Sierra Leone's Truth and Reconciliation Commission and Special Court for Sierra Leone: A Citizen's Handbook" (New York: National Forum for Human Rights and the International Center for Transitional Justice, 2003).

lay down arms did not come easily for ex-combatants. In addition to fearing prosecution or revenge, many RUF fighters had spent their childhoods at war and faced uncertain prospects for reuniting with their families and integrating into civilian life and gainful employment.

From the start, a combination of internal and external normative and strategic factors drove a pronounced restorative orientation at the TRC. In some regards, domestically, the TRC was established in an atmosphere that was relatively favorable to reconciliation. Civil society activism preceded the end of the war often at significant personal risk. These included anti-war demonstrations of over 30,000 people in front of Sankoh's home to end the war. Important voices within the country justified a restorative approach given the vast challenges facing the country. The Interreligious Council was particularly important, having gained visibility through its members' earlier travels to war-affected areas to urge the RUF to release children in custody. Humper, describes a process to reach out to RUF militants and listen to their terms of surrender, including trips upcountry to speak to mobilized RUF and visits to captured RUF leader Sankoh in prison.[60] During these visits, Humper emphasized the importance of approaching Sankoh as an equal, and giving him the chance to talk.[61] The Interreligious Council was active in calling for a peace process and took part in UN negotiations to set up a TRC.

The war itself also led to a mushrooming of civil society actors invested in peace-building – a trend that continued at the end of the war. Over time, however, with the exception of a select group of actors – notably the Interreligious Council – Sierra Leonean civil society sectors and activists were increasingly marginalized from the peace process. Eventually, only a very selective group of civil society actors was able to participate in the Lomé peace talks, principally the Interreligious Council.[62]

As was the case in South Africa, the decision to set up a truth commission was originally pragmatic in Sierra Leone. Eleven years of civil war had left the country in a state of severe poverty and underdevelopment.[63] The war had caused large-scale displacement and destroyed the judicial

[60] Humper, interview.

[61] Ibid. Humper is adamant that the RUF should be treated with dignity, stressing that the rebels had fought for a cause. He maintains that the RUF fighters were not "pagans" and that religion still provided a rare inroad to negotiations.

[62] Simone Datzberger, "Peace-building and the Depoliticization of Civil Society," *Third World Quarterly* 36, no. 8 (2015), pp. 1592–1609.

[63] Since the end of the war, Sierra Leone has ranked as one of the three most underdeveloped countries on the UN Human Development Index, facing severe unemployment. Immediately after the war, Sierra Leone was the lowest. The UNDP Human

system and much of the country's infrastructure and agriculture. The country also faced a unique challenge of how to reintegrate the large population of youth who fought in the war, many of whom had started fighting as young as eight years old and had spent most of their lives in combat. Prolonged social displacement – where children often became child soldiers or spent their childhood in neighboring countries – caused further marginalization, leaving youth without skills and social support structures. Many were afraid to return to their communities; others did not want to go back to a submissive position after fighting. For many Sierra Leoneans, the reintegration of youth was a security concern and struck emotional chords, given the large-scale victimization of children.

In light of these factors, the TRC was established in a social climate that was relatively favorable to ex-combatants. The marginalized and youthful demographics of many ex-RUF and government soldiers also facilitated an understanding of the war as a youth crisis, which was symptomatic of broader societal ills, rather than the actions of one group. While ethnic tensions existed and had to an extent contributed to the war, the conflict generally did not follow ethnic lines.[64] In this context, activists embedded calls for a TRC within domestic traditions of restorative justice and cited the South African TRC as a familiar reference point for civil society.[65]

Together, these factors influenced the TRC to take a strongly restorative orientation, tied to several key aims.[66] First, the Commission sought to contribute to the reintegration of ex-combatants. The TRC embarked on a sustained outreach effort to include ex-fighters. Article 9 of the Lomé Accord granted "absolute and free pardon" to Sankoh and to all combatants and collaborators in respect to "anything done by them in pursuit of their objectives up to the time of the signing of the present agreement."[67] It also recognized the RUF as a political actor, promising that the "Government of Sierra Leone shall accord every facility to the RUF to

Development Index, released on November 2011, put the country at 180. Available at: http://hdrstats.undp.org/en/countries/profiles/sle.html.

64 For some interviewees, the cross-cutting nature of the conflict was the only positive legacy emerging from the war, making it easier, in their view, to move forward, in contrast to more "intractable" intergroup conflicts. For example, Osman Gbla, professor of political science at Fourah Bay University, interview by author, Freetown, Sierra Leone, July 24, 2009; and Joe A. D. Alie. See also Laura Stovel, *Long Road Home: Building Reconciliation and Trust in Post-war Sierra Leone* (Mortsel, Belgium: Interstentia, 2010).

65 Bishop Joseph Humper and Josephine Thompson Shaw, interviews by author.

66 The TRC's mandate encompasses several broad goals, including producing a report on human rights violations beginning in 1991, providing a forum for victims and perpetrators, and recommending policies to facilitate democratization and reconciliation, and to prevent future violations.

67 The Lomé Peace Accord. Available at: www.sierra-leone.org/lomeaccord.html.

transform itself into a political party and enter the mainstream of the democratic process."[68] It pledged that within thirty days of the agreement, the Sierra Leone government would take all "necessary legal steps" to let the RUF register as a political party.

The establishment of the SCSL further entrenched the TRC's non-punitive orientation. Over time, international politics concerning the TRC intensified, a factor that would significantly affect its policies and local buy-in. Details having to do with Sierra Leone's cease-fire and amnesty provisions for the RUF, humanitarian operations, socioeconomic distributions, human rights, DDR, and the establishment of a new army were agreed relatively fast at Lomé.[69] The Lomé Peace Accord did not set out a mandate for the TRC, and included little information as to its composition.[70] Within two weeks of the Lomé agreement, personnel from the United Nations High Commission for Human Rights visited Sierra Leone to begin consultations on the TRC's design, submitting proposed legislation. While Article XXVI of the agreement calls for the Commission's membership to be drawn from "a cross-section of Sierra Leonean society with the participation and some technical support of the International Community,"[71] as Chris Mahony and Yasmin Sooka have argued, the Kabbah government and external actors were insufficiently engaged in and committed to the support of the TRC post-Lomé.[72] Although the OHCHR took on a greater role in designing the TRC, the OHCHR also marginalized government and civil society from central participation in the TRC's design.[73] Another consequence of the TRC's limited resources compared to the SCSL was the number of competent personnel the Commission could afford.[74] Although the TRC employed two West African specialists to serve as consultants, the TRC struggled to find staff who could write and were computer literate. Under budgetary constraints, the TRC relied on temporary and part-time personnel to complete critical tasks.

Undercutting the Lomé Accord's amnesty provision and raising questions vis-à-vis the TRC's guarantees of confidentiality, officials within the

[68] Ibid. [69] Sooka and Mahony, "The Truth about the Truth."

[70] Report of the Sierra Leone Truth and Reconciliation Commission, Vol. 1, 2004 Accra: GPL Press, pp. 23–24.

[71] SL-TRC Report, Vol. 1, pp. 23–24.

[72] See Sooka and Mahony, "The Truth about the Truth." See also Chris Mahony, "A Political Tool? The Politics of Case Selection at the Special Court for Sierra Leone," in *Evaluating Transitional Justice: Accountability and Peace-building in Post-Conflict Sierra Leone* (London: Palgrave, 2015), pp. 77–100.

[73] Ibid.

[74] The TRC was largely dependent on the UNOHCHR, UNDP, and the UN Peacekeeping Mission for funding rather than enjoying state financial support.

Commission took a cautious view of the Court, expressing the concern that trials would pose a threat to peace and impose on Sierra Leonean culture and conflict resolution mechanisms.[75] TRC staff also expressed a fear that the SCSL could subpoena the TRC's material and override its guarantees of confidentiality. Some members of the SCSL, in turn, criticized the TRC for offering what they alleged to be an inadequate approach, inconsistent with international legal norms and obligations.[76] These tensions increased over time, reaching their apex during the high-profile trial of CDF Kamajor leader, Chief Samuel Hinga Norman. Norman's prosecution was already a sensitive matter and contentious, given his role in the civil defense of the country and domestic perception as a national hero.[77] In a highly publicized trial, Norman requested to speak in front of the TRC, but the SCSL refused.[78] The TRC stressed the importance of allowing Norman to testify at the Commission; however, the SCSL prosecution responded that both the interests of justice and the integrity of its proceedings might be put at risk. In addition, SCSL officials criticized Norman's motivations, accusing him of seeking personal attention and political controversy. SCSL Judge Geoffrey Robertson denied the TRC's request, on the basis that Norman's invitation to testify would contradict his right to the presumption of innocence before the Court and might prejudice the jury. In a widely appealed and controversial decision, the SCSL made arrangements for Norman to give a confidential statement to the TRC but both Norman and the TRC refused.[79]

Most of the SCSL officials criticized Norman's motivations, accusing him of seeking personal attention and political controversy. Although

[75] William Schabas, "Conjoined Twins of Transitional Justice: The Sierra Leone Truth and Reconciliation Commission and the Special Court," *Journal of International Criminal Justice* 2 (2004), p. 1083.

[76] Ibid.

[77] Lansana Gberie, "The Civil Defence Forces Trial: Limit to International Justice?" in *The Sierra Leone Special Court and Its Legacy: The Impact for Africa and International Criminal Law*, ed. Charles Chernor Jalloh (Cambridge: Cambridge University Press, 2013), pp. 624–641. See also Tim Kelsall, *Culture under Cross Examination: International Justice and the Special Court for Sierra Leone* (Cambridge: Cambridge University Press, 2013).

[78] See William A. Schabas, "The Relationship between Truth Commissions and International Courts: The Case of Sierra Leone," *Human Rights Quarterly* 245, no. 4 (2003) p. 1041; Sarah Williams, "Amnesties in International Law: The Experience of the Special Court for Sierra Leone," *Human Rights Law Review* 5 (2005), p. 278.

[79] SCSL President Geoffrey Robertson later offered a compromise that Norman could give a written sworn affidavit testimony to the TRC and answer questions from the TRC through writing. See The Special Court for Sierra Leone, *Decision on the Request by the TRC of Sierra Leone to Conduct a Public Hearing with the Accused* (October 29, 2009), available at www.sc.sl.org.

both the TRC and the SCSL shared an interest in popular engagement, public confusion about the relative mandates and demarcations of each body presented a greater challenge to the TRC, which had less resources and whose methodology depended to a large degree on public participation. A number of TRC commissioners and civil society organizations argued that the international community favored and bestowed more authority on the SCSL, arguing that the Kabbah administration had been pressured to request an SCSL and that a South African (amnesty) model would have been better.[80] Local uncertainty over the differences between the two bodies, and that some TRC officials were also tied to SCSL, increased tensions and generated conflicts of interest. The TRC's initial headquarters in Pademba Road, site of Freetown's high security prison, and informal exchanges between the two bodies fed into a widespread view among ex-combatants that the TRC was a "feeder court" for the SCSL.[81] The TRC's final report confirms its disillusionment with the two-track experience, stating that the TRC had been established as an "alternative" to criminal justice, and that the SCSL's creation abandoned the amnesty provisions at Lomé. The TRC faults the international community for signaling to "combatants in future wars that peace agreements containing amnesty clauses ought not to be trusted," and thereby undermining the "legitimacy of such national and regional peace initiatives."[82]

Significantly, over time, the TRC's concerns about the SCSL also led it to reevaluate – and further entrench – aspects of its own work, particularly its position on confidentiality. Despite a series of early efforts by the United Nations and Sierra Leonean and international organizations to work out a complementary relationship and preempt problems, both bodies eventually abandoned talks. Instead, both sought to advance their work largely by turning inward and establishing and defining

[80] The Sierra Leone TRC Working Group reveals tensions between international and Sierra Leonean civil society members on both issues. "Searching for Truth and Justice in Sierra Leone," p. 7.

[81] Kelsall recalls, "It was common to see representatives from the Court and the TRC lunching together in Freetown." "Truth, Lies, Ritual," p. 381. Shaw remarks that ex-combatants confused not only the TRC and SCSL but also both of these institutions with DDR, which prevented many from signing up for disarmament. "Linking Justice with Reintegration?" p. 121. While Schabas argues that popular confusion between the two bodies was to be expected, in the view of numerous TRC commissioners, the establishment of the SCSL and the presence of internationals at the TRC deterred ex-combatants from coming forward to the TRC and moderated the statements of others. Schabas, "The Relation between Truth Commissions and International Courts," pp. 1064–1065. This was an especially prevalent view among Sierra Leonean commissioners. See "Searching For Truth and Reconciliation in Sierra Leone," pp. 6–8, and the Sierra Leonean TRC Report, Volume 2, Chapter 1.

[82] Sierra Leonean TRC Report, Volume 2, Chapter 1.

their own institutional differentiation and spheres of influence. The International Center for Transitional Justice and the United Nations organized a series of early workshops. Priscilla B. Hayner and Paul van Zyl, together with the US Institute of Peace and International Human Rights Law Group, the Office of the High Commissioner for Human Rights, and the United Nations Mission for Sierra Leone (UNAMSIL), initiated efforts to "work out the relationship" and institutionalize a set of guidelines.[83] While SCSL officials made clear that the Court was only interested in the "big fish" and that the SCSL would use its own resources to investigate its cases, the TRC sought to reassure the public by further distancing itself from the SCSL.[84] As the TRC's report recalls, during its operation, the Commission could not rule out that at any given point the SCSL would try to seize information from its archives, and if a conflict arose, that international actors would award primacy to and take the side of the Court.[85] While the TRC statute never formally stated that self-incriminating evidence would not be used for legal proceedings,[86] strict confidentiality became its de facto policy.[87] The net result was the development of a two-pronged transitional justice approach, and an ad hoc division of labor, in which the SCSL focused on criminal guilt and the TRC focused on peace-building and democratization, with a particular emphasis on sexual violence and youth.[88] Somewhat ironically, given their strained relationship, this tension also led to a similar hierarchical discourse of guilt at both institutions, with the SCSL focusing on "those who bear the greatest responsibility," and

[83] Schabas, "The Relation between Truth Commissions and International Courts." See also Rebekka Friedman and Andrew Jillions, "The Pitfalls and Politics of Holistic Justice," *Global Policy* 6, no. 2 (2015), pp. 141–150.

[84] Key members of the SCSL publicly stated that they supported the TRC and that they would not use evidence collected during its hearings for prosecution. Chief Prosecutor David Crane also stated on numerous occasions that they were not interested in child soldiers and that the TRC was more suited for dealing with youth offenders. See interviews/publications. See also the TRC Report, Chapter 6, "The TRC and the Special Court."

[85] Ibid. [86] Unlike the Ghanaian and South African commissions, for example.

[87] Humper was an important figure in calling for complete confidentiality and immunity for ex-combatants – an orientation that became more entrenched over time. See also Schabas, "The Relationship between Truth Commissions and International Courts," p. 1048.

[88] While the minimum age of offenders at the Special Court for Sierra Leone was fifteen years (as opposed to ICC's minimum age of eighteen years), UN and Special Court for Sierra Leone officials repeatedly publicly expressed the view that prosecuting child offenders was not in the Special Court's jurisdiction and that the TRC was better placed to deal with youth perpetrators. See, for example, Special Court for Sierra Leone, Prosecutor, David Crane's interview with the UN Office for the Coordination of Humanitarian Affairs, IRIN (September 25, 2012), available at: www.irinnews.org/InDepthMain.aspx?InDepthId=31&ReportId=70568.

the TRC encompassing society more broadly (victims, witnesses, and perpetrators).[89] This differentiation, as I will cover in greater detail in the subsequent chapter, influenced the TRC's narrative stance and approach to testimony, creating clashes over the questions of individual commitment and responsibility.[90]

Second, where the TRC took a nonpunitive orientation, it contributed to transitional justice and post-conflict reconstruction in other ways, particularly through its self-conception as an instrument of democratization. The TRC tied testimony to a broader conception of civic nation-building.[91] TRC officials presented the Commission as a people's forum, which would provide a voice and opportunity to articulate recommendations for post-war reconstruction. Statement taker, Josephine Thompson-Shaw, remembers:

> Immediately after the war, some people were saying there's no need for a TRC. President Kabbah said "let us forgive and forget; let us move on with our lives." But we had to sensitize the people – "it's not just moving on with our lives; we must make sure this doesn't happen again. We want to avoid these mistakes in the future. We must make sure that you and I, all of us, have a say in the future of the country."[92]

The TRC's self-conception as an instrument of democratization took on additional meaning in the context of the war and the suspension of civil liberties. Commissioners promoted the TRC as a return to peaceful politics and a rejection of the war.[93] In this process, the TRC put emphasis on giving a voice to marginalized groups, particularly women and

[89] While the minimum age of offenders at the SCSL was fifteen years, UN and SCSL officials repeatedly publicly expressed the view that prosecuting child offenders was not in the Special Court's jurisdiction and that the TRC was better placed to deal with youth perpetrators. See, for example, David Crane's interview with the UN Office for the Coordination of Humanitarian Affairs, IRIN (September 25, 2012), available at: www.irinnews.org/InDepthMain.aspx?InDepthId=31&ReportId=70568.

[90] Although the TRC examined the role of senior actors like Foday Sankoh, President Kabbah, Samuel Hinga Norman, and Charles Taylor, it made clear throughout its report and proceedings that its role was not to judge the legitimacy of the RUF. TRC officials also took this position. Humper argued that the purpose of the TRC was not to "scapegoat" or "cast blame." Humper, interview.

[91] The Sierra Leonean TRC Report, Chapter 1, p. 25.

[92] Shaw, interview, See also the Sierra Leonean TRC Report.

[93] While some argued that the amputations served practical functions, preventing civilians from mining diamonds, which would support government troops, and creating fear and allowing the rebels to take full control of the diamond mines, others argued that amputations had a symbolic meaning. For David Keen, in response to the then election slogan that the people "had power in their hands," the RUF's amputation of hands was meant to prevent voting. He also hypothesizes that amputation, in particular of elders and intellectuals, was a way for previously marginalized youth to assert their new social power (the hand used for writing symbolizing the intellectual's previous source of status). *Conflict and Collusion.*

youth. Referring to the initial reluctant participation of women, Thompson-Shaw recalls:

> A few times it seemed women really wanted to give statements, but mostly when we asked the question, "What would you like the government to do for you?" So when they know they had a stake in the process and they would have a voice, they had something burning. Whenever that question was attached, they knew they could make recommendations to improve their lives, they wanted to talk.[94]

Sierra Leonean youth worker Michael Charley, who helped administer the UNICEF-run children's hearings, shared a similar experience:

> One of the key incentives for the children was not actually about direct benefits coming to them but that the children knew that they would eventually make recommendations that would lead to reparations, that would increase their education, that would enhance their communities and remove their potential for conflict ... From the onset of the campaign it was made clear that it was not about direct physical benefits but about the community and moving forward.[95]

Lastly, the TRC sought to use hearings and disseminate its report to raise awareness and generate solidarity and responsibility for victims of the conflict among populations, who had been less affected by the war.[96] It also emphasized reaching the next generation – who would no longer remember the destructiveness of the war.

Methodology

The TRC's methodology and its preparation of its findings reflected this pedagogical focus. Early on, the TRC took a holistic orientation, emphasizing the importance of public engagement and interlinking various transitional justice goals. The TRC stressed the need for an integrated approach, calling for stages of transitional justice and endorsing a plurality of mechanisms:

> If the Commission had not intended to pursue a reparation policy for victims, truth-telling without reparation could conceivably be perceived by the victims to be an incomplete process in which they have revealed their pain and suffering without any mechanism being put in place to deal with the consequences of that pain. Similarly, reparations without truth-telling could be perceived by the beneficiaries as an attempt to buy their silence. Restorative justice requires not only truth telling, but also reparations which will strengthen the reconciliation process.[97]

[94] Thompson-Shaw, interview. [95] Charley, interview.
[96] TRC staff stated their primary target audience to listen was urban classes in the capital, who had only experienced RUF violence toward the end of the war.
[97] The Sierra Leonean TRC Report, Volume 1, Chapter 3.

The TRC's methodology incorporated both didactic and participatory procedures. Asserting an "inalienable right to truth," it prioritized the production of a detailed history and long-term analysis of the conflict.[98] The Commission's primary methodology consisted of statement taking, most of which were collected in confidence, and which it used to write its report. The TRC offered an analysis of systematic patterns of abuses over time in a lengthy root causes chapter, focusing on underlying political, economic, and social antecedents of the war.

At the same time, and similar to the South African Commission, the Sierra Leonean TRC linked truth-seeking to reconciliation and employed a pedagogical and participatory methodology. The TRC's narration of the conflict uses "window cases" to illustrate particular issues or patterns of events. The Commission prepared its reports for commemoration projects and educational purposes, particularly school curricula.[99] The TRC produced a total of three publications, including versions for primary and secondary school children, and made abbreviated versions available for distribution among civil society and NGOs.[100]

This participatory and restorative emphasis was also manifest in other realms of its work. The TRC held hearings in different parts of the country, focusing in particular on ex-combatants. The Commission recommended a variety of skills training and education programs and community service for ex-combatants, e.g., rebuilding schools and hospitals, to prove themselves and "win the hearts and minds."[101] Because of the high number of children involved in the war, it was the first truth commission to set up separate children's proceedings under the auspices of UNICEF for youth. The Commission also held a series of focus groups to target different stakeholders, especially gender-related violence.

The TRC also placed emphasis on its recommendations and reform process, calling for institutional and jurisdictional reforms and for compensation.[102] These included reparations in housing, skills training, health care, education and agricultural assistance, and symbolic reparations, such as reburials, memorials, and remembrance ceremonies.

[98] Ibid. [99] Ibid., pp. 147–148.

[100] As in the Citizen's Report briefing produced by the National Forum for Human Rights and the International Center for Transitional Justice on the TRC and Special Court for Sierra Leone, to increase public accessibility and minimize confusion. James-Allen, Lahai, and O'Connell, "Sierra Leone's Truth and Reconciliation Commission and Special Court."

[101] As Priscilla Hayner notes, perpetrators gave more than 13 percent of testimonies, higher than in front of any other commission. Hayner, "The Sierra Leone Truth and Reconciliation Commission."

[102] *Witness to Truth: Report of the Sierra Leone Truth and Reconciliation Commission* (Accra: Graphic Packaging Ltd, 2004), Volume 2, Chapter 3, "Recommendations on Governance."

Importantly, the TRC sought to use civic engagement to reinforce democratization and build civic trust.[103] As I will argue in the next chapter, this multitiered approach also fed into later negative evaluations of the TRC as the lack of follow-up delegitimized the Commission's work. A particularly widespread critique given the TRC's didactic self-perception is that many at the grassroots level did not understand the TRC's purpose and mandate, or were not aware of its existence altogether.

Reconciliation

The TRC's progress in interpreting its mandate of reconciliation was slow and even members of the Commission criticized it as incomplete.[104] Stark disagreements emerged between TRC officials over what reconciliation should entail and the Commission's contribution. As Varney remembers, the Commission was still "debating what reconciliation should mean until right at the end of the TRC. No programme on reconciliation was developed until October 2003 – right at the end ... It was too little too late."[105] Eventually, however, the TRC settled on a broader conception of democratic reconciliation between society and state. While the Commission expressed the hope in its foreword that a truth-seeking process would facilitate healing and interpersonal reconciliation by providing a "forum for both the victims and perpetrators" and getting a "clear picture of the past," it identified these more intimate and internal processes as beyond the TRC's purview.[106] The report distinguishes between individual healing and national reconciliation, arguing that healing and accountability benefit reconciliation, yet are separate,[107] and defining national reconciliation as a long-term process ("rather than an event"), which will "take time and will need to continue even beyond the present generation."[108]

[103] The Commission argued that reparations were critical not only as a form of justice and compensation but also to create civic trust and social and political capital:

> A sincere commitment from the Government to the execution of the proposed Reparations Programme would give a clear sign to the victims that the State and their fellow citizens are serious in their efforts to re-establish relations of equality and respect. Acknowledging the wrongdoing done to victims, engaging with those victimized and disempowered will lead to members of society having a renewed faith in the democratic process. This leads to the restoration of civic trust and a sense of ownership for the nation.

The Sierra Leonean TRC Report, Volume 2, Chapter 4.

[104] James-Allen, Lahai, and O'Connell, "Sierra Leone's Truth and Reconciliation Commission and Special Court," p. 9.

[105] Ibid. [106] The Sierra Leonean TRC Report, Chapter 1, p. 24. [107] Ibid., p. 2.

[108] Ibid., p. 15.

In a similar vein, the report's tripartite conception of reconciliation distinguishes between the national, community, and individual levels. The report argues that while individual reconciliation would require victims and perpetrators to meet, national reconciliation would not require perpetrators to express remorse or the victim's forgiveness.[109] Community reconciliation occurs between the community and the perpetrator, and is a long-term project, which requires communal acceptance of past wrongs, and the support of chiefs. National reconciliation, where the TRC put most of its emphasis, "begins by creating the conditions for an immediate cessation of the armed conflict and the return of the country to peace."[110] Reconciliation necessitates amelioration of socioeconomic living conditions, strong institutions, and a comprehensive reparations program.[111] The Commission provided for the continuation of reconciliation projects after its closure, notably through the establishment of District Reconciliation Committees in 2003 in partnership with the Interreligious Council.

Conversations with TRC officials further brought out this long-term understanding. Humper added a fourth type of reconciliation: "intra-reconciliation" (occurring within the individual). In his assessment, while the TRC contributed to national reconciliation by encouraging dialogue and creating a historical record, communal reconciliation should occur later at the grassroots level. While NGOs and academics have often criticized the TRC's (lack of) impact on communal reconciliation and interpersonal reconciliation between victims and perpetrators, pointing out that many ex-combatants have yet to return to their former communities, intra-reconciliation is an internal healing process and cannot be measured by the restoration of a previous status quo. Healing was a personal process, which individuals must come to at their own time and volition. The objective of national reconciliation was to create a "space" for these processes so that individuals can feel at home anywhere in the country.[112]

While much of the recent ethnographic research on Sierra Leone has argued that the TRC did not bring about interpersonal reconciliation and healing, the TRC's own self-understanding and procedures were

[109] The Sierra Leonean TRC Report, Volume 2, Chapter 1. [110] Ibid.

[111] The TRC stated that given its short lifespan, it could only explore reconciliation through "sensitization" and high-profile "events," including reconciliation and memorial ceremonies, and workshops with civil society to discuss drivers and preconditions for reconciliation. The Sierra Leonean TRC Report, Chapter 7, Volume 3B.

[112] Humper, interview. As other members of the Commission remarked, rifts within communities also played a part in contributing to the war and individuals should not be forced to return to their communities of origin, and should be able to start a new life if this is what they choose.

arguably less geared to bring about these goals. The Commission recognized that public testimony and investigating the past could be psychologically painful, justifying its truth-seeking agenda instead for the sake of societal reconciliation.[113] Although some TRC officials shared that in their experience, testifying and receiving acknowledgment were generally beneficial for participants, the Commission noted the uncertain psychological impact of testimony on participants and took measures to mitigate the possibility of re-traumatization.[114] The TRC also tended not to bring together victims and perpetrators (although it tried to accommodate victims who requested that the perpetrator be present), and held separate focus groups for different categories of people, particularly women and child soldiers.[115]

Narrative

The TRC's narrative stance reflects its nonpunitive orientation, emphasizing explanation over blame, and highlighting collective victimization and responsibility.[116] The loss of individual and societal agency and the extraordinary circumstances of the war are central to the TRC's narrative and run through its report. Calling for a process of moral reflection and national dialogue, Humper refers to the TRC as a "national mirror": "We are one nation and the TRC is a mirror. You come, you pass by and you see your reflection."[117] The TRC's Report calls for a process of

[113] TRC Report, Chapter 1.

[114] Chapter 3 of the TRC Report begins with the mantra, "truth hurts but war hurts more." The TRC Report and officials working at the commission presented reconciliation and truth-seeking as "painful" processes, explicitly stating that reconciliation would be most difficult for victims and war-affected communities. In response to the same question, Executive Secretary of the Human Rights Commission, Abraham John, replied,

> Well I think so, but you know there are different theories on whether testifying actually helps people heal. Some people think talking about the past can reopen wounds, even re-traumatize them. We are all programmed differently psychologically and you can't generalize. What will work for one person will hurt another. It's a big debate in transitional justice and not so simple.

Interview by author, Freetown, Sierra Leone, August 6, 2009. The TRC also had psychologists on staff to counsel and assess individuals after testifying. In addition, the TRC implemented measures to address sexual violence, e.g., women had the choice to testify in front of female commissioners, and in cases of rape, testimonies were collected in confidence and anonymously, unless individuals expressed the preference to testify in public.

[115] The Sierra Leonean TRC Report, Chapter 1, p. 30.

[116] Ibid., Chapters 1, 3, and Foreword.

[117] Humper, interview. In Humper's words, "The TRC exposes all of us, regardless of who we are, from generation to generation we have been involved. All of us are collectively responsible, so all of us must now join together in rebuilding Sierra Leone."

understanding and learning to create a basis for future peace: "It is only through generating such understanding that the horrors of the past can effectively be prevented from occurring again. Knowledge and understanding are the most powerful deterrents against conflict and war."[118]

The themes of empirical self-correction as a deterrent against future violence and collective progress are consistent throughout the TRC's narration and bolstered its restorative stance, notably its dealings with perpetrators. In promoting the TRC, officials emphasized the destructiveness and senselessness of the war, highlighting that the conflict did not follow ethnic lines. It stressed that the war affected all of society, leaving "no victors," and divided families, pitting "brother against brother." While the TRC named individual perpetrators, it cautioned against the attribution of blame and taking sides, considering, for example, whether the RUF had just cause for its mobilization. As this stands in important contrast to other commissions, particularly the CVR, the following passage is quoted at length to highlight the TRC's nonpunitive approach:

> At the outset, it seems important to state that the Commission is not called upon to assess the justness of the conflict itself. It may be argued by some that those who initiated the attempts to overthrow the Momoh regime were justified in taking up arms. The preamble of the *Universal Declaration of Human Rights* states: 'Whereas it is essential, if man is not to be compelled to have recourse, as a last resort, to rebellion against tyranny and oppression, that human rights should be protected by the Rule of Law. Accordingly, human rights law seems to acknowledge that in extreme conditions, there is a "right of rebellion". . . . Governmental change, in principle, is to be effected at the ballot box. Sometimes, however, after long years of dictatorship, this aspiration may seem unlikely or even impossible. The Commission need not determine whether the conditions mentioned in the preamble of the *Universal Declaration of Human Rights* for the right of rebellion were indeed fulfilled. But, as this Report explains elsewhere, there is little doubt that the words "tyranny" and "oppression", and the failure to protect human rights by the Rule of Law, were appropriate descriptions of Sierra Leone in March 1991.[119]

The TRC's training of staff also reflects this neutral stance. The Commission instructed statement takers to let perpetrators "speak freely" and not to ask "leading questions" or "judge."[120] It urged staff to remember that perpetrators were also victims and acknowledged the many "grey areas" of war. It reiterated that perpetrators should also be free to talk and give recommendations as future stakeholders.[121]

Where the TRC took a stance against taking sides, it emphasized the long-standing root causes of the conflict. Tracing social hierarchies to

[118] The Sierra Leonean TRC Report, Chapter 1, p. 2. [119] Ibid., Chapter 3, p. 86.
[120] Ibid., Chapter 5, pp. 184–186. [121] Ibid.

British rule, the Commission faulted the colonial manipulation of the chieftaincy system for intentionally creating "two nations in the same land" and undermining the legitimacy of chiefs. The TRC also created a profile of victims, highlighting the gendered nature of abuses. It found, for instance, that while 59.6 percent of general violations and 89.1 percent of forced recruitments were committed against adult males, rape and sexual slavery were committed exclusively against females. The TRC notes the youthful demographics of female victims: 44.9 percent of child victims were female; and 25 percent of victims of forced recruitment, rape, and sexual slavery were young children. The report identifies the RUF, the Armed Forces Revolutionary Council (AFRC), and the SLA (when it operated with the AFRC) as the primary organizations that committed violations against children.

Finally, the Commission put emphasis on generating social understanding for the motivations and experiences of ex-combatants. The report highlights the social-psychological dimensions of conflict, noting, in particular, generational tensions and participation in violence as a way of settling scores.[122] Throughout its report, the TRC stressed that youth ex-combatants were also victims, pointing out that the RUF kidnapped and drugged many of its fighters, and that children carried out "crazed violence."[123] Portraying the conflict as "stolen childhoods and stolen dreams," the Children's report maintains that children were simultaneously victims and perpetrators in an "adult war" and were "forced to fight for a cause they did not understand."[124] It states that children were often drugged before fighting and recruited into the armed forces after witnessing the murder or abuse of family members. The Report concludes that all children were victims in the Sierra Leonean war: "Who suffers the greater horror, the child who is violated, or the child who is forced to become a perpetrator? We are the victim, the perpetrator and the witness, all at once."[125]

Testimony

The TRC collected a total of 7,706 statements; of these, it took 36 percent from women and 5 percent from children. It took statements in fifteen different languages, although the majority was taken in Mende (40 percent), Krio (39 percent), and Temne (12 percent). While public

[122] TRC agents emphasized the demography of ex-combatants as marginalized youth, pointing out that the RUF pulled most of its fighters from "migrant youth, roaming the countryside," and the targeted nature of violence and degrading treatment of traditional authorities and intellectuals. Humper, interview.

[123] UNICEF Sierra Leonean TRC Youth Report, p. 24. [124] Ibid. [125] Ibid.

hearings represented the most high-profile aspect of the Commission's work, most individuals participated by giving private statements. The TRC held separate focus groups and sessions for different categories of people, particularly for women and youth.[126] TRC statement takers were able to cover the majority of chiefdoms – however, as the TRC admits in its report, due to accessibility and security constraints, it collected less than ten statements from a number of chiefdoms, and did not cover nine chiefdoms at all. Fambul Tok would later target some of these regions, particularly Kailahun, Koinadugu, and Pujehun, as regions, which the TRC had overshadowed.[127]

For ex-combatants who participated at the TRC, testimony was often a chance to explain or clarify their actions to further their reintegration and societal reacceptance. In a survey, conducted by the Sierra Leonean NGO Pride, ex-combatants gave the following explanations for testifying at the TRC: "'I hope to be free from people when I say the truth,' 'The TRC will give us a chance to explain why we fought,' 'the truth will help families and victims forgive us,' and 'it will let our families accept us in good faith.'"[128] According to the report, 72 percent of ex-RUF raised allegations of forced recruitment. Many claimed that they were drugged and forced to commit acts of violence against people they knew.

In some regards, the TRC also encouraged a less personal approach to testimony. Statement takers instructed perpetrators not to provide details of their crimes to avoid re-traumatizing victims. They urged young people especially to use their testimony as an opportunity to make broader recommendations and have a say in post-conflict governance. Victims' testimonies in front of the TRC were also often general, focusing on their community's experiences and needs. According to Thompson-Shaw, this was especially the case for women: "Most of the time when women spoke the stories were general. Only one or two times the stories were personal, like rape or murder of family. But mostly the stories were general – I had

[126] The Sierra Leonean TRC Report, Chapter 1, p. 30. Michael Charley, UNICEF Youth Programme Officer, who also worked on the Children's TRC. He also explained that children always had a family member with them when testifying to support them, and where this was not possible were assigned an adult mentor to ease them through the process. Interview by author, Freetown, Sierra Leone, July 24, 2009. In the case of children's testimonies, fear of stigmatization led the TRC not to release their testimonies. As one statement taker explained, "You never know who that child might grow up to be and how the past will haunt them." Josephine Thompson-Shaw, TRC Statement Taker, interview by author, Freetown, Sierra Leone, Sierra Leone, August 6, 2009.

[127] The Sierra Leonean TRC Report, Volume 1, Chapter 4.

[128] Post-conflict Reintegration Initiative for Development and Empowerment (Pride), "Ex-Combatant Views of the Truth and Reconciliation Commission and the Special Court in Sierra Leone" (Freetown, Sierra Leone, PRIDE in partnership with the International Center for Transitional Justice, 2002), p. 12.

to run away, the war came on this day, we all suffered, and so on."[129] Shaw argues that women were reluctant to speak until they were offered the opportunity to make recommendations, and in these cases, the recommendations tended to be social rather than personal: "They would tell us, 'I want them to build schools, I want them to build a hospital, I want education for my children.' Sometimes, they would say, 'I want money to start my business,' but usually they don't ask for anything personal, but for social amenities for the children and the community."[130]

Conclusions

The TRC was established in a complex and in many ways, uncertain domestic climate. Pragmatic concerns over the challenges facing the country and a domestic and regional legacy favoring reconciliation gave weight to a restorative agenda among sections of Sierra Leonean civil society. At the same time, the TRC's orientation became more entrenched over time, particularly in light of concerns over the SCSL's impact on its proceedings. The TRC's restorative orientation shaped various aspects of its work, including its methodology, narrative, conception of reconciliation, and collection of testimonies.

Leading into the next chapter, and central to later criticisms of transitional justice, critics inside and outside of the country have contested both the causes and the end of the war. The RUF's agency – whether in fact it had a choice in surrendering – has played a determining role in the SCSL's case of RUF interim commander, Issa Sesay. Also of interest is the diplomatic contribution of Sierra Leonean civil society in negotiations with the RUF – a factor which we will see in the next chapter, emerges again in an intense politics of legitimacy of transitional justice.

Feeding into Sierra Leone's transitional justice process, the end of the war has also renewed discussions about the drivers and causes of the war. External academics, journalists, and Sierra Leonean government officials

[129] Thompson-Shaw, interview.

[130] While the TRC sought to incorporate gender-sensitive measures (e.g., hiring female statement takers and not releasing names of rape victims), like others, Thompson-Shaw notes that women rarely discussed sexual violence. Thompson-Shaw, interview. Although the TRC claims that contrary to the Commission's expectations, a large number of women were willing and wanted to speak about sexual violence, as others have argued, women were hesitant to speak about experiences of rape for cultural and social reasons. See in particular, Chris Coulter, *Bush Wives and Girl Soldiers: Women's Lives through War and Peace in Sierra Leone* (Ithaca: Cornell University Press, 2009), p. 180.

have often focused on the economic drivers of the conflict.[131] Journalist and media accounts have frequently capitalized on the hedonism and criminal mentality of the RUF, depicting the conflict as urban gang warfare and opportunism.[132] Focusing on the RUF's involvement in diamond mining, Sierra Leonean academic and journalist Lansana Gberie has argued that while Sierra Leoneans consistently puzzled over the motives and "depths of depravity" of the rebels, a more important question is what could have "sustained the level of intensity and violence that plagued such a materially poor country?"[133]

Many within Sierra Leonean civil society and more ethnographically inclined scholars have criticized the emphasis on economic drivers of the war. They posit that diamonds are significant because of the highly unequal social system and the low tax revenue and corruption resulting from Sierra Leone's lucrative extractive economy.[134] A combination of class politics and hierarchical community structures, youth marginalization, and a "crisis of education" had pervasive effects on all aspects of economic, social, and political life. Noting the often-personalized character of violence, these accounts have emphasized psychosocial factors in driving ex-combatant participation in the war, arguing that the RUF played into micro-level social and personal grievances.[135]

131 These studies highlight Charles Taylor, external diamond companies, and Sierra Leone's Lebanese community as direct beneficiaries in the conflict. See Gberie, *A Dirty War in West Africa*; Mats Berdal and David M. Malone, eds., *Greed and Grievance: Economic Agendas in Civil Wars* (Boulder, CO: Lynne Rienner, 2000); Paul Collier and Anke Hoeffler, "On Economic Causes of Civil War," *Oxford Economic Papers* 50 (1998); and Paul Collier, "Economic Causes of Civil Conflict and Their Implications for Policy" (Washington, DC: World Bank, 2000).

132 Robert D. Kaplan, "The Coming Anarchy," *The Atlantic Monthly* (1994) and Douglas Farah, "They Fought for Nothing, and that's What They Got," *Washington Post* (September 1, 2001).

133 Gberie, *A Dirty War*, p. 180.

134 David Keen and Paul Richards cite a complex mixture of economic need and profit and fear and resentment. Peters, *War and the Crisis of Youth* and Keen, *Conflict and Collusion*. See also Roy Maconachie and Tony Binns, "Beyond the Resource Curse? Diamond Mining, Development, and Post-Conflict Reconstruction in Sierra Leone," *Resource Policy* 32 (2007).

135 Zack-Williams, "Child Soldiers," p. 78. Macartan Humphreys and Jeremy M. Weinstein note the high number of female fighters in the RUF (25 percent), arguing that RUF "combat wives units" and recruitment of females were targeted policies, in which the RUF played upon the unequal access to wives. "Who Fights? The Determinants of Participation in Civil War," *American Journal of Political Science* 52, no. 2 (2006), p. 576. See also Chris Coulter, *Bush Wives and Girl Soldiers*. Myriam Denov adds an interesting perspective to the issue of agency and youth combatants. *Child Soldiers: Sierra Leone's Revolutionary United Front* (Cambridge: Cambridge University Press, 2010). For orphans and displaced youth, the army also provided safety and a social network, as military life offered a kind of "surrogate family." Keen, *Conflict*

These narratives have implications for peace-building and transitional justice. For many government officials, embodied in the Kabbah administration's "forgive and forget" discourse, moving forward and economic development should take priority and developing a deeper understanding of the RUF would not be productive.[136] Ethnographically oriented analysts, on the other hand, emphasize studying and taking seriously subjective understandings of ex-fighters. In their view, engaging and understanding ex-combatant motivations and concerns are essential both to facilitate academic understanding, and to further their reintegration and peace-building. Krijn Peters and Paul Richards argue that the key to conflict resolution is agrarian justice and opportunity, and call for the reform of customary land and marriage law.[137] While communal authorities and civil society in the post-TRC period have, by and large, upheld the Commission's non-punitive reintegrative objectives, criticisms of its short-term orientation and formalistic methodology have mobilized local actors to carry out local reconciliation and peace-building. As I will argue in the next chapter, by tying testimony to communal practices of reciprocity and collective labor, community reconciliation has given ex-combatants an opportunity to prove themselves. In the view of my informants, it has also, at least relative to formal mechanisms, provided a long-term framework for reconciliation, making it valuable and self-reinforcing over time.

and Collusion, p. 47. Micro-level accounts tend to emphasize the ideology of the RUF. Paul Richards refers to the RUF as "revolutionaries," who were inspired by the notion of a "Third Way," citing the influence of Gaddafi's "Green Book" and RUF training in camps in Benghazi. *Fighting for the Rainforest*. In these understandings, experiences of deprivation and humiliation also explain some of the extreme brutality of the war.

136 Oxford development economist Paul Collier cautions that interviews with ex-combatants in Sierra Leone are not useful, stating that ex-combatants have an economic interest in misrepresentation and warning that their testimonies will be predetermined:

> The parties to a civil war do not stay silent: they are not white mice observed by scientists. They offer explanations for their actions. Indeed, both parties to a conflict will make a major effort to have good public relations. The larger rebel organizations will hire professional public relations firms to promote their explanation, and the governments which they are opposing will routinely hire rival public relations firms. –Collier, "Economic Causes of Civil Conflict," p. 1.

137 Krijn Peters criticizes the literature's disregard of RUF voices. While RUF leaders enriched themselves, lower-level combatants gained little from the conflict. In his findings, former RUF did believe that they were fighting for a cause, emphasizing in particular agricultural development and redistribution. While most of Peters' interviewees acknowledged that the RUF had failed, Peters argues that post-war reintegration of the RUF has worked best where agrarian reform created economic opportunities for former fighters. Krijn Peters and Paul Richards, "Why We Fight: Voices of Youth Combatants in Sierra Leone," *Africa: Journal of the International Africa Institute* 68 (1998), pp. 183–210. See also Richards, "To Fight or to Farm?"

5 Localism and Pragmatic Solidarity in Sierra Leone

Since the end of the war, Sierra Leone has faced complex challenges of recovery. In a small country, measuring approximately 28,000 square miles and with a population of just over 6 million inhabitants, the war left immense legacies. Chronic underdevelopment,[1] unemployment,[2] and corruption[3] have carried over from the civil war. This post-war context provides a significant critical backdrop in structuring local experiences of the country's recent high-profile transitional justice institutions. In this chapter, I emphasize the importance of endogeneity in evaluating transitional justice. Where prolonged experiences of violence and marginalization, especially in rural areas, had already eroded civic trust and political capital, slow progress in implementing the TRC's recommendations and its linking of testimony to inducements generated a crisis of expectations, particularly among victims. A backdrop of continued communal marginalization and atomization of affected populations (particularly victims) also colored transitional justice experiences and generated significant dissatisfaction among affected communities and survivors.

A closer analysis, however, reveals a multifaceted picture in which local actors and community organizations have mobilized to take forward the aims of peace-building and reconciliation. Rather than stall reconciliation efforts, concern over the international character of transitional justice and the severe challenges facing the country motivated local agents to organize in favor of locally led peace-building and reconciliation. In this chapter, I describe a complex and dynamic process that emerged largely

[1] Only 42 percent of the rural population has access to an improved water source and the current average life expectancy at birth is forty-five years. Although on the rise, gross national income as of 2013 is 680 USD per capita. Measured in 2012. Available at: http://data.worldbank.org/country/sierra-leone.

[2] Sierra Leone's youth unemployment rate at 60 percent is among the highest in West Africa. Available at: www.worldbank.org/en/country/sierraleone/overview.

[3] Sierra Leone continues to come out at the bottom of Transparency International's Global Corruption Barometer. Transparency International, Global Corruption Barometer 2013 (Berlin, Germany, 2013). Available at: www.wingia.com/web/files/news/61/file/61.pdf.

out of contention over the scope and nature of transitional justice. On a surface level, recent civil society peace-building and reconciliation efforts, notably Fambul Tok, also advanced a broadly restorative orientation, linking testimony to reintegration and emphasizing youth empowerment and the fostering of generational bonds. At the same time, grassroots efforts also represent a critical reevaluation among sectors of civil society, taking up a commitment to localism and capacity-building in the post-TRC era. Informal processes, I will argue, filled a crucial void left in the wake of politicized and short-term formal processes, and created ownership and a meaningful ongoing opportunity for community reconciliation. In this context, I will argue that informal communal mechanisms functioned also as an outgrowth of formal processes. If anything, formal justice processes mobilized space for local and tradition-based practices to take hold.

Civic Trust, Pragmatic Solidarity, and a Crisis of Expectations

They spent millions to reintegrate the ex-combatants in the DDR process. If they could just spend a small fraction of this on the victims, it would make such a difference. It is not fair. We have a permanent disability; it is for life. Our children are our breadwinners. We are like children. Looking at me, people say, "that man is finished." Sometimes it is hard to get food here.

–Alhaji Jusu Jaka, Chair of the Sierra Leone Amputees and War-Wounded Association.[4]

Our people are poor in Sierra Leone, we have to reconcile, we don't have a choice.

–Sierra Leonean journalist and Fambul Tok officer, Pel Koroma.

Sierra Leone's eleven-year civil war caused a devastating loss of life and severely damaged the country's infrastructure and social fabric. The messy nature of the war, where RUF insurgents, military combatants, and civilian defense forces committed atrocities against civilians, and occasional collaboration between protagonists, left a high degree of societal insecurity and mistrust. In Kailahun, where the war began and ended, a long backdrop of state marginalization and neglect reinforced fatalism in authority structures and collective action. At the same time, personalized experiences of violence and the use of child soldiers strained the societal fabric and social norms, particularly intergenerational relations. The war left a large population of migrant youth, many of whom were afraid or unwilling to return to a subordinate status. Displacement

[4] Jaka, interview.

and loss of family members further ruptured traditional family and educational support structures.[5]

While the TRC sought to address some of these legacies by linking its proceedings to democratization, youth engagement, and a participatory reform process, lack of follow-up and the slow implementation of the Commission's recommendations undermined its legacy. Concerns over the appropriate follow-up to the Commission came up as early as 2005, when the TRC Working Group Report warned of a "bumpy start" to the "follow-up phase."[6] The report described a widespread frustration over the TRC's delay in making the report available. It warned that individuals felt "betrayed," calling the lag an "anticlimax," and raising the concern that the government was "doctoring the report."[7] Chief Investigator, Howard Varney, called the delay "potentially fatal," at the time stating that the Commission's momentum was lost and its work was delegitimized.[8] Officials also warned that the Commission's work would be irrelevant without results – and that "people will turn against the whole idea of a TRC."[9]

By 2009, when my research for this project began, the lack of progress in carrying out the TRC's recommendations had severely affected public perceptions. In historically marginalized areas, such as Kailahun, slow implementation of reparatory justice reinforced a larger experience of government neglect and indifference. Inhabitants of the region emphasized the persistence of the root causes of the war, and pointed out its pervasive legacies, including physical manifestations, which served as daily reminders of the war.[10] In the village of Bomaru on the Eastern Liberian border,

5 Fambul Tok representative in Kailahun, interview by author, Kailahun, Sierra Leone, July 13, 2009. In war-affected areas, such as Kailahun, families were often separated, and fled to Freetown, Guinea, or Liberia. Handicap International official Bobo Cakpindi, who spent his childhood as a refugee in Guinea, recalled his experience coming back a decade later, with some of his cohorts more fluent in French than in their mother tongue. Bobo Cakpindi, Handicap International official, interview by author, Kailahun, Sierra Leone, July 13, 2009.

6 Ibid. Copies of the report had only arrived in August 2005. Paul James-Allen, SheKu B. S. Lahai and Jamie O'Connell, "Sierra Leone's Truth and Reconciliation Commission and Special Court: A Citizen's Handbook" (New York: National Forum for Human Rights and the International Center for Transitional Justice, 2003), p. 2.

7 Copies of the report had only arrived in August 2005.

8 James-Allen, Lahai, and O'Connell, "Sierra Leone's Truth and Reconciliation Commission," p. 11.

9 Interview with Daisy Marion Bockarie in the Sierra Leone Working Group on Truth and Reconciliation, "Searching for Truth and Reconciliation."

10 Teachers bemoaned the lack of state funds for education and that families cannot educate and feed their children. In Kailahun, CORD-Sierra Leone staff members pointed to the now empty RUF "slaughter house" in the town square and a wall that still had bloodstains. Vandi Dauda, Abie Morray, and Foday Momoh Amara, Officials at CORD-Sierra Leone Development NGO, interview by author, Kailahun, Sierra Leone, July 12, 2009.

marking the site of the RUF's first attack, residents expressed ambivalence toward the TRC's memorial pavilion. Community members alleged that residents in Freetown blamed them for the war, citing the memorial as their last contact with the TRC. A health-care worker living in Bomaru from Kenema shared that the government had stationed him in the village for several years, but that he has yet to receive a salary.[11] He treats patients in the village and they house him and give him food, yet he does not have medical supplies to offer people, including antiretroviral treatment. As was the case in other communities in Kailahun, villagers in Bomaru stated that they were still in the "emergency relief" stage, contrasting the present situation to the fertile potential of the land and agriculture before the war. At present, poor roads and the lack of basic waterproof and airproof storage facilities spoil produce before it gets to the market. Resentment was also high over foreign food imports a decade since the end of the war, which created more dependence on foreign aid, rather than capacity and infrastructure for sustainable development.[12] Failure to provide basic opportunities in subsistence agriculture in war-affected areas significantly damaged the reputation of the TRC. Local residents perceived the lack of follow-up as a governmental failing, thereby undermining democracy.

Victims' marginalization in all parts of the country continues to be particularly acute. Although the TRC took steps to explain that it had no funding to carry out recommendations and was independent of the government, victims frequently charged that the TRC had not "delivered," particularly in the realm of reparatory justice. As the chair of the Sierra Leone Amputees and War-Wounded Association, Alhaji Jusu Jaka notes, for amputees who testified at TRC hearings, the lack of reparations has been a bitter pill to swallow: "We were expecting immediately after the recommendation report, the government would implement it but nothing has come."[13] At the Grafton War-Wounded Camp, amputees who had testified at the TRC stressed that they had participated in good faith and revealed intimate stories with little result. They saw the implementation of the TRC's recommendations as a test of government and societal commitment, which had failed, sending a message to vulnerable populations that it had not taken their needs seriously nor heard their voices.[14] In

[11] Mr. Salieh, interview by author, Bomaru, Sierra Leone, July 13, 2009.

[12] Bomaru Focus Group, Bomaru, Sierra Leone, July 7, 2009.

[13] Alhaji Jusu Jaka, chair of Sierra Leone Amputees and War-Wounded Association, interview by author, Freetown, Sierra Leone, August 7, 2009.

[14] Amputees interviewed in Grafton were still waiting for reparations – all had to pull their children out of school to help contribute to the family income. For Sunni Savinam, age sixty-nine, widower and father of nine, the only way to subsist was to send his children to beg in Freetown on Fridays before Muslim prayer services. His eldest son, age twenty-nine, has taken on the responsibility as primary caretaker for the younger children.

Figure 5.1 War Memorial in Bomaru, Sierra Leone, commemorating the victims of the RUF's first attack in the country on March 23, 1991. Photo taken by author in July 2009.

war-affected villages in Kailahun, amputees shared this disillusionment, stating that they never heard from the TRC after testifying.

Disappointment over reparatory justice and the everyday struggles of victims also fed into societal perceptions of reintegration. On the one hand, as I noted in Chapter 4, although many Sierra Leoneans were not familiar with the TRC's hearings and findings, the TRC's nonpunitive and restorative stance generated less controversy. Interviewees, particularly in rural areas, tended to express similar views of the causes of the conflict and echoed the TRC's narrative stance, describing the conflict as a "war that profited nobody," and "destroyed the country." Although intellectuals and academics often supported prosecutions – emphasizing the contribution of trials to reestablish the rule of law and as a means of deterrence – victims and war-affected communities in Kailahun and Grafton frequently endorsed a nonpunitive orientation.[15] Interviewees

[15] Some residents of villages in Kailahun stressed that punishment was less important for those who committed atrocities, although some agreed that the SCSL should focus on the highest perpetrators in the conflict. Individuals who testified at the TRC stated that reconciliation was the "Sierra Leonean way" and that "God has put the capacity of

Figure 5.2 Grafton Village, Sierra Leone, with residents from the Polio, War-Wounded, and Amputee Camps. Photo taken by author in July 2009. The residents asked for the photo to be taken to raise awareness to their isolation in the camps and present plight.

agreed that reconciliation was inevitable, and "the only way forward" for future development and peace. When asked why they testified at the TRC, residents in Grafton shared their hopes that their participation would give their communities and families a better future.[16] Inhabitants of rural areas in Kailahun referred to "stages of conflict transition," looking at reconciliation as a precondition for long-term capacity-building and sustainable development.

Significantly, the TRC's pragmatic orientation toward ex-combatants also extended to victims. At the Grafton War-Wounded Camp, victims stated that it was not society's role nor in its interest to punish crimes of this magnitude. Some found solace that justice would come eventually,

forgiveness inside us." See also Gearoid Millar. Truth Telling in Sierra Leone: Post-war Needs and Transitional Justice," *Human Rights Review* 12 (2011), pp. 524–529.

16 Grafton group interview, Grafton War-Wounded Camp, Grafton, Sierra Leone, July 7, 2009.

and inspiration for reconciliation in religion.[17] Another common concern was that criminal justice monopolized scarce resources, which could be invested into development. Interviewees also distinguished between levels of guilt, taking a similar position to the TRC that children were foremost victims, and differentiating between "those who bear the greatest responsibility" and lower-level combatants. Grafton resident Sunni Savinam, who lost both hands to the RUF attack on Freetown and testified in front of the SCSL and the TRC, recalls: "The person who cut my hand was a rebel, a small boy. It happened on Friday, January 22. But the boss is [RUF commander] Issa Sesay. If Sesay is locked in jail I am very happy for that but not the one who cut my hand, who was just a small boy."[18] For Savinam, the child's involvement in the RUF was not his fault, and he hopes that he can finish his schooling. In his view, forcing a child to maim was also a crime against the child, who would have to carry this legacy for life.[19]

At the same time, disillusionment over reparatory justice and continued structural problems have severely tested the boundaries of social tolerance. Widespread concern that the TRC's proceedings targeted reintegration over the needs of victims undermined social capital. Victims, such as Jaka, complained about having to bear a disproportionate burden for societal reconciliation:

> These people [the ex-combatants] have already stolen the country's money and goods and committed violence for the eleven years of the war and then they were very well paid during the DDR process to make them self-reliant. They spend it right away and have the criminal mentality – they will just loot somewhere else when it runs out. It's like putting water on the sand with them.[20]

While the plight of child soldiers has generated considerable domestic and international attention and sympathy, victims have generally been less visible in the public sphere. They often face social stigma and, in a primarily rural economy that relies heavily on collective labor, have

[17] At Grafton, victims expressed reassurance that perpetrators are in "God's hands now." As put by Jaka, "Maybe they can't be identified by the Special Court but God will punish them. The final maker of every human being in the world needs to make the final judgment so they will face their judgment day. They may have escaped here but their maker will take action on them." Jaka, interview. See also Millar, "Ah Lef Ma Case Fo God."

[18] Sunni Savinam, sixty-nine-year-old amputee, widower, and father of nine, interview by author, Grafton War-Wounded Camp, Grafton, Sierra Leone, July 7, 2009.

[19] Ibid.

[20] Jaka, interview. Timothy Kelsall also found that the TRC's hearings were focused much more on the reintegration of ex-combatants rather than victims. "Truth, Lies, Ritual: Preliminary Reflections on the TRC in Sierra Leone," *Human Rights Quarterly* 27 (2005), pp. 361–391.

internalized a view of themselves as burdens to their communities and families.[21] At Grafton, Savinam contrasted the lush green surroundings and quiet atmosphere to his inability to work – stating that the location is "peaceful," but that he did not see a future here for himself and his children.[22] Amputees, who lived with their former communities, also described stigma and marginalization. In villages in Kailahun, amputees spoke of "infantalization," as they could not sufficiently carry their weight and contribute to collective work.[23] As I will detail shortly, when discussing reparations, victims frequently brought up the range of programs to reintegrate combatants, for instance, skills training, education, and the UN-led DDR process. Some complained that perpetrators had better living conditions in prisons at the SCSL, compared to victims in their communities.[24]

These criticisms have unleashed a politics of blame at the elite level. Government officials have criticized the TRC as shortsighted, faulting it for its "lack of a follow-up strategy," failing to secure sufficient funding, and more generally for making promises and raising hopes without long-term planning.[25] TRC officials commonly argued that insufficient internal government support stifled the Commission's public impact and irreversibly delegitimized the process. Secretary of the Human Rights Commission, Abraham John, cites a broader frustration over the international influence over the Commission:

21 Many amputees have been relocated to disability camps. In the case of Grafton Amputee Camp, amputees were initially resettled as part of the TRC's collective reparations program to avoid stigma and give them farmland, along with other disabled populations, including widows and polio victims. While the Norwegian Council provided financial support during their first six months of residency, today, most are socially isolated and find it impossible to earn a living. Other residents of the camp include individuals with polio, widows, and victims of wartime rape and their children. The physical and social isolation of victims has also kept them out of the everyday experiences of the general population.

22 Savinam, interview.

23 Amandu Kante, interview by author, Bomaru, Sierra Leone, July 7, 2009.

24 Donors spent a total of 80 million USD for DDR, paying each combatant 150 USD for handing in their weapon. However, while the United Nations estimates that approximately 72,490 combatants were disarmed, fewer than half that number of weapons has been collected. See the UN DDR Sierra Leone Country Programme Report, available at: www.unddr.org/countryprogrammes.php?c=60. For a discussion on the victims' perception of DDR in other contexts, see Lars Waldorf, "Just Peace? Integrating DDR and Transitional Justice," in *Transitional Justice and Peace-building on the Ground*, ed. Chandra Lekha Sriram Jemima García-Godos, Johanna Herman, and Olga Martin-Ortega (New York and London: Routledge, 2013), pp. 66–67. See also Wendy Lambourne on Sierra Leone, "Transitional Justice and Peace-building after Mass Violence," *International Journal of Transitional Justice* 3, no. 1 (March 2009), p. 42.

25 See, for example, Dr. Lansana Nyalley, deputy minister of education, youth and sports, interview by author, Freetown, Sierra Leone, August 16, 2009.

I know that the TRC had a lot of problems – administrative and financial – which affected its ability to reconcile victims and perpetrators. It was done in my view in a superficial way. I don't want to be part of the conspiracy theory that it was all done by external actors, but there was not enough financial internal support. I think if there had been more internal government support, it would contribute to the depth of the reconciliation process.[26]

While in some cases, the government did implement programs that reflected the TRC's recommendations, as in its "mainstreaming youth initiative," it did not generally link these to the Commission or its recommendations.[27]

Civil Society, Community Reconciliation, and Localism

If we do not reconcile, we can't develop. If we have war grudges, we can't reconcile. So with the children, we are teaching them that the war came as a result of mistakes that we made ourselves. And that we had the impact. And that your uncle did something wrong to your father.

Masiver Bilahai, secondary school principal, who runs peace workshops and foster care initiatives with rural children and former child soldiers in Kailahun.[28]

I, as a chief, used to tell them that if we don't come out and tell our stories, forget about everything, development will not come to our communities.

–Chief Maada Alpha Ndolleh, District Chief of Kailahun district and Fambul Tok representative in Kailahun.[29]

Manifestations of a complex and shifting relationship between the TRC and Sierra Leonean civil society appeared early on during the initial planning of the TRC. In August 1999, the TRC Working Group was created as a coalition of human rights NGOs, professional groups, and development organizations under the direction of the National Forum for Human Rights. Human rights activist John Caulker founded the Sierra Leonean human rights organization, Forum of Conscience, in 1996, as the organizing point of the Working Group. The Working Group's purpose was to "involve Sierra Leonean civil society in the TRC process and to ensure that civil society's concerns would be addressed in the design of

[26] John, interview. Some TRC staff also cited the insufficient level of commitment of international commissioners, who "left as soon as the job was over," as barriers to the TRC having a meaningful political impact. See James-Allen, Lahai, and O'Connell, "Sierra Leone's Truth and Reconciliation Commission and Special Court," p. 8. See also Beth Dougherty, "Searching for Answers: Sierra Leone's Truth and Reconciliation Commission," *African Studies Quarterly* 8 (2004), pp. 39–56.

[27] Youth programs also existed at the centralized level, where the government undertook programs to "mainstream youth" into decision-making, including "child ambassadors" to government.

[28] Bilahai, interview.

[29] Interview by author, Kailahun, Sierra Leone, July 12, 2009.

the TRC Act and in the ways in which the Commission was going to undertake its task."[30] While the resumption of violence after the Lomé Accord initially stalled meetings, the Forum and the Human Rights Section of the United Nations Mission in Sierra Leone (UNAMSIL) met again in the early 2000s to conduct sensitization and public education on the TRC.

Tensions quickly surfaced between the Working Group and the TRC. The TRC attributed inadequate public awareness of its work and objectives to the "poor management" of the Working Group.[31] Key members of the Working Group expressed concern over the international influence over the TRC, the sidelining of Sierra Leonean civil society, and the TRC's overall level of popular engagement, especially in rural areas. Disappointment mounted that the TRC had helped reinforce and generate new elites through its partnership with a select group of civil society. Tensions also mounted where the TRC and international actors failed to acknowledge important parallel and preceding civil society efforts.[32]

Significantly for procedural reconciliation, however, despite – or because of – this strained and uneven relationship, the TRC would come to offer an important mobilizing focus for victims' groups and civil society campaigns. Already during the TRC's operation, amputees in Sierra Leone drew international headlines, boycotting the TRC until it set out provisions to guarantee their demands.[33] In 2002, Caulker helped establish the Sierra Leone Amputees and War-Wounded Association for victims to have a platform at the TRC. Through meetings between amputee representatives and the TRC, both groups reached an agreement on March 15, 2003. The TRC recruited two members of the amputee association as assistant statement takers, taking its first statements in the Freetown Amputee Camp on March 19, 2003. Chair of the association, former businessman Alhaji Jusu Jaka, who lost both arms during the 1999 RUF invasion of Freetown, has become a well-known figure domestically and abroad for his campaigns on behalf of victims. While the organization focuses primarily on amputees in the Murray Town camp in Freetown, it has expanded its focus to include victims' issues on the national level.[34]

[30] The Sierra Leonean TRC Report, Volume 1, Chapter 5. [31] Ibid.

[32] See, for instance, Simone Datzberger, "Barefoot Soldiers for Social Justice, Food Security and Peace," *Africa at LSE* (2012), Available at: http://blogs.lse.ac.uk/africaatlse/2012/01/11/sierra-leone-barefoot-soldiers-for-social-justice-food-security-and-peace/.

[33] These included housing, a monthly allowance in cash, rice, education for children, a reintegration allowance, medical treatment, and assistance with transport.

[34] Joint sensitization campaigns between the TRC and the Amputee Association ran from April 3 to 6, 2003, in Bo, Kenema, Kono, Makeni, and Masiaka. TRC staff and

Rifts between the TRC and some segments of civil society grew stronger as the TRC carried out its work. Caulker became an important figure in taking steps to localize transitional justice. Although he initially served on the TRC Working Committee, over time, Forum of Conscience became increasingly critical of the TRC's management and policies.[35] It cited the TRC's lack of "partnership" with communal authorities, and insufficient engagement of local culture and traditions as particularly grave shortcomings.[36] While Forum of Conscience originally worked in support of the TRC, Caulker eventually distanced himself, establishing the community reconciliation project Fambul Tok in 2007.[37] Emphasizing local ownership and communal traditions, Fambul Tok ceremonies utilize local practices of conflict management and work through a decentralized system of local authorities and representatives.[38] In an ethnically diverse country, Fambul Tok serves as an umbrella framework to encourage dialogue and interest in reconciliation and help communities revive their own restorative practices.[39]

This realignment was not universal. For some advocacy groups, the TRC provided an important reference point. As Kailahun secondary

representatives of the Amputee Association of Freetown worked together to encourage amputees to give statements to the Commission.

35 These criticisms also emerged among some of the Sierra Leonean commissioners and staff.

36 This is also Tim Kelsall's finding. See Kelsall, "Truth, Lies, Ritual." See also the Sierra Leone Working Group on Truth and Reconciliation, "Searching for Truth and Justice in Sierra Leone: An Initial Study of the Performance and Impact of the Truth and Reconciliation Commission" (February 2006). Commissioner William Schabas controversially defends the TRC's public impact:

> After all, most European law students have trouble explaining the distinctions between the European Court of Human Rights and the European Court of Justice. Who can really expect uneducated, illiterate peasants in the countryside of Sierra Leone to do better? ... To the extent that the people of Sierra Leone understand that the two bodies exist, and that they have some shared objectives, such as accountability for human rights violations, then the message has been delivered and "sensitization" achieved.

"The Relationship between Truth Commissions and International Courts: The Case of Sierra Leone." *Human Rights Quarterly* 25 (2003), pp. 1064–1065.

37 After four months of community consultations and sensitization across Sierra Leone's fourteen districts, Forum of Conscience began its first pilot project in March 2008 in Kailahun given its significance in the history of the war.

38 Fambul Tok procedures include a series of truth-telling bonfire ceremonies, where victims and offenders are given the chance to testify at ceremonies often accompanied by local traditions: ritual cleansing and the optional offering of forgiveness. These are often followed by other initiatives, notably the drawing of a peace tree as a site for future conflict resolution, sports events, youth recordings of testimonies for broadcast on local radio, and communal farming projects, wherein recently reconciled individuals work side by side.

39 Fambul Tok benefits from financial and research support from the American organization Catalyst for Peace. The Center for Justice and Peace-building at Eastern Mennonite University also supports the organization.

school principal Masiver Bilahai, who ran peace sessions with youth and foster programs, maintained, both the TRC and community reconciliation efforts played important roles in Sierra Leone's post-conflict recovery, and should not be seen as alternatives: "We all do our part to rebuild our country after the war."[40] In his view, the TRC has served as a catalyst for community reconciliation and peace-building, reviving interest in traditional mechanisms of redress and dispute resolution.[41] The post-war period has seen a general increase of NGO activity and activism, focusing on peace-building and youth integration. Individuals connected to the TRC have staffed some of these organizations, particularly in Freetown, where advocacy groups formally linked themselves to the Commission to carry out their campaigns. In November 2007, the Sierra Leonean parliament enacted the National Human Rights Commission Act to produce a completion strategy for the implementation of the TRC's recommendations. This led to the establishment of the Human Rights Commission, which has taken on a de facto role as the TRC's follow-up committee, drawing on the TRC's findings and agenda and conducting research and monitoring current human rights issues in the country. In August 2008, the government of Sierra Leone and the United Nations implemented the National Commission for Social Action (NaCSA), to implement recommendations related to reparations.[42] While these ties to the Commission were strongest in Freetown, they also extended to more remote war-affected areas. In Kailahun, a range of organizations have emerged throughout the region, often under Sierra Leonean professionals from Kailahun or individuals who had moved to the region from different parts of the country to help in post-conflict reconstruction.

Less directly, important normative and discursive continuities have carried over between the TRC and local peace-building efforts. While important actors, notably Fambul Tok, distanced themselves from international transitional justice, contrasting their grassroots focus to centralized formal processes in Freetown, local peace-building and reconciliation processes have often shared the TRC's restorative orientation, emphasizing reintegration and reconciliation over criminal punishment.[43] Community

[40] Masiver Bilahai, Kailahun secondary school principal and youth worker, interview by author, Kailahun, Sierra Leone, July 14, 2009.

[41] Saidu Conton Sasay, NaCSA, interview by author, Freetown, Sierra Leone, August 18, 2009.

[42] Reparations' payments, averaging 80 USD per victim, are part of the 4.55 million USD Sierra Leone Reparations Program, funded by the UN Peace-building Fund. Available at: http://reliefweb.int/report/sierra-leone/sierra-leone-victims-receive-compensation.

[43] Teachers in Kailahun stated that it was better to "let bygones, be bygones," and "nobody is pointing fingers here." Plan International official, interview by author, Kailahun, Sierra Leone, July 12, 2009.

organizations have often taken a similar pragmatic stance toward youth, arguing that children were foremost victims and were "forced" and "indoctrinated" to participate in violence. I was frequently told that "These are our own children who committed the atrocities" and "You cannot disown your own child" and that the "government used the youth to destroy their own country."[44]

The fear that speaking openly about the war would generate self-incriminating evidence and lead to prosecutions also continued to be a challenge for grassroots reconciliation, and like the TRC, community organizations took steps to mitigate this. For Kailahun district chief and Fambul Tok representative, Maada Alpha Ndolleh, "sensitizing" people to participate in Fambul Tok reconciliation was a process of confidence-building and reassurance that testifying would not lead to incrimination:

> Before they start talking, confessing, they say, "You just want to arrest us and take us to Freetown." But before doing that, the chief, as district chairman, has to talk to them to give them the confidence. Because here we have the Special Court and they are afraid that at the end of the day, we will come out and arrest them. So I give them the confidence that nothing will happen to you. If anything happens to you, you can just blame me, Chief Ndolleh. We tell them that we are doing this because we just want our community to develop.[45]

To pave the way, Ndolleh described his own testimony at the first Fambul Tok bonfire in Kailahun Town, admitting that during the war he had stolen from his niece and her husband out of hunger. He publicly apologized and embraced her family.[46] Here, as well, community authorities capitalized on the collective externalities of reconciliation, promoting reconciliation as the "only way forward," and necessary for future peace and development.[47]

Despite these thematic continuities, however, local peace-building efforts indicate a subtle but important critical reorientation over the

[44] It was commonly argued that it did not make sense to hold a grudge against our own "sons and daughters," and that "our children, who were taken from us have finally returned." Bilahai, interview.

[45] Ndolleh, interview.

[46] Similarly, Bilahai emphasized leading by example for his pupils, reconciling with his own family members after the war.

[47] As Sierra Leonean journalist and Fambul Tok officer Pel Koroma put it, "Our people are poor in Sierra Leone, we have to reconcile, we don't have a choice." Interview by author, Freetown, Sierra Leone, August 18, 2009. In Kailahun, Ndolleh encouraged his constituents to take part in Fambul Tok ceremonies to generate a stable foundation for economic growth:

> If we don't come together and talk about what happened, I, as a chief would tell them, development will not happen in our community. If you're silent about it the community will not grow. But if you talk, ask for forgiveness, repent, we have a chance. Each of us knows if we don't forgive this person, our country will not develop. –Ndolleh, interview.

means and drivers of transitional justice. As part of this shift, grassroots efforts have put greater emphasis on the procedures and agents of transitional justice, emphasizing the importance of an organic and sustainable approach that would revitalize local culture and bonds. They commonly asserted that the focus on formal and criminal individual accountability was Western and not meaningful given the emphasis on community and close social ties in Sierra Leonean society. Community groups and participants juxtaposed the intimate link of culture and identity against international transitional justice as a measure of legitimacy and a resource for reconciliation. Fambul Tok, in particular, redirected ownership to the community by articulating and institutionalizing a link between reconciliation, poverty reduction, and development into its practices and encouraging generational repair and empathy.

This discourse was especially potent in areas marginalized from the TRC – and from the state. In Kailahun, the high-profile TRC proceedings juxtaposed against a lack of post-war reconstruction and state policies in rural areas. Residents described a "frozen peace" with simmering problems beneath the surface.[48] Where many cited youth's inability to "solve their problems" as a cause of the war, the lack of reintegration of former child soldiers was especially concerning. Interviewees argued that former combatants were still "drifting," and had little economic opportunity.[49] Some criticized the short-term orientation of international reintegration efforts, e.g., the UNDP or Red Cross technical skills training for ex-RUF, for creating a supply of technical laborers but failing to lead to gainful employment. As a former RUF, who now works as a motorcycle taxi driver, commented, "How many carpenters do we need in one village?"[50]

Rather than stall reconciliation efforts, however, frustration over the lack of youth integration and communal reconciliation created an impetus for local actors to take stock of peace-building and reconciliation and distance themselves from international processes. In Kailahun, a growing sense that the region was on its own bolstered regional and community identifications. Pending challenges, coupled with criticisms

48 "A hungry man is an angry man, a busy man is a content man" and "an idle mind is the devil's nest" were common refrains.

49 Referring to the widespread phenomenon of ex-RUF driving motorcycle taxis, for development worker Matthew Ambrose Moigua, "I'm telling you, if there were no bikes, there would be a lot of harassment, a lot of armed robbery" (Moigua, interview). For a longer discussion on the relation of economic opportunity and reintegration, see Krjin Peters, "From Weapons to Wheels: Young Sierra Leonean Ex-Combatants Become Motorbike Taxi Drivers," *Journal of Peace, Conflict and Development* 10 (2007), pp. 1–23.

50 Former RUF combatant from Kailahun, age thirty-two, interview by author, Kailahun, Sierra Leone, July 12, 2009.

of the international influence over transitional justice, invigorated local efforts, reinforcing a broader emphasis to turn inward among civil society and communal leaders. In Bomaru, villagers recalled their first participation in a Fambul Tok ceremony. As in other villages in Kailahun where perpetrators and victims inhabited the same communities, tensions between villagers were stifling – preventing them from speaking to each other and participating in communal life. Rifts resulting from the war had impeded social relations to the point that villagers, who relied on collective agricultural labor, found it hard to do vital communal work, such as farming and building houses. An elderly man described a "miserable atmosphere" – citing a regular occurrence, where a rape victim would go out of her way to avoid contact with an ex-RUF member. Schoolteacher Sensy J. Musah recalls Fambul Tok's arrival in which it spoke with the villagers about reconciliation. Initially, they were skeptical: "What is this reconciliation? we asked them." Eventually, however, a primary motivation for villagers to participate in Fambul Tok reconciliation ceremonies was to improve their economic situations. After six years of not speaking, the community took part in a series of Fambul Tok reconciliation ceremonies, gathering the following week to build a road to bring agricultural produce to the markets and repairing the homes of war victims. Over time, rifts within the village became less tense as communal work restored a degree of social trust and normalcy in everyday life. Reconciliation served as a form of social capital, which became meaningful and self-generating when proven through action and bringing collective benefit.

This reorientation in favor of local peace-building and reconciliation has generated its own momentum as organizations and individuals liaised with each other in different regions. At the organizational level, Forum of Conscience put together workshops between traditional authorities and youth and installed and trained "youth ambassadors" to help plan reconciliation programs in their villages. Less formally, individuals, such as Bilahai, have taken up a commitment to peace-building within their own communities, focusing on peace education and dispute management training, setting up foster homes for orphans, tutoring and reeducation programs for ex-combatants, and matching up adult mentors to marginalized youth.

As Fambul Tok staff themselves acknowledge, however, the turn toward localism has come with risks. Although Fambul Tok officials have taken steps to tackle prewar hierarchies by empowering youth and fostering intergenerational repair, the organization has also invested in and worked through the chiefdom system to localize reconciliation efforts. While providing ownership and legitimacy and contributing to peace-building at the micro levels, the revitalization of community traditions and authority structures has further distanced local actors and political structures from the center and runs a risk of reinforcing prewar social hierarchies and inequalities.[51] It has also tended to generate less participation on historically marginalized issues, particularly sexual violence, and from subgroups that have historically been disenfranchised, notably, war-affected women.[52]

Navigating Agency: Individual Responsibility and Community Reconciliation

The navigation of accountability and responsibility in Sierra Leone remains a complex issue and continues to surface in present-day community reconciliation work. As was the case at the TRC, for ex-combatants, public testimony at Fambul Tok presented an avenue for reintegration and acceptance into their former communities.[53] Recalling his participation in a Fambul Tok ceremony in Kailahun, an ex-RUF member emphasized to me the importance of generating social understanding of the conditions which drew former insurgents into combat:

EX-RUF MEMBER: *I was so happy when I heard the war was over. Overwhelmed but so happy. Although our houses were burnt and we didn't have places to dwell and we had to come back and reestablish ourselves so it was very hard especially for those who had been away.*

AUTHOR: *Did you feel isolated from other people?*

EX-RUF MEMBER: *When our brothers and sisters came from exile [referring to civilian refugees who had gone to Liberia and Guinea], there was this distinction between us. They considered us to be part of the rebels, they thought we were the fighters, those responsible, when really, we were victims ourselves. They thought I was a rebel because I was with the RUF, but I was also a civilian. They were taking us to be*

[51] Others have made similar arguments in reference to the chiefdom system and current access to justice. See Paul Jackson, "Whose justice in Sierra Leone? Power, Security and Justice in Post-Conflict Reconstruction," in *Evaluating Transitional Justice: Accountability and Peace-building in Post-Conflict Sierra Leone*, ed. Kirsten Ainley, Rebekka Friedman, and Christopher Mahony (Basingstoke: Palgrave Macmillan, 2015), pp. 197–215. In the same volume, see Rebekka Friedman, "Restorative Justice: Promises and Limitations," in *Evaluating Transitional Justice: Accountability and Peace-building in Post-Conflict Sierra Leone*, ed. Kirsten Ainley, Rebekka Friedman, and Christopher Mahony (Basingstoke: Palgrave Macmillan, 2015), pp. 55–76.

[52] Fambul Tok representatives in Kailahun, interview by author, Kailahun, Sierra Leone, July 13 and 14, 2009.

[53] Post-conflict Reintegration Initiative for Development and Empowerment (Pride), "Ex-Combatant Views of the Truth and Reconciliation Commission and the Special Court in Sierra Leone" (Freetown, Sierra Leone, PRIDE in partnership with the International Center for Transitional Justice, 2002).

different people, and we were taking them to be different people. But for now things are a little bit OK.

AUTHOR: *How did you deal with these divisions?*

EX-RUF MEMBER: *From the family level. We had elderly people that came and talked to us to tell us to come together, forgive each other, do what is right. They helped people understand that I was still a civilian, still a victim, even though I had been with the rebels, I was still one of them – a civilian.*

AUTHOR: *Were you afraid that people wouldn't accept you?*

EX-RUF MEMBER: *Yes, I was afraid. Very much afraid. They were saying they have established a Court, whether you fought or did not fight, if you had been with them [the RUF], everyone could be arrested and prosecuted.*

AUTHOR: *Why did you decide to tell your story through Fambul Tok?*

EX-RUF MEMBER: *It's good for me to say something about myself and my activities so other people's minds will be clear about my actions and it's also good for the next man, as maybe I'm taking him as something bad or good, but now his position can be clear. So it's important for us to come together so we no longer have this misunderstanding. If there is no dialogue between us we would never have known his or her position. So it's always important to have dialogue between ourselves.*[54]

While public testimonies provided an opportunity for former fighters to express goodwill, as others have remarked, critical interrogation of individual accountability has often been missing from individual narratives. Jon Elster argues that the acknowledgment of personal wrongdoing may be too much to bear. Perpetrators deny wrongdoing not only strategically but to retain a moral image of themselves: "Very soon, rationalizations, justifications, and excuses take over – not merely to provide a defense in the courts but to preserve the agent's self-image as a moral being."[55] Although many have not returned to their former communities, most former child soldiers have stayed in the country, having to deal with both the psychological impact of their participation and navigating an understanding of themselves and their actions in relation to their present-day opportunity structures and former communities.[56]

What is distinctive within Sierra Leone, however, is the consolidation of a specific post-war narrative structure that has embedded the loss and retrieval of individual agency within the country's post-war recovery

[54] Former RUF from Kailahun, age thirty-two, interview by author, Kailahun, Sierra Leone, July 12, 2009.

[55] Jon Elster, *Closing the Books: Transitional Justice in Historical Perspective* (Cambridge: Cambridge University Press, 2004), p. 241. See also Trudy Govier, "A Dialectic of Acknowledgment," in *Reconciliation (s): Transitional Justice in Postconflict Societies*, ed. Joanna Quinn (Montreal and Kingston, London, and Ithaca: McGill-Queen's University Press, 2009), pp. 43–44.

[56] Abdullah Mustapha argues that ex-combatants practice "self-punishment" by not returning to their communities. Director General, Central Intelligence and Security Unit Office of the President, National Security Secretariat, interview by author, Freetown, Sierra Leone, August 15, 2009.

process. In Northern Sierra Leone, Rosalind Shaw argues that ex-combatants who wanted to establish themselves into civilian life needed to self-identify as victims.[57] To gain the trust and support of their former communities as well as international humanitarian agencies, personal narratives of ex-combatants exhibited certain commonalities. A common theme is for ex-combatants to avoid speaking about any violence beyond their initial abduction, and to emphasize their nonvoluntary entry into the war: "ex-combatants construct a moral personhood affirming that their 'hearts' (Temne *ta-buth*), or inner dispositions are not the 'warm' or 'angry' hearts of fighters. They were not acting for themselves, as many expressed it: their agency was subsumed by their commanders."[58]

Both the TRC and community authorities have perpetuated this narrative.[59] In reference to Fambul Tok, Ndolleh explained: "We come to hear the stories. They will tell us, 'Yes, I did that, but I did that because of the war,' 'I did that because of command,' 'I did that but it was not our fault,' so we forgive him."[60] Through testimony, individual actions become conceptualized as a mistake and public oration presents an opportunity for clarification. In the process, individual agency is renegotiated away from the individual and toward the collective, attributed to forces beyond the individual's control. In South Africa, Peter Wilson likens the TRC's narration of the past to the construction of civic nationalism in European nation-building experiences:

> Truth commissions publish reports which share a similar form with nationalist narratives in the way they render a discontinuity with the past . . . Unlike some nationalist visions of the past in, say, Britain or France, the new South African nation is not naturalized by reference to its ancientness, but in its affirming of the uniqueness of the present. The new South African identity is constructed upon a discontinuous historicity, where the past is not a past of pride, but of abuse . . . pride is only to be found in resistance, by those struggling to recover an "authentic" democratic tradition.[61]

[57] Rosalind Shaw, "Linking Justice with Reintegration? Excombatants and the Sierra Leone Experiment," in *Localizing Transitional Justice: Interventions and Priorities after Mass Violence*, ed. Rosalind Shaw and Lars Waldorf (Stanford, CA: Stanford University Press, 2010), pp. 124–125.

[58] Ibid., p. 125.

[59] As Shaw argues, this discourse is not just learned from international humanitarian and transitional justice actors but also draws upon "longstanding local modes of personhood, power, and agency, in which 'big people's' (in this case, commanders) power is manifest in their capacity for extension, for acting through the vehicle of their subordinates." "Linking Justice with Reintegration?," p. 125.

[60] Ibid.

[61] Richard A. Wilson, *The Politics of Truth and Reconciliation in South Africa: Legitimizing the Post-Apartheid State* (Cambridge, UK: Cambridge University Press, 2001), pp. 16–17.

In Sierra Leone, this other-ing has taken on distinct dynamics. The Sierra Leonean post-war narrative emphasizes severe social, political, and economic strain, resulting from a long history of external exploitation and the marginalization of youth. In a stifling context, this narrative presents the war as a societal illness and collective plague, in which Sierra Leonean society strayed from social norms and imploded inward. War time atrocities are as "not human," and juxtapose against pre-war and present-day social values. The war is not "normal" in Sierra Leone's history or "typically Sierra Leonean," where "Sierra Leoneans are a gentle people" and "not violent." Commonly attributing war time brutalities to drugs, the frenzy of war, and brainwashing, the rediscovery of the country's pre-war traditions and rebuilding of its social fabric become a way forward to collectively attain peace. Emblematic is the child soldier who is at once a victim of the conflict and worthy and capable of redemption.

The post-TRC period has seen a gradual but significant reassessment of responsibility and commitment.[62] As Fambul Tok officials in Kailahun put it, "If every RUF was a victim, then who are the perpetrators?" Interviewees frequently criticized the "one step" orientation toward testimony, challenging the TRC on its own mantra that "reconciliation is a process, not an event." A common view was that the Commission's emphasis on victimization and restitution had generated a sense of individual entitlement, trumping the communal emphasis on restoration and making amends. For some, the TRC had generated a sense of entitlement.[63] Minister of Youth, Sports, and Education, Dr. Lansana Nyalley, described his disappointment with ex-combatant reintegration:

> The aspect of reconciliation as a panacea, that lasted and is done and is finished is what amazes me ... Reconciliation was supposed to be a process, not an event. That you come in, you confess, you're forgiven, you go. It shouldn't be that way. We have to sit again and again and again and again and keep talking about it to the point that it becomes conversational. You may say, "it's done," but I may still be remembering. Because it's like you stand up there and say that it "wasn't my fault, I was on the drug, let's move on." To me that's not satisfying. We don't even know the potential of this person – they did it once, will they do it again, will they reoffend? How do we know that the person has changed, that they will be reintegrated? ... Only when we revisit it frequently, only when we go back to the community and repay something. Even if it's only community service, even if it's only teaching. Even going to a member of that particular family and helping them with something, even if it's only farm work.[64]

[62] Shaw describes a narrative of collective suffering and victimhood. She notes that combatants who wished to reintegrate also needed to locate themselves as "victims" or civilians. "Linking Justice with Reintegration," p. 125.

[63] Sasay, interview. [64] Nyalley, interview.

Reconciliation, it was argued, should be the "first step" of a "series of solutions," where the magnitude of war crimes requires a holistic and multifaceted recovery process.

These criticisms highlight a consistent tension between the assumption of individual responsibility and blame, on the one hand, and communal reconciliation and peace-building, on the other. One consequence has been a greater emphasis among civil society and community leaders on nonformal mechanisms. For Fambul Tok, navigating the tension between reconciliation and accountability requires an understanding of responsibility that is demonstrated, rather than expressed, and continues over time. Truth-telling was just a first step – a ritualistic turning point – to put the war in the past and start a longer-term process of proving individual commitment.[65] Fambul Tok was an important actor in institutionalizing this conception of reconciliation as responsibility into practice through its procedures, tying reconciliation to physical work and giving back to the community.[66] At the micro level, ex-combatants had a chance to prove themselves to their communities through their everyday behavior and actions, thereby demonstrating a capacity for reform and building trust.[67] In Fambul Tok's view, the TRC's linking of testimony to inducements, notably reparations for victims, and reintegration for ex-combatants, had created an instrumental understanding of reconciliation. The expectation of follow-up had led to individual disappointment and eroded social capital by fostering a perception of participation as strategic and disingenuous. One of Fambul Tok's current practices in Kailahun is that after testifying ex-combatants must do something for others, especially victims, for instance, helping with farmwork or rebuilding homes. It insisted that communities show support for reconciliation to make it more meaningful and generate ownership, establishing a criterion that communities must wholly or partially fund their own reconciliation processes.[68]

[65] While the TRC sought to institutionalize the reintegration of ex-combatants into civilian life through its recommendations, calling for ex-combatants to engage in community work, this largely happened with former military soldiers, many of whom now serve in the current military and police corps. Where current soldiers have been involved in a variety of communal work to improve civil–military relations, e.g., building schools and roads, ex-RUF combatants have mainly gone through UN-run skills training and reeducation programs, focused more on their future livelihood rather than in their social reintegration and repair of social relations.

[66] For Fambul Tok staff, the benefit of local as opposed to centralized formal mechanisms, i.e., the TRC and the SCSL was the chance to prove goodwill over time.

[67] Ndolleh, interview.

[68] To this end, Fambul Tok covers half the costs of a ceremony and the village covers the other.

Conclusions

Peace-building and reconciliation are active fields in post-war Sierra Leone, yet the contribution of formal transitional justice to these efforts has been dynamic and complex. On the one hand, the nature of the war and post-war context and a lack of follow-up limited the TRC's broader social and political impact. Where prolonged violence and political neglect and corruption had undermined civic trust and political capital in remote regions, slow progress in reparatory justice and severe post-war problems further damaged the legitimacy of the TRC and contributed to broader alienation and disillusionment. Although the TRC's discourse of reconciliation as a prerequisite for development and peace resonated in a war-weary society, its short-term and rushed methodology also undermined solidarity and awareness of its work.

Significantly, as we shall see in contrast to Peru, in Sierra Leone, where the RUF faces less stigmatization, the TRC's historical findings have generated less debate. Much more in Sierra Leone, however, victims are less conspicuous in the public sphere and many remain marginalized and suffer social isolation. In a backdrop of long-standing restorative practices and returning child soldiers, while the TRC's restorative orientation garnered some social support, over time, a discourse that ex-combatants had not proven themselves and followed their testimonies with action tempered popular tolerance and openness to reconciliation.[69] This disenchantment, coupled with inadequate long-term follow-up and severe underdevelopment, led to criticisms of formal transitional justice and opened space for alternative orientations and voices.

On the other hand, despite – or in some ways, because of – these criticisms, the TRC played an important role in mobilizing civil society. The TRC helped propagate a discourse of political rights and duties, social and individual responsibility, and reconciliation, which present-day organizations have used to frame and legitimize their objectives. Fambul Tok is an important example of a complex and multidimensional relationship between formal and informal justice. While Fambul Tok distanced itself from the TRC – and international transitional justice in general – it also shared core orientations of the TRC, tying reconciliation to communal recovery and economic development, youth empowerment, and intergenerational repair, and emphasizing personal testimony and

[69] For an interesting discussion on perpetrators and responsibility, see Jon Elster, who argues that individuals deny wrongdoing to retain a moral self-image. As time passes, they cannot deal with the weight of their actions: "Very soon, rationalizations, justifications, and excuses take over – not merely to provide a defense in the courts but to preserve the agent's self-image as a moral being." *Closing the Books*, p. 241. See also Govier, "A Dialectic of Acknowledgment," pp. 43–44.

hearings as vehicles to build social understanding and solidarity. At the same time, in Sierra Leone, community leaders and civil society have consciously distanced themselves from international processes, reinforcing the importance of long-term grassroots processes. Plugging into a criticism that ex-combatants should follow testimony with actions, and that they must prove repentance over time, Fambul Tok, in particular, invested reconciliation back into the community, and took an applied approach, following reconciliation ceremonies with communal development and practices of reciprocity. Importantly, however, as I will argue, in contrast to Peru, where contention over formal justice often strengthened centralized democratic politics, the Sierra Leonean TRC helped propagate a normative discourse and politics of reconciliation. Given Sierra Leone's long and contentious history of colonialism and external interference in the country, criticisms that the TRC sidelined local civil society and Sierra Leonean culture and traditions reinforced a larger interest in communal reconciliation and tradition-based practices. While grassroots initiatives, notably Fambul Tok, strengthened communal reconciliation and peace-building, they have had less of an impact on national integration, reinforcing instead a turn toward localism and the decentralization of authority structures.

6 The Shining Path and Political Violence: The Establishment of a Punitive Human Rights–Based Approach

> *The official [state] memory is a simple but effective narrative, where Peru was a peaceful country until Sendero (the Shining Path) appeared, and the military waged a counter-campaign in defense of peace. The official discourse has allowed a partial vision, where victims of terrorism or the epoch of terrorism is a discourse that implies that the victims of the state were not victims.*
>
> – *Félix Reátegui, CVR researcher and sociologist.*[1]

The armed conflict in Peru killed an estimated 69,280 people, surpassing the number of deaths in all foreign and civil wars in Peru's 182 years of independence.[2] Two decades of political violence internally displaced over 600,000 people and destroyed more than 400 peasant communities.[3] Experiences of violence varied sharply across the country: Peru's coastal population and capital were relatively cut off from military violence and experienced attacks by the Shining Path and Movimiento Revolutionario Túpac Amaru (MRTA) relatively late into the conflict. In contrast, civilians in Peru's rural hinterlands suffered political violence at the hands of both Shining Path militants and the armed forces. These diverging experiences left very different legacies and created sharply diverging perspectives on how to best address conflict-related atrocities and move forward.

Taking a closer look at the establishment and procedures of the Comisión de la Verdad y Reconciliación (CVR), in this chapter, I will argue that it took a distinct punitive and human rights–based approach. As in Sierra Leone, contextual factors strongly shaped the Commission's proceedings and domestic reception. The CVR's retrospective establishment after the state's military victory over the Shining Path, a polarized domestic climate, strong stigmas surrounding the Shining Path, and very different regional legacies of violence polarized transitional justice and created a tense relationship between the Commission and large portions of society. In addition, the CVR's commitment to criminal justice further strained its relationship to the armed forces. In this context, the Commission's normative agenda, coupled with mounting tensions and

[1] Félix Reátegui, CVR researcher, interview by author, Lima, Peru, December 1, 2011.
[2] Ibid. [3] CVR Report, Volume 1, Chapter 3.

public pressures, led it to prioritize victims' rights and cultural pluralism over reintegration and engagement of protagonists.

History of the Conflict

The Peruvian armed conflict began in Ayacucho, Huamanga, in the south-central Peruvian Andes. Geographically insignificant and isolated, but home to the majority of victims of the conflict and many former Shining Path militants, Huamanga played a significant role in the colonial history of Peru.[4] Following a sustained Inca rebellion against the Spanish, Francisco Pizarro settled the region with a small number of Spaniards from Lima and Cusco, officially founding the province on April 25, 1540. Venezuelan military leader, Simón Bolívar, named the city in 1825 after the historic Battle of Ayacucho in the nearby Pampa de la Quinoa, which marked the last armed standoff between the Spanish and the *independistas* (independence forces). Throughout the eighteenth century, Ayacucho was a site of indigenous revolts against the Spanish, with descendent of the last emperor, Túpac Amaru II, leading the most well-known uprising in 1780. While the state's suppression of the revolution exterminated the rest of the Inca royal family, as the first large rebellion in the Spanish colonies the insurrection inspired later revolts. After independence, the development of a two-tier feudal society further entrenched neocolonial divisions in the province.[5] Race and class factored into a system of harsh repression from large landowners as governmental neglect magnified popular discontent. In rural areas, a policy of forced assimilation through Spanish "modernization" schools institutionalized the depreciation of indigenous identity. A hierarchical class structure internalized these divides, creating an urban *mestizo* (mixed) upper class amid an indigenous peasant majority.[6]

The Shining Path originated as an eccentric and obscure fringe group in Huamanga. Although it was eventually classified as one of the world's deadliest revolutionary forces[7] and branded as a terrorist organization

[4] Various indigenous groups inhabited the region, including the Wari, Chanka Nazca, and, later, the Inca. The Inca Empire was at its height before the arrival of the Spanish, covering a vast and diverse territory from present-day Colombia to Chile.

[5] For an excellent overall analysis, see Jaymie Heilman, *Before the Shining Path: Politics in Rural Ayacucho, 1895–1980* (Stanford: Stanford University Press, 2010).

[6] See Antonia Zapata Velasco, Nelson Pereyra, and Rolando Rojas Rojas, eds. *Historia y Cultura de Ayacucho* (Lima, Perú: Instituto de Estudios Peruanos, UNICEF, and DED Servicio Alemán de Cooperación Social-Técnica Programa Servicio Civil Para La Paz, 2008).

[7] Gustavo Gorriti, *The Shining Path: A History of the Millenarian War in Peru* (Chapel Hill: University of North Carolina Press, 1999).

within and outside Peru,[8] few had heard of the movement before the 1980s in Peru or globally. The Shining Path's rise did not follow the pattern of Marxist movements in other Latin American universities, which focused more on academic study and gaining intellectual influence.[9] For some observers, the rise of the Shining Path and Peru's descent into political violence were counterintuitive.[10] Where established literature expects democratic transitions to defuse tensions by allowing for a peaceful expression of discontent through formal channels, the Shining Path's emergence in the Andes paralleled the growth of a large and influential legal left.[11] It came to prominence during Peru's most extensive democratic transition and after a sustained period of economic growth.[12] The Shining Path took an almost solitary role among Peru's active left, opposing the country's first long-term economic, social, and political reforms, and spread without foreign support from impoverished areas to more affluent regions in the jungle and along the coast.[13]

The Shining Path's symbol and leader, philosophy professor Abimael Guzmán Reynoso, was born in the city of Arequipa but educated in Lima, completing bachelor degrees in philosophy and law. In 1962, the rector of the university, Dr. Efrain Morote Best, recruited Guzmán to teach philosophy at the Universidad Nacional de San Cristóbal de Huamanga (UNSCH) in Ayacucho and encouraged him to study Quechua. At the

[8] Including by the Peruvian government, the US Department of State, Canada, and the European Union: David Scott Palmer, "Introduction," *The Shining Path of Peru*, ed. David Scott Palmer (London: C. Hurst & Co. Ltd., 1992), pp. 1–32.

[9] Ibid., p. 1. The clandestine character of the Shining Path augmented its mysterious origins: unlike the MRTA, the Shining Path did not give public speeches and generally did not engage with academic researchers at the time.

[10] Jeff Goodwin and Theda Skocpol, "Explaining Revolutions in the Contemporary Third World," *Politics and Society* 17 (1989), p. 495; Ted Robert Gurr, *Why Men Rebel* (Princeton, NJ: Princeton University Press, 1970). Peruvian journalist and Shining Path expert Gustavo Gorriti argues that the Peruvian military was aware of the insurrection and allowed the Shining Path to gain strength because its energies were consumed elsewhere, and as leverage against the civilian government. Gorriti, *The Shining Path*, pp. 45–49; Gustavo Gorriti, interview by author, Lima, Peru, December 3, 2010.

[11] This period saw the establishment of universal suffrage, free press, and an increase in governmental services, particularly in public education and rural development. Palmer, "Introduction," pp. 1–2.

[12] Jo Marie Burt argues that conventional political science understandings of insurgency, emphasizing structural conditions and "failed states," drew on European histories of Weberian state-building, where states eventually consolidate and institutionalize order in the market and society, creating a functional bureaucracy to control territory and maintain a legitimate monopoly of force. She contends that many Latin-American states are better understood as weak states, which do not collapse but never provide for their citizens. Burt, *Violencia y Autoritarismo: Bajo La Sombra de Sendero y la Dictadura de Fujimori* (Lima, Peru: Institute of Peruvian Studies, 2009), p. 30.

[13] Bruce H. Kay, "Violent Opportunities: The Rise and Fall of 'King Coca' and Shining Path," *Journal of Interamerican Studies and World Affairs* 41 (1999), pp. 97–127.

UNSCH Guzmán became increasingly active in left-wing political circles, attracting a following of young academics and activist students; however, he left the university after a tenure as department head in the mid-1970s and went underground.

The Shining Path emerged quietly and garnered little initial attention. In January 1979, the Peruvian police arrested Guzmán, along with several leftist politicians and union leaders, following an urban strike by the Peruvian General Confederation of Workers. Despite leads that Shining Path insurgents were preparing an armed insurrection from Ayacucho, the security services failed to elicit information from the professor.[14] Growing pressure from prominent advocates protesting his innocence, including Guzmán's family members within the military, led to a quick release.[15] Few noticed the Shining Path's first attack. On May 17, 1980, one day before the general elections, five hooded men entered the electoral registration office in the Andean village of Chuschi, tying up the administrator before setting fire to the registry and ballots.[16] Several hours later, the army arrested the youths and took them to the nearby town of Cangallo. The Peruvian government replaced the ballot boxes and the incident blew over.[17]

The Shining Path was founded as a communist party with the objective of overthrowing the Peruvian state and replacing "bourgeois democracy" with "new democracy." Taking up Maoist theories of guerrilla warfare, it planned a revolution from the countryside, espousing violence as the way forward and engaging in the Maoist practices of purging and "self-criticism."[18] State weakness and the marginalization of rural areas played important roles in the group's emergence and consolidation of power. The Shining Path's beginnings in remote outposts in the 1980s allowed it to quickly develop its forces and simultaneously push the government into a reactive response.[19] The government's heavy-handed and frequently indiscriminate military response further hurt the civilian population.[20] In the 1980s, a deepening economic crisis resulted in inflation and a decline in the production of goods and services. Disease and

[14] Gorriti, *The Shining Path*, p. 2. [15] Ibid. [16] Ibid., p. 17.

[17] Even the Ayacuchan press did not mention the incident until four days later, and even then gave it little importance.

[18] Tom Marks, "Making Revolution with Shining Path," in *The Shining Path of Peru*, ed. David Scott Palmer (London: C. Hurst & Co. Ltd., 1992), pp. 193–196. See also Marisol de la Cadena, "From Race to Class: Insurgent Intellectuals *de provincia* in Peru, 1910–1970," in *Shining and Other Paths: War and Society in Peru, 1980–1995*, ed. Steve J. Stern (Durham and London: Duke University Press, 1998), pp. 22–59.

[19] Palmer, "Introduction," p. 2.

[20] Ibid. Carlos Iván Degregori, *Qué Difícil es Ser Dios: El Partido Comunista del Perú – Sendero Luminoso y el Conflicto Armado Interno en el Perú: 1980–1999* (Lima, Peru: Institute of Peruvian Studies, 2010).

a sharp drop in living standards gave the Shining Path new opportunities, to the government's detriment. Under rapid economic liberalization, the government's abandonment of food subsidies and its opening of markets to external competition wreaked havoc among the poor.[21] While Peru functioned as a democratic state in that it held elections and was protective of free press and association, the government labeled and put large portions of territory under military control as "emergency zones." In these marginalized areas, the military held power, rather than elected representatives, and the state suspended civil liberties and political participation.[22] In this context, the Shining Path represented the Peruvian state as fascist and reactionary,[23] and established its stronghold in marginalized areas through a combination of patronage and fear.[24]

Education, class, and status also played significant roles in the Shining Path's recruitment of militants. Guzmán himself was a "dedicated and intelligent student from a lower middle-class background and an irregular family situation, who advanced by dedication and self-discipline rather than natural brilliance."[25] The majority of Shining Path members were marginalized indigenous youth and often first-generation university students. Frustrated expectations resulting from increased educational exposure and non-correlative opportunities increased the Shining Path's ideological appeal.[26] The late Peruvian anthropologist and ex-CVR commissioner, Carlos Iván Degregori, emphasized the pedagogical nature of the Shining Path, noting its "revolution of manuals" and distribution of Marxist literature.[27]

The UNSCH played an influential role in the mobilization of the Shining Path.[28] Although the Shining Path would eventually establish a presence in student councils throughout Peru, as Latin America's third-oldest university and the region's only general university, the UNSCH

[21] John Simpson, *In the Forests of the Night: Encounters with Terrorism, Drug-Running and Military Oppression* (London: Random House, 1993), p. 87.

[22] Burt, *Violencia y Autoritarismo*. For a comprehensive discussion, see Miguel La Serna, *The Corner of the Living: Ayacucho on the Eve of the Shining Path Insurgency* (Chapel Hill, NC: University of North Carolina Press, 2012).

[23] Cynthia McClintock, "Theories of Revolution and the Case of Peru," *The Shining Path of Peru*, ed. David Scott Palmer (London: C. Hurst & Co. Ltd., 1992), p. 228.

[24] Degregori, *Qué Difícil es Ser Dios*. [25] Palmer, "Introduction," p. 9.

[26] De la Cadena, "From Race to Class," p. 24. McClintock, "Theories of Revolution," p. 234. Degregori points out that the Shining Path discourses had a strong influence among rural Andean youth, who had experienced social and economic dislocation. Degregori, *Qué Difícil es Ser Dios*.

[27] Degregori, *Qué Difícil es Ser Dios*, p. 41. Similarly, Gustavo Gorriti describes the personality cult surrounding Guzmán – his doctrinaire use of ideology and his disciplined and methodological leadership. Gorriti, *The Shining Path*.

[28] Orin Starn, "Maoism in the Andes: The Communist Party of Peru-Shining Path and the Refusal of History," *Journal of Latin American Studies* 27 (1995), p. 404.

had historically functioned as a symbol of modernity in Ayacucho and had a prestigious image, attracting external support and donations from European countries as well as young, ideologically driven professors from across Peru.[29] During a time of radicalization of Peruvian universities, the UNSCH embraced and stepped up its historical role as a "bastion of antifascist resistance."[30] The Shining Path was especially popular among faculty in the Department of Anthropology, gaining a following of "cosmopolitan professors" who set up *escuelas populares*, or working-class schools, in the countryside.[31]

While the Shining Path grew in both the territory it controlled and recruits during the 1980s, its university support base began to decline. In Ayacucho, divisions appeared between "foreign" and "native" faculty and students. After a campus battle left sixty people gravely injured, the Shining Path's longtime public face, *Frente de Defensa del Pueblo*, condemned the action.[32] With this loss of university support, the Shining Path shifted focus to the countryside. In March of 1980, it formed a political and military "Revolutionary Directorate" and held its "First Military School," beginning a systematic tactics and weapons training program. During this period, its discourse of equality and provision of services and order found some support among the peasant population.[33] Florencia Mallon refers to a "political honeymoon," where the Shining Path filled a void left by state neglect and repression [34] before its adoption of increasingly brutal and violent measures.[35]

[29] Degregori, *Qué Difícil es Ser Dios*, pp. 132–133. The Shining Path gained particular control over the Universities of Huancayo and La Cantuta, and the National University of Engineering and National University of San Marcos in Lima.

[30] Ibid., p. 140. [31] Ibid., pp. 139 and 133. [32] Ibid., p. 141.

[33] Kimberly Susan Theidon, "Justice in Transition: The Micropolitics of Reconciliation in Post-war Peru," *The Journal of Conflict Resolution* 50 (2006), p. 439.

[34] Florencia E. Mallon, "Chronicle of a Path Foretold? Velasco's Revolution, Vanguardia Revolucionaria, and 'Shining Omens' in the Indigenous Communities of Andahuaylas," in *Shining and Other Paths: War and Society in Peru, 1980–1995*, ed. Steve J. Stern (Durham and London: Duke University Press, 1998), p. 122.

[35] Gonzalo Portocarrero, *Razones de sangre: Aproximaciones a la violencia política* (Reasons of blood: Approximations of political violence) (Lima, Perú: Pontificia Universidad Católica del Perú, 2012); CVR Report, Volume 4, Chapter 1; Degregori, *Qué Difícil es Ser Dios*. De la Cadena, "From Race to Class"; Iván Hinojosa, "On Poor Relations and the Nouveau Riche: Shining Path and the Radical Peruvian Left," in *Shining and Other Paths: War and Society in Peru, 1980–1995*, ed. Steve J. Stern (Durham and London: Duke University Press, 1998), pp. 60–83. In the same volume, see also Ponciano del Pino, "Family, Culture, and 'Revolution': Everyday Life with Sendero Luminoso," in *Shining and Other Paths: War and Society in Peru, 1980–1995*, ed. Steve J. Stern (Durham and London: Duke University Press, 1998), pp. 158–192. This pattern extended to several of Peru's jungle regions as well. In Ashaninka villages, the Shining Path initially enticed men to join the movement with offers of guns or knives. Eventually, however, it forced conscripts to enlist, sometimes ordering new members to commit

The dynamics of the Peruvian armed conflict varied over time. Unlike other South American insurgencies, where state agents committed violence against often middle-class political dissidents, the majority of victims in Peru were Quechua-speaking indigenous peasants and represented an impoverished demographic. Ethnicity, like ideology, became a political tool in a struggle for power, politicized in a vacuum of state neglect and social discrimination. Where the Shining Path became known for its display of mutilated bodies, the armed forces often hid their victims, using disappearances to cover extrajudicial interrogations and as a form of terror. Sexual violence and child conscription were widespread.

The MRTA played a less well-known but still important role. Named after the eighteenth-century rebel leader Túpac Amaru II and his ancestor, the last Inca leader, the MRTA formed out of the union of the Marxist-Leninist Revolutionary Socialist Party and the militant arm of the Revolutionary Left Movement. Unlike the Shining Path, the MRTA attempted to ally with other leftist organizations. Victor Polay Campos and, later, Néstor Cerpa Cartolini led the MRTA. With a following of several hundred members, including former Peruvian military officials, its stated aims included the establishment of a communist state and the elimination of imperialist elements from Peru. Although the MRTA gained attention for high-profile acts, in general it retained a more self-restrained image compared to the Shining Path.[36] A combination of military victories, clashes with the Shining Path, the imprisonment of its leadership, and a loss of support from the left led to its decline.[37]

The Peruvian state, including political parties, the military, police, and other armed security forces, was responsible for the remainder of deaths. The *Grupo Colina* death squad became particularly notorious for crimes it committed under former President Alberto Fujimori and Peruvian Head of National Security, Vladimiro Montesinos.[38]

Civilians were in the crossfire throughout the conflict, and faced accusations from both the state and the Shining Path on grounds of suspected collaboration. The state played an active role in mobilizing peasants.[39] The Shining Path's retaliation in these cases was swift and violent, as in the Lucanamarca massacre in 1983, in which militants tortured and

brutalities and take part in massacres in their own communities and other Ashaninka villages.

[36] The MRTA's members generally wore military clothing and publicly explained their actions and objectives.

[37] The Shining Path peaked in 1988 and then began to slowly decline.

[38] The *La Cantuta* massacres, in which state actors killed innocent young people, later became a defining moment in Peru's transitional justice process, featuring heavily in Fujimori's conviction.

[39] Theidon, "Justice in Transition," p. 440.

massacred sixty-nine men, women, and children.[40] As Kimberly Theidon points out, while the militarization and arming of the peasants helped bring an end to the conflict, it also initiated one of its bloodiest phases – the "internal war fought by intimate enemies" – leading to a bloody campaign of personalized violence.[41] The consequence of the peasants' enlistment was a rapid escalation of violence within communities, marked by paranoia and self-preservation against perceived sympathizers, which pitted villagers against each other. Tactical defeats of the Shining Path led to greater reprisals from the group. This division of loyalties also occurred in the capital, particularly in shanty towns, where the conflict displaced more than 100,000 civilians.[42]

The Peruvian armed conflict came to an end slowly, as a consequence of the Shining Path's increased use of violence and its loss of civilian control, as well as a change in state tactics. Although the Belaúnde and García administrations in the early 1980s and 1990s oversaw periods of high state violence, the Shining Path's reprisals and indiscriminate violence against civilians isolated it from the general population.[43] Degregori describes the militarization of the peasants as a "Pandora's box." The Shining Path had foreseen an armed conflict between the peasants and the state, yet by underestimating the peasants and their capacity for independent agency sowed the seeds of its own defeat.[44] The Shining Path's increasingly extreme actions – for example, its closing of markets and burning of Catholic churches and symbols – isolated it from the peasants.[45] Additionally, the Shining Path's disregard of existing authorities and communal structures and its tendency to work through those on the margins further threatened established communal power structures

[40] The massacre, according to Guzmán, was meant to serve as a warning and reinforce the Shining Path's willingness to shed blood. See the CVR Report, Volume 5, Chapter 2; and Carlos Iván Degregori, "Harvesting Storms: Peasant *Rondas* and the Defeat of Sendero Luminoso in Ayacucho," in *Shining and Other Paths: War and Society in Peru, 1980–1995*, ed. Steve J. Stern (Durham and London: Duke University Press, 1998), pp. 128–157.

[41] Theidon, "Justice in Transition." See also Rolando Forgues, *Perú: Entre el Desafío de la Violencia y el Sueño de lo Posible* (Lima, Peru: Librería Editorial Minerva, 1993).

[42] Degregori, *Qué Difícil es Ser Dios*.

[43] In Lima and Ayacucho, citizens recall scenes of victims' bodies left in public and dogs hung up from streetlights. See Degregori, *Qué Difícil es Ser Dios*, p. 89.

[44] Burt, *Violencia y Autoritarismo*, p. 36. Carlos Iván Degregori, interview by author, Lima, Peru, February 28, 2011. Interviewees often distinguished between types of support, e.g., passive support, including providing housing and feeding Shining Path militants, versus active participation.

[45] In her study of Villa El Salvador, Jo-Marie Burt finds a similar dynamic in urban areas, describing violent Shining Path power struggles as it sought to establish its hegemony against the left-wing opposition. She notes the Shining Path's "culture of fear" and its loss of support after its main leaders were arrested in 1992. *Violencia y Autoritarismo*, pp. 39–40.

and increased suspicion.[46] At the same time, its mounting brutality against civilians and the extravagant lifestyles of its leaders led to a loss of morale among lower-level militants.[47]

In rural parts of Ayacucho, the entry of armed forces in late 1982 marked a turning point. Although the first three years of military presence saw an escalation of military violence, a growing number of peasants decided to work on the side of the armed forces.[48] Recognition that its heavy-handed military response was hurting the counter-insurgency, along with heightened human rights advocacy and pressure from Peruvian civil society, led the government to shift to a less militarized response.[49] As the state increasingly enlisted and armed the peasant populations, the administration also took a populist turn under Fujimori.[50] In 1992, the Fujimori government found and arrested Guzmán in a safe house in Lima. The sight of Guzmán captured and displayed in a public cage, followed by his military trial in which he proclaimed the end of the struggle, largely decapitated the movement. In October of 1992, in his speech in front of the UN General Assembly, Fujimori read a letter from Guzmán calling for peace talks. Guzmán's followers initially suspected fabrication or that authorities had extracted the letter through torture. Eventually, however, as Guzmán made more public statements, many began to accept his resignation. Shining Path militants were divided after Guzmán's arrest. While some denounced him, others stayed loyal, leading to a fracture between those who continued the armed conflict without Guzmán, Sendero Rojo (Red Path), and those who did not, Sendero Negro (Black Path). The group

[46] Degregori, *Qué Difícil es Ser Dios*, p. 42; Mallon, "Chronicle of a Path Foretold?"

[47] The recollections of a female ex-Shining Path member illustrate this disillusionment. While she was initially attracted for ideological reasons as a twenty-one-year-old university student, she became increasingly critical of the Shining Path, remembering the leaders' large, leisurely meals while the rank and file went hungry. For her, the arrival of an eleven-year-old child combatant in her unit was a turning point, leading to her disillusionment. Interview by author. Lima, Peru, February 23, 2011. On the Shining Path's use of children, see del Puno, "Family, Culture, and 'Revolution'. "

[48] José Coronel, "Violencia política y respuestas campesinas en Huanta" (Political violence and peasant responses in Huanta), in *Las rondas campesinas y la derrota de Sendero Luminoso* (Peasant patrols and the defeat of the Shining Path), ed. Carlos Iván Degregori, José Coronel, Ponciano del Pino, and Orin Starn (Lima, Perú: IEP, 1996), pp. 29–116; Orin Starn, "Senderos inesperados: Las rondas campesinas de la sierra sur central" (Unexpected paths: Peasant patrols in the South Central Sierra), in *Las rondas campesinas y la derrota de Sendero Luminoso* (Peasant patrols and the defeat of the Shining Path), ed. Carlos Iván Degregori, José Coronel, Ponciano del Pino, and Orin Starn (Lima, Perú: IEP, 2006), pp. 227–262.

[49] However, this period was marked by an increase in human rights abuses and lack of due process for suspected captured insurgents in Lima.

[50] Fujimori became well known for his visits to the provinces and patronage of peasants.

splintered after the capture of interim leader Oscar Ramírez in 1999. While the Shining Path has continued sporadic activity from the jungle, it is no longer deemed to be a threat.[51]

The Establishment of a Multipronged Transitional Justice Approach

Transitional justice in Peru was an ambitious and public set of efforts. Interim president Valentín Paniagua established the CVR by executive decree in February 2001. The CVR initially had seven commissioners, but enlarged into a twelve-person body in September 2001, after President Toledo took office. Salomón Lerner Febres, a philosophy professor and later president of the Andean Region of the Union of Universities for Latin America, chaired the Commission. The remaining eleven commissioners were also Peruvian nationals. They included political scientist and former politician, Rolando Ames Cobián; Father Gastón Garatea Yori; late anthropologist and Shining Path specialist, Carlos Iván Degregori; priest, José Antúnezde Mayolo; national security official and retired air force lieutenant general, Luis Arias Grazziani; executive director of the Andean commission of jurists, Enrique Bernales Ballesteros; engineer and former rector of the UNSCH, Alberto Morote Sanchéz; engineer and politician, Carlos Tapia García; lawyer and former congresswoman, Beatriz Alva Hart; Evangelical minister, Father Humberto Lay Sun; and sociologist and ex-executive secretary of the National Human Rights Coordinator, Sofia Macher Batanero. Luis Armando Bambarén Gastelumendi served as an observer. The CVR presented its final twelve-volume report to President Toledo on August 28, 2003.

As in Sierra Leone, the CVR operated alongside war crimes trials. A special prosecutor responsible for investigating human rights crimes under Fujimori filed the first charges against members of *La Colina*. The Inter-American Court of Human Rights also played an important role in Peru's criminal justice process.

Parallel grassroots restorative processes have also taken place in villages in the Sierra and Amazon regions. Some of these initiatives preceded the CVR, drawing on traditional restorative practices.[52] Where Peru lacks an official reintegration process, community leaders – and, in some cases,

[51] While the Movimiento por Amnistía y Derechos Fundamentales (Movement for Amnesty and Fundamental Rights) tried to register as a political party on a platform of liberating Guzmán and granting a general amnesty to ex-Shining Path, the Peruvian government denied its registration.

[52] Theidon, "Justice in Transition."

Evangelical Christian groups – have helped reintegrate ex-Shining Path members into communities.[53]

Historical Context and Aims: Advancing a Punitive Human Rights Agenda

From its inception, the CVR took a strong orientation in favor of human rights and criminal justice. It is significant that the Peruvian government established the CVR retrospectively after a military victory against the Shining Path. State agents involved in the conflict and the military remained powerful, retaining a significant support base among the middle classes. In consequence, the military had fewer incentives to cooperate with the Commission and tended to see the CVR as a threat to and violation of the military's prestige.

The CVR also followed an armed conflict that had affected various parts of Peruvian society very differently. While villages in the Andes suffered violence at the hands of both the Shining Path and the military for several decades, urban classes in the capital and the coast mainly witnessed Shining Path violence, and that relatively late into the conflict. Prolonged experiences of political violence in historically marginalized rural regions increased inequality between rural and urban areas and within urban areas, particularly metropolitan Lima, which absorbed a large population from Peru's hinterlands. In Ayacucho, in particular, the military's tactic of disappearances and mutilation of bodies augmented the legacies of violence for families who continue to seek information on missing relatives. As I will detail in Chapter 7, the effects of political violence have been wide ranging, including a high incidence of mental health problems and posttraumatic stress, and a general fatalism and lack of trust in authority and institutions.

This picture contrasts sharply with post-war Lima. For Peru's coastal populations, who had been less exposed to military violence, the Shining Path remains the face of the conflict and bears a strong stigma.[54] While

[53] José Coronel Aguirre argues that this process preceded the CVR where communities could not afford to "wait for the state." José Coronel Aguirre, interview by author, Ayacucho, Peru, January 12, 2011. Some also note the conversion of former Shining Path members to Evangelism as a factor facilitating reintegration. In Ayacucho, Theidon describes a process whereby ex-Shining Path asked for pardon from their former communities. She emphasizes the normalization of relations through the communal working of land and the reestablishment of bonds of reciprocity and trust. Theidon, "Justice in Transition," pp. 445–454. For more on Evangelism and the Shining Path, see Theidon, "Intimate Enemies," pp. 357–359.

[54] While this view was prevalent among middle and upper classes and the economic elite, it also extended to the left and academic and civil society circles, where the Shining Path's violent and extreme ideology and tactics, its failure to accept other political actors as

inequality and poverty within the capital also rose due to population growth and an increase of *pueblos jóvenes* (shanty towns), the capital's economy has seen a significant rebound since the end of the conflict, with Lima becoming a growing center of international investment.[55] These different experiences polarized transitional justice and generated strong suspicions of the CVR. As Peru's economic recovery gradually eased the traumatic memory of the Shining Path, the human rights community's emphasis on investigating the past and establishing accountability ran against the discourse of government officials and elites that it is time to "*pasar la página*" (turn the page) and move on to a more prosperous future.[56] Degregori describes a "*memoria salvadora*" (savior memory) – a view that the state and the armed forces had saved the country from terrorism and that the loss of civilian lives was the cost that society had to pay to save the country from further chaos and destruction.[57] This "black and white history" politicized public discussions, stigmatizing not only insurgent groups but also those who disagreed with the official narrative.[58]

The CVR also emerged in the presence of strong regional and international normative support for criminal justice. Unlike the Sierra Leonean context, where the influence of the South African TRC and domestic traditions of restorative justice generated greater normative and social support for reconciliation and amnesty, the CVR plugged into a larger regional legacy linking truth commissions to struggles for justice and

legitimate, and its secretive character had isolated it. Degregori notes that state and media portrayals of the Shining Path and their equating of criticism of state policies with support for terrorism led to the suppression of critical views, even among academia and civil society. *Qué Difícil es Ser Dios*, p. 43. Burt refers to a "culture of authoritarian consensus." Burt, *Violencia y Autoritarismo*, pp. 325–327. Residents of Lima remember the 1980s and 1990s blackouts, attacks on infrastructure, and bombings and kidnappings in Lima. For many, for example the Japanese Embassy Hostage Crisis in 1996, where fourteen MRTA members captured hundreds of senior diplomats, government, military officials, and businessmen, is emblematic of the conflict.

55 This is a result of the conflict and a high rate of rural to urban migration, particularly from affected provinces. The population of Lima has doubled in the last decade. Nevertheless, Peru's economic growth has remained constant in a turbulent regional context. Peru did not experience the financial collapses seen in Argentina and Uruguay in the late 1990s and early 2000s. The Peruvian economy grew 0.9 percent, and reached one of the fastest growth rates in the world at 8.8 percent in 2010. Since 2004, the country has seen a 28.4 percent decline in poverty. USAID/Peru, "Peru: Economic Growth" (February 2011), p. 1, available at: www.usaid.gov/pe.

56 Degregori, *Qué Difícil es Ser Dios*.

57 Degregori, interview. The state's "instrumentalization of fear" during the Fujimori years and its criminalization of those who questioned the official narrative of the Shining Path further entrenched this discourse.

58 Reátegui, interview. See also Cynthia E. Milton, "Defacing Memory: Untying Peru's Memory Knots," *Memory Studies* 4, no. 2 (2011), pp. 190–205.

democratization. International and domestic pressures in favor of prosecution reinforced this orientation. The CVR came into being during a period of high-profile international activity in international criminal justice, first through the establishment of the International Criminal Tribunal for the former Yugoslavia (ICTY) and the International Criminal Tribunal for Rwanda (ICTR), and then with the ratification of the Rome Statute for the International Criminal Court (ICC) in 2002. These developments, in the view of commissioners, had entrenched a mounting international norm in favor of individual accountability and conditional state sovereignty.[59] As Peru's political situation stabilized, public scrutiny of the treatment and trial of Shining Path and MRTA prisoners increased. While many Shining Path and MRTA insurgents were already serving sentences, heightened human rights activism toward the end of the conflict led to a series of retrials of previously sentenced Shining Path and MRTA militants.[60]

The major impetus for criminal justice, however, came in 2000, following a tainted presidential campaign. After the discovery of corruption in the Fujimori administration, the former president fled the country and faxed his resignation from Japan.[61] While the Fujimori government had passed a general amnesty law in 1995, the Inter-American Court of Human Rights outlawed the ruling in March of 2001. In February of 2001, Peru reached an accord with the Inter-American Court in which the government agreed to investigate and determine criminal responsibility.

Finally, Peruvian civil society played an active role in campaigning against impunity. In contrast to Sierra Leone – in part because the CVR did not operate alongside an international tribunal – the Commission did not view itself as an alternative to criminal justice, but rather as one of the main bodies responsible for bringing about prosecutions. The establishment of the CVR as the sole new transitional justice institution put a certain onus on the Commission from the start, in which it saw itself as responsible for carrying out multiple goals and accountable to a range of stakeholders. As Lerner recalls, even if the CVR had wanted to avoid retributive justice, amnesty was never a possibility given domestic aversion to the Shining Path and international and regional pressure to prosecute. Relaying an incident

[59] Salomón Lerner Febres, interview by author, Lima, Peru, February 10, 2011; Enrique Bernales, CVR commissioner, interview by author, Lima, Peru, March 1, 2011.

[60] Many had been hastily sentenced in trials presided over by judges who wore hoods to avoid retribution by insurgent groups.

[61] Peru's sudden political transition was more of a response to middle-class worries about corruption rather than violations during the conflict. See Leigh A. Payne's discussion on how corruption can change public perceptions of national heroes. *Unsettling Accounts: Neither Truth Nor Reconciliation in Confessions of State Violence* (Durham and London: Duke University Press, 2008), p. 96.

in which an ex-militant requested amnesty in exchange for intelligence, he explained: "Even if I had been in favor of amnesty, of course I could never agree to it. It was not an option."[62]

Together, these factors pushed the Commission away from amnesty and toward human rights and criminal justice. The CVR itself emerged as a historical commission, with the mandate to look into conflict-related human rights abuses and disappearances and to acknowledge and give a voice to victims. Reflecting the opposition of key state parties to reconciliation, the CVR's mandate did not mention reconciliation until 2001, when Paniagua's successor, President Alejandro Toledo, added it to its name and mandate. While many within the Commission felt uncomfortable with the political connotations of reconciliation and its association with impunity, as I will detail shortly, the CVR decided to redefine reconciliation in a manner that would suit its broader objectives.

The conception of the CVR as an instrument of human rights became more entrenched as it began its work and went through its own learning curve of political and social feasibility, particularly in reference to the Shining Path. Throughout its operation, the Peruvian media closely monitored the Commission's language and characterization of the Shining Path.[63] Also important was the Commission's discovery of the magnitude of crimes.[64] Taking note of the scale and racial nature of violence, the CVR increasingly emphasized the geographic concentration of violence and its "ethnic undertones."[65]

The CVR prioritized several objectives. Its first goal was to acknowledge and empower victims and populations in marginalized parts of the country. Early on, the CVR identified the marginalization of rural areas and indigenous populations to be root causes of the conflict, and set raising awareness and furthering social justice as key objectives. As Degregori argued, testimony at the CVR was intended to offer a "double" symbolic reparation, affirming the status of participants as agents and as citizens of the country.[66] This was especially important where individuals testified in

62 Lerner, interview.

63 In a tense illustrative moment, after Commissioner Sofia Macher referred to the Shining Path as a "political party," a vocal media campaign accused the CVR of taking a pro-terrorist position, prompting a series of high-profile investigations. On July 15, 2002, a Congressional Committee summoned Lerner to defend the application of the term "political party" to the Shining Path. See "Theidon, Intimate Enemies, p. 325."

64 Ibid. See also Lerner, interview; and Dr. Beatriz Alva Hart, CVR commissioner, interview by author, Lima, Peru, February 4, 2011.

65 In the CVR's analysis, "If the ratio of victims to population reported to the CVR with respect to Ayacucho were similar countrywide, the violence would have caused 1,200,000 deaths and disappearances. Of that number, 340,000 would have occurred in the city of Lima." CVR Report, Volume 1, Chapter 3.

66 Degregori, *Qué Difícil es Ser Dios*.

a language other than Spanish: "Because his [the participant's] silence was broken, and because his voice was heard in silenced languages in the public sphere."[67]

The CVR's second objective was democratization and the generation of social solidarity. As I will outline further in this chapter, the CVR made recommendations, assigned individual criminal responsibility, and sought to raise awareness and enshrine respect for cultural pluralism. The Commission took a strongly pedagogical approach, seeking to raise awareness and generate solidarity for a historically "invisible" population.[68] As was the case in Sierra Leone, the CVR identified the populations most removed from the conflict – middle classes in the capital and coastal cities – as its target audience.[69]

Procedures and Methodology

The CVR was a mixed-method commission, combining rigorous truth-seeking with public hearings. Yet, while the CVR consulted external representatives and studied other models, commissioners emphasized the importance of keeping the CVR a Peruvian institution and adapting externally derived procedures to suit its context and goals.[70] The CVR deliberately employed only Peruvian commissioners,[71] and its initial planning was mainly a closed process. For a year prior to the Commission's establishment, Lerner and his wife, Rosemary Rizo-Patrón, both philosophy professors at the Pontificia Católica del Perú (PUCP), held workshops to define various terms and objectives of the Commission. The Commission's primary inspiration came from Guatemala.[72] Both countries had in common the historical oppression and systematic violence against an indigenous population. The Guatemalan Commission's focus on the establishment of an objective historical record and identification of systematic

[67] Ibid. [68] Lerner, interview.

[69] Lerner referred to the CVR's "moral" mandate as a form of consciousness-raising.

[70] For example, consultation with the International Center for Transitional Justice.

[71] Lerner also shared his view that foreign staff would not have been able to understand and relate to the Peruvian conflict and context in the same way. After an initial discussion with the government over the appropriate backgrounds of the commissioners and whom the commissioners should represent (whether regions of the country, political positions, or sides of the conflict), a decision was reached to choose commissioners based on their moral standing and contribution to social justice. CVR officials maintained that it would have been politically explosive to place protagonists on the Commission. Instead, they installed a former general and an Ayacuchan professor from UNHCR as commissioners. The presence of both caused significant criticism. Professor Morote was related to a Shining Path leader and had worked at the UNSCH. Interviewees in Ayacucho often criticized the presence of the general.

[72] Ibid.

patterns also influenced the CVR, as did its emphasis on truth-seeking over reconciliation. Many of the CVR's procedures reflect this didactic influence. The CVR collected 16,917 testimonials, and held additional focus groups and public hearings. It also consulted academic specialists and read classified documents. Many consider the Commission's report to be the most extensive recollection of the history of Peru, spanning a total of nine volumes, with abbreviated versions available for history curricula and younger audiences. The CVR prepared its findings for educational and awareness-raising purposes, particularly the photo archive and exposition *Yuyanapaq* ("to remember" in Quechua) in the Museum of the Nation in Lima.

While the CVR drew on restorative procedures, becoming the only Latin-American commission to use public testimonies and hearings, according to the Commission, hearings had two objectives. The primary objective was to dignify victims by providing a platform and acknowledgment, thereby reaffirming their status as rights bearers before the state. Commissioners emphasized the symbolic meaning of hearings. For many participants from rural backgrounds, testimony at the CVR provided their first opportunity to speak publicly and receive acknowledgment. The second objective was to raise awareness and increase solidarity for victims.[73] To this end, the Commission held thirteen public audiences in different locations and aired live hearings on television and radio.

The CVR put less emphasis on reintegration and engagement of combatants. Although the CVR provided an opportunity for all sides of the conflict to testify, most spoke to the Commission in confidence. The CVR required ex-militants to "auto-criticize" as a condition of testifying; in other words, former Shining Path and MRTA members had to renounce the movement and their role in it.[74] The CVR's relationship with the armed forces was particularly thorny. For more on the the CVR's relationship to the armed forces, see Rebecca Root, Transitional Justice in Peru, New York: Palgrave Macmillan (2012), p. 85 and Rebekka Friedman, "Implementing Transformative Justice: Survivors and Ex-Combatants at the Comisión de la Verdad y Reconciliación in Peru," Ethnic ad Racial Studies" (2017). The CVR's position on how to deal with military crimes remained unresolved until the end of its operation. After prolonged internal disagreements over the extent to which prosecutions should have access to and use information gleaned during testimonies, eventually, the Commission decided that it would list the names of perpetrators and the details of crimes, but that it

[73] CVR hearings were broadcast on television. Condensed versions of the report were also made available in hard copy, for example, the Hatun Willakuy volume.

[74] Rolando Ames Cobián, interview by author, Lima, Peru, February 7, 2011.

would not relate specific abuses to individuals.[75] While the CVR laid out "plans for the treatment of prisoners, incarcerated for political violence, and plans for their rehabilitation,"[76] to date the CVR was not tied to an official reintegration program.

Finally, the Commission prioritized its provision of recommendations. The Commission's report includes a chapter of reforms, covering a range of topics, including democratization, judicial and institutional reforms, civilian–military relations, decentralization, governance, rural development, cultural pluralism, and representation. Its Program of Integral Reparations identifies symbolic reparations, reparations in mental and physical health, reparations in education, economic (individual) reparations, and collective reparations. Individual reparations apply to relatives of victims of death or disappearance, those left mentally or physically incapacitated, victims of unjust imprisonment and sexual violence, and children who were products of sexual violence.[77] Collective reparations include the reconstruction of productive infrastructure, institutions, basic services, and employment in communities and areas affected by political violence.[78]

Reconciliation

The CVR offered a "contractual" understanding of reconciliation, tied to justice and civic rights. Sociologist and CVR researcher Félix Reátegui describes the CVR staff's original aversion and discomfort with the term: "Reconciliation for us carries an association of impunity, of mutual amnesties in civil wars for strategic reasons . . . Especially in Latin America, it is understood as the necessity of being in peace with the armed forces, where reconciliation means forgetting."[79] Eventually, however, the CVR decided to embrace its new mandate and to redefine reconciliation on its own terms.[80] CVR officials decided early on that interpersonal reconciliation between victims and perpetrators would be beyond the scope of the Commission.[81] The CVR Working Group conceived reconciliation to be private to individuals and

[75] For more on the CVR's contribution to prosecutions, see Eduardo González Cueva, "The Peruvian Truth and Reconciliation Commission and the Challenge of Impunity," in *Transitional Justice in the Twenty-first Century*, ed. Naomi Roht-Arriaza (Cambridge: Cambridge University Press, 2006), pp. 190–205.

[76] *Hatun Willakuy*, abbreviated version of the CVR (Lima, Perú: Comisión de Entrega de la Comisión de la Verdad y Reconciliación, February 2004), p. 412.

[77] Ibid., p. 420. [78] Ibid., p. 421. [79] Reátegui, interview. [80] Ibid.

[81] Rosemary Rizo-Patrón links interpersonal reconciliation with pardon and repentance – personal and "asymmetrical" processes which are not necessarily "reciprocally oriented to the past." Rosemary Rizo-Patrón, CVR Working Group Minutes, p. 74. See also Rosemary Rizo-Patrón, "Between Conflict and Reconciliation: The Hard Truth," *Human Studies* 30, no. 2 (2007), pp. 115–130.

inappropriate in the public sphere. Whereas interpersonal reconciliation between two parties would require forgiveness, only individuals themselves can decide whether to reconcile and outsiders cannot encouraged reconciliation.[82]

The Commission's final report distinguishes between levels (what it calls "dimensions") of reconciliation, including a political dimension between the state, society, and political parties; a social dimension, referring to institutions and civil society; and an interpersonal dimension, which occurs at the community level.[83] The CVR identified its focus to be national reconciliation, which it defines as future-oriented, and rests on the establishment of a new sociopolitical framework built on pluralism and justice. Distancing its understanding from the South African restorative conception, it warns that the aim of reconciliation in Peru should not be to restore previous political and economic structures and social conditions, many of which underpinned the conflict.[84] It defines reconciliation as conditional upon democratic accountability, individual and group rights, social and criminal justice, reparations, and institutional reforms.[85] Horizontally, contractual reconciliation should address the root causes of conflict, establish social ties, and generate solidarity.[86] Vertically, reconciliation should reinforce civic rights and political accountability.[87] Economic and criminal justice are both a precondition and an outgrowth of reconciliation.[88]

Narrative

The CVR took a broad historical view, emphasizing the root causes of the conflict. While it identified the Shining Path's decision to wage a "popular war" as the immediate trigger of Peru's two decades of political violence, it outlined the long-standing social, political, and economic antecedents that gave rise to the movement.[89] These include an underlying context of state neglect and marginalization, unequal employment and educational opportunities, weak institutions, government corruption, underdevelopment, deep-seated racism and cultural discrimination, and the legacies of colonialism and neocolonialism. The CVR also put emphasis on identifying

[82] Lerner, interview. See also Salomón Lerner Febres, *La Rebelión de la Memoria: Selección de Discursos, 2001–2003* (Lima, Perú: CEP, IDEH-PUCP, Coordinadora Nacional de Derechos Humanos, 2004).

[83] *Hatun Willakuy*, p. 411.

[84] M. Giusti notes that reconciliation cannot aim to reestablish an original relation or framework, as prior political and social structures "cultivated the perverse process that led to its destruction." CVR Working Group Minutes.

[85] *Hatun Willakuy*, p. 412. [86] Ibid., p. 411. The Spanish word is "*refundación.*"

[87] Giusti, CVR Working Group Minutes, p. 70. [88] Ibid., pp. 69–70.

[89] *Hatun Willakuy*.

patterns of victimization and blame, putting weight on the demographics of victimization. Over 40 percent of conflict-related deaths occurred in the department of Ayacucho, 79 percent of the victims lived in rural areas and engaged in livestock activities (as compared to only 29 percent of Peru's total population according to the 1993 census), 75 percent spoke Quechua or other native languages as their mother tongue (as compared to only 16 percent of the national average at the time), and 68 percent of the war's victims did not complete secondary education (as compared to 40 percent of the general population).[90] The Commission concluded that ethnicity was important in determining the probability of being a victim and in the type of violence that victims experienced.[91]

Similarly, the CVR assigned direct blame. The Commission found the Shining Path to be responsible for 54 percent of abuses reported, the armed forces for 37 percent, and smaller groups, including the MRTA, for the rest.[92] Taking a strong moral stance on "secondary responsibility" and "double outrage" throughout its work, the CVR cites indifference and public apathy as causes of the conflict.[93]

Unlike the Sierra Leonean TRC, which suspends judgment on the legitimacy of the RUF, the CVR identifies the Shining Path as a terrorist organization. Commissioners, by and large, shared this view. For Lerner, the Shining Path's use of terrorism destroyed the political process and Peru's civic community and made the Shining Path illegitimate from the start.[94] For other CVR staff, treating the group as a political actor would give it more credit than it deserved. Degregori describes the Shining Path's ideology as a "political religion" that quickly fell apart without a leader.[95] He and other commissioners argued that private interviews and statement-taking with militants did not lead to profound answers. Rolando Ames Cobián recalls the CVR interview with Guzmán as "uninteresting" and "banal," maintaining that Guzmán had little to say away from his followers and political support base.[96] Some took the view that ex-Shining Path had not repented after their prison terms and

[90] Ibid.

[91] The role of ethnicity came up consistently in interviews as well. Interviewees raised the ethnic profile of the majority of victims and the ethnic undertones of violence. For instance, many remarked that ethnic slurs accompanied physical violence.

[92] CVR Report, Volume 1, Chapter 3.

[93] Ibid., pp. 9–11. Lerner's preface to the CVR report asserts a "general guilt, the guilt of omission that involves all those who did not ask during the years of violence." *Hatun Willakuy*, p. 10. See also CVR Preface (Primera Edición), p. 9.

[94] In Lerner's view, deeper engagement with insurgents might have been more publicly acceptable if the CVR was only dealing with the more moderate MRTA. Lerner, interview.

[95] Degregori, interview. See also *Qué Difícil es Ser Dios*.

[96] Rolando Ames Cobián, interview.

that public hearings with former Shining Path would not have benefited reconciliation.

Testimonies

Victims provided most of the CVR's testimonies. The CVR held its first hearing in Ayacucho. Ayacuchan victims' rights activist Mamá Angélica, whose campaigns on behalf of her missing son had made her a well-known domestic and international figure, gave the first testimony at the CVR. While victims tended to share personal experiences of atrocities at hearings, as in Sierra Leone, most testimonies went beyond sharing a personal story and demanded civil and legal redress.[97] Especially in areas that had experienced military violence, many victims came forward to speak about and register missing family members.

Protagonists featured less prominently in the CVR's work. The CVR held hearings with the police and *rondas campesinas* (peasant patrols). In public hearings in Ayacucho, while the *Rondas* and the police expressed regret, they emphasized that they did not institutionally condone violence against civilians and portrayed abuses as isolated, rather than systematic.[98] Many of the MRTA's testimonies emphasized the challenge of mitigating circumstances and the difficulty of distinguishing combatants from civilians.[99] The military and the Shining Path did not participate in public hearings.[100] The Shining Path leadership came to a decision in prison that militants should not give public testimonies. Those who chose to speak to the CVR did so anonymously, through confidential interviews. The CVR's relationship with the military grew especially tense. While some senior military members and former government leaders appeared before the Commission, many refused to participate. Participation was sensitive in the context of open trials and, as I will discuss in more detail in Chapter 7, many took offense at their depiction and treatment as an actor in an internal conflict alongside insurgent groups. Tensions increased following the

[97] Degregori, *Qué Difícil es Ser Dios*, p. 283; Lisa J. Laplante and Kimberly Susan Theidon, "Truth with Consequences: Justice and Reparations in Post-Truth Commission Peru," *Human Rights Quarterly* 29 (2007), pp. 228–250.

[98] Videos of CVR Hearings, obtained from IDEHPUCP.

[99] Nelson Manrique argues that the MRTA had a history of exposing its practices to local public questioning in the jungle. Unlike the Shining Path, the MRTA submitted to autocriticism in front of the Ashaninka communities, and later the CVR. "The War for the Central Sierra," in *Shining and Other Paths: War and Society in Peru, 1980–1995*, ed. Steve J. Stern (Durham and London: Duke University Press, 1998), p. 213.

[100] Fujimori rejected Lerner when he went to Japan to collect a statement from the former president.

indictment of high-ranking military officers, some of whom are on trial and cannot leave the country.

Conclusions

The Peruvian armed conflict took a devastating toll on human life and social, political, and economic development and infrastructure. Two decades of political violence divided the country. Varying and unequal experiences of violence in Peru have distinctively spilled into and shaped its truth-seeking and transitional justice processes.

In this chapter, I argued that the nature of political violence in Peru and regional and domestic contextual factors pushed the CVR to take a strong orientation against impunity and in favor of victims' rights and criminal justice. As the first Latin American commission to use public hearings, the CVR prioritized empowering and dignifying victims and raising awareness and solidarity over reintegration. The Commission's punitive and human rights orientation became more entrenched over time, reflecting and further reinforcing tensions with protagonists.

Leading into the next chapter, as in Sierra Leone, the end of the Peruvian armed conflict has prompted tense questions about the causes of and responsibility for political violence.[101] Here, as well, two narratives and lenses of analysis have interrogated the rise and persistence of the Shining Path. Economically oriented analysts have emphasized the role of resources and political opportunity structures in driving the emergence of the Shining Path.[102] The Shining Path's base in the Huallaga Valley in the northeast of the country is responsible for more than 70 percent of Peru's cocaine production. Revenue from the illegal production and the coca trade, coupled with a failing legal economy and decreased government services, allowed the Shining Path to mobilize and gain strength.[103] In this vein, the collapse of Peru's coca economy and the state's aggressive institutional reforms led to the Shining Path's eventual decline.[104]

Another – often Peruvian and ethnographic – literature has focused on the psychosocial aspects of insurgency. This scholarship highlights a broader backdrop of grievances, arguing that economic incentives and

[101] While the Shining Path operated in secrecy during the conflict, the MRTA waged a "media war," giving press conferences and inviting journalists. In contrast to the Shining Path, the MRTA projected an image of a "heroic guerilla" and a "*guerra limpia*" (clean war). Degregori, interview. For more on the MRTA's auto-criticism, see the CVR's interview with former MRTA director Alberto Galvez Olaechea. CVR Report, Chapter 2.

[102] Kay, "Violent Opportunities," p. 99.

[103] Palmer, "Introduction," p. 7.

[104] Kay, "Violent Opportunities," p. 100.

state neglect cannot solely account for individual and group motivations.[105] At the micro level, the Shining Path recruited in a context of deep generational breaches. Differential access to education and internal migration exacerbated social rupture. For Degregori, educated youth "had eyes," "they saw things that adults could not see," gaining respect through their exposure and indoctrination.[106] Knowledge offered a channel of social mobility and a "form of control," through which the Shining Path was able to make sense of an oppressive history and provided a way forward.[107] Often, the Shining Path took advantage of tensions and relative disparities within communities, appealing to and playing upon inequalities. It targeted those with ambition but who existed on the margins, notably youth, women, and the poor.[108]

Linking into questions of reconciliation, these varying narratives have become important again in evaluations of transitional justice in Peru. Attributing the underlying causes of the conflict largely to state neglect, racism, and indifference, the CVR sought to strengthen democratic institutions and accountability, and generate civic trust, social awareness, and solidarity. The Commission put less emphasis on engaging and understanding the micro-level motivations of former insurgents and protagonists. As I will detail in Chapter 7, the CVR emerged as part of a larger orientation in favor of human rights and rule of law following the discovery of massive corruption under the Fujimori regime. In this context, the Commission introduced its work as part of a greater turn toward truth and accountability, designed to provide justice for victims and combat impunity. Unlike the Sierra Leonean TRC, although the CVR originally took a more inclusive stance, the Commission eventually concentrated most of its efforts on creating visibility for victims and the marginalization of rural and indigenous populations. Also in contrast to the Sierra Leonean Commission, the CVR played a central part in furthering criminal justice, reinforcing a strained and generally antagonistic relationship with protagonists of the conflict, particularly the military and the Shining Path. As time passed and tensions with protagonists heightened, the CVR's punitive stance further entrenched, and took precedence over an inclusive platform that would provide space for individuals from different sides of the conflict to testify.

[105] At the time, Ayacucho had one of the highest rates of illiteracy in the country, second only to neighboring Apurimac.

[106] Degregori, *Qué Difícil es Ser Dios*, p. 79. [107] Ibid.

[108] On women in the Shining Path, see Robin Kirk, *The Monkey's Paw: New Chronicles from Peru* (Amherst, MA: University of Massachusetts Press, 1997); and Isabel Coral Cordero, "Women in War: Impact and Responses," in *Shining and Other Paths: War and Society in Peru, 1980–1995*, ed. Steve J. Stern (Durham and London: Duke University Press, 1998), pp. 345–374.

7 Memory Activism and the Politics of the Past

The establishment of the CVR came at a significant time in Peruvian history. In many regards, Peru's two decades of political violence remained shrouded in secrecy. The military frequently carried out covert counterinsurgency campaigns, and the Shining Path tended to shun interviews and public engagement. The CVR began its work during a time of rapid democratization and a turn toward accountability, manifest in the retrials of previously sentenced Shining Path prisoners and the indictment of high-profile government and military officials.

More so than the Sierra Leonean TRC, the CVR had important normative and discursive effects in Peru. The Commission increased awareness of military violence, providing a critical mobilizing point for civil society. The CVR also helped consolidate an overall norm of truth-seeking, even among sectors opposed to its work. Also differently than in Sierra Leone, where civil society groups frequently turned inward and distanced themselves from national politics, in Ayacucho advocacy groups have often focused their campaigns on Lima, working through and thereby reinforcing the political process. Although not uniform, this process has significantly strengthened procedural reconciliation, even while often heightening conflict and exposing ongoing ethnic, racial, and class cleavages.

At the same time, as was the case in Sierra Leone, the nature of the Peruvian conflict and the slow implementation of the CVR's recommendations have also undermined its work. In remote parts of the country, prolonged experiences of military violence and state neglect had left a high degree of mistrust and resentment. In turn, the concentration of military violence in rural provinces further distanced experiences of violence from the emotional identifications and reference points of the coastal populations and middle classes. In this polarized social climate, the CVR's investigations have led to considerable backlash and ignited a vocal politics of memory, which continues into the present.

Political Violence and Civic Trust: Justice as a Precondition for Reconciliation

When reconciliation is achieved, it won't be necessary to talk about it. But this will come from concrete state changes in people's lives. We live in a place where the state is sick. Every single aspect of life – health, employment, education and development – is affected by the state. Reconciliation will take place in the long-term; it will come from people within when they have opportunities.

–Law Student, age 21, UNSCH, Ayacucho.[1]

How can you say that building a school or well or better roads, what the state should do for us anyways, is a reparation? This is already our right to development – it is what the state should do for us already.

–Widow, Cayara.[2]

Located 2,761 meters above sea level in the south-central Peruvian Andes, Ayacucho's capital is a lively mountain town. Eleven years after the military termination of the conflict, however, the region bears heavy legacies of political violence. A range of NGOs is actively working on forensic investigations, exhumations, reparations, *memoria histórica* (historical memory), and mental health.

As I detailed in Chapter 6, while one of the CVR's key objectives – which it embodied in its methodology and procedures – was to generate civic trust, the Peruvian context posed significant constraints. In Ayacucho, in particular, a prolonged and heavy-handed military presence and the region's long-term marginalization had severely damaged political and social capital. Both marginalization and decades of political violence at the hands of military agents had left a strong fear of authority structures. Although Ayacucho experienced high Shining Path and military violence, interviewees frequently distinguished between the two, arguing that Shining Path violence was merely a symptom of wider disenfranchisement and oppression. There was often a qualitative difference in discussions of military violence, in which affected communities saw military violence as less discriminate, particularly in light of widespread practices of rape and extrajudicial disappearances.[3] As an engineer and development officer in Ayacucho remembers:

[1] Interview by author, Ayacucho, Peru, October 21, 2010.
[2] Interview by author, Cayara, Peru, October 13, 2010.
[3] Although my interviewees often disagreed over Fujimori's legacy and responsibility, interviewees in Ayacucho consistently identified the state as the main culprit and the Shining Path as a symptom of structural violence and state neglect. This applied also to victims of the Shining Path. On Fujimori's populism and the poor, see Patricia Oliart, "Albert Fujimori: 'The Man Peru Needed?'" in *Shining and Other Paths: War and Society in Peru, 1980–1995*, ed. Steve J. Stern (Durham and London: Duke University Press, 1998), pp. 415–421. The Shining Path had deeper roots in the south, and the state invested less in post-conflict reconstruction. See interview with José Coronel Aguirre. On the differing

> Yes, Sendero Luminoso [the Shining Path] and any group who committed violence were bad, but we can never forget the sexual violence [of the military]. The women will carry that with them for the rest of their lives. Many cannot have children . . . Every time they see a uniform, every time they hear loud noises, they are scared.[4]

Military violence also left a lasting and engrained mistrust of the state. In the words of a young Ayacuchan woman who worked for the reconciliation organization *Paz y Esperanza* (Peace and Hope): "It's not about whether one is worse than the other, but that the state should have protected us [from the Shining Path]. They weren't there when we needed them. Instead they turned on us."[5] "They treated us like enemies," recalls an engineer in Huancapi, reflecting on her agricultural visits to villages in Victor Fajardo during the conflict.[6] To ANFASEP (Asociación Nacional de Familiares de Secuestrados, Detenidos y Desaparecidos del Perú, National Association of Relatives of Kidnapped, Detained and Disappeared of Peru) official Maribel Ascarza, "They [the military] killed us as if we weren't part of Peru." In an interview in Cangallo, eighty-year-old Rosa María pulled out photos of her son – a scientist, who was killed by the military. She, like others who lost family members, expressed bewilderment over the state's targeting of her son: "He was a scientist. What did he have to do with politics? What did he ever do against the state?"[7] In contrast to Shining Path militants, who intentionally displayed their victims in public as an example or to create fear, the military often conducted covert operations, keeping families in limbo and leading them to hang on to hope that their loved ones would return and to continue to search for their remains. Interviewees frequently referred to disappearances as the worst type of violence, allowing no closure. The lack of information on missing persons also kept families from filing for reparations, perpetuating a sense of victimization and helplessness vis-à-vis the state.[8]

Years of political violence also eroded trust at the micro level. In rural communities, where lower-level former Shining Path and state collaborators coexisted with victims and their families, fear of self-incrimination

legacies of the war in southern versus northern Ayacucho, see Kimberly Theidon, *Intimate Enemies: Violence and Reconciliation in Peru* (Philadelphia: University of Pennsylvania Press, 2012), pp. 321–322.

4 Interview by author, Huancapi, Peru, October 16, 2010.

5 Ana Milagros Quiroz Vargas, Paz y Esperanza (Peace and Hope, NGO), interview by author, Ayacucho, October 20, 2010.

6 Interview by author, Huancapi, Peru, October 16, 2010.

7 Rosa María García Caldrón, interview by author, Cangallo, Peru, October 16, 2010.

8 Suspicion that the military knows the whereabouts of the remains but refuses to offer information has further worn down civic trust.

and betrayal continue to strain communal relations. Local NGOs and academics described an atmosphere of self-censorship and a "culture of fear," where individuals monitored what they openly said or were deliberately vague.[9] The messy nature of the conflict, where former Shining Path militants switched sides and became part of the *rondas* (supported by the state) or served as political representatives, augmented communal suspicions.[10] Victims of Shining Path violence noted their hesitancy to speak openly about their experiences in Ayacucho, given the high number of victims of military violence and relatives of Shining Path members inhabiting the region. The net effect, as lawyer and ANFASEP official Yuber Alarcón Quispe put it, is a confused and "closed" society with multiple narratives and a "torn social fabric."[11] Interviewees often stressed the "indirect victims" of the conflict, where family hurts passed down to subsequent generations.[12]

The ethnic undertones of the conflict further magnified the legacies of political violence. In Ayacucho, a backdrop of state marginalization and degradation of indigenous culture and identity continues to politicize personal grievances, reinforcing a sentiment that the decades of Shining Path violence and reprisals were only an episode in a longer history of violations. The region's present struggles and marginalization magnified perceptions of persecution, including among younger people who had not

[9] Theidon describes ambiguity as a "resource" to facilitate the reintegration of *arrepentidos* (repented ex-militants), who turned themselves in to communities and showed their sincerity through remorse, rather than discussion of their actions. "Justice in Transition: The Micropolitics of Reconciliation in Post-war Peru," *The Journal of Conflict Resolution* 50 (2006), p. 451.

[10] Lurgio Gavilán Sánchez, *Memorias de un soldado desconocido* (Memories of an unknown soldier) (Lima, Perú: Instituto de Estudios Peruanos, 2012). José Coronel, "Violencia política y respuestas campesinas en Huanta" (Political violence and peasant responses in Huanta), in *Las rondas campesinas y la derrota de Sendero Luminoso* (Peasant patrols and the defeat of the Shining Path) ed. Carlos Iván Degregori, José Coronel, Ponciano del Pino, and Orin Starn (Lima, Perú: Instituto de Estudios Peruanos, 2006), pp. 29–116. In Cayara, charred homes and a high number of female-headed households evidenced the killing of boys and men during the conflict, and present-day rural to urban migration as husbands and sons have relocated to find work so that they could send money to their families. Critics continue to contest details of the Cayara massacre. Ayacuchan Special Prosecutor Carlos Escobar claims that the military executed at least thirty villagers before removing their bodies from the scene. See Amnesty International's coverage, including "Peru: The Cayara massacre" (September 1989). See also the CVR's coverage of the Cayara massacre and the extra-judicial military disappearances of alleged suspicious persons.

[11] Alarcón Quispe, interview by author, Ayacucho, Peru, October 12, 2010. See also Jelke Boesten on continuities of sexual violence after the armed conflict. Jelke Boesten, "Analyzing Rape Regimes at the Interface of War and Peace in Peru," *International Journal of Transitional Justice* 4 (2010), pp. 110–129.

[12] UNSCH students referred to a "broken cord and society in disharmony." UNSCH Anthropology Student Focus Group, Ayacucho, Peru, October 21, 2010.

directly experienced the conflict. The state's continued neglect of the region fed into perceptions that the state and capital sanctioned military abuses. At the same time, opposition to the CVR's work and official denials of the scale of abuses further entrenched a depreciation of indigenous lives.[13] This despair was particularly acute among the young, many of whom did not remember the political violence. Young people cited ethnic discrimination and racism as barriers to reconciliation, complaining of the persistence of prejudices against those of indigenous descent as "inferior" and "backwards."[14] In an unequal class structure, while education presented a rare vehicle for social mobility, prospects for gainful employment were limited and the region's only university bore a historical stigma on account of its former ties to the Shining Path. Relaying an earlier arrest of a student on suspicion of subversion, for a faculty in the Anthropology Department, censorship has stifled critical thinking among students: "We can barely breathe here ... What kind of children are we going to have? We put words in their mouth and they tell us what we want to hear."[15]

Slow progress in implementing the CVR's recommendations, particularly in reparatory justice, augmented disillusionment. Interviewees pointed out that they did not "hear from the Commission again" – that they did not receive the final report and were not aware of its findings. The importance of individual over collective and symbolic reparations came out particularly strongly.[16] For many survivors, individual reparations provided crucial economic support to the *afectados* (those affected) and a direct form of recognition.[17] Victims frequently criticized collective

[13] See Salomón Lerner's recent article, "¿Por Qué Incomoda la Memoria?" *La República* (September 16, 2012).

[14] UNSCH Law and Anthropology Focus Groups. Many brought up social and professional discrimination on account of their Ayacuchan identity when they traveled or looked for work, especially in Lima, where they felt stigmatized for coming from a "red" (subversive) area, as a barrier to reconciliation. In their everyday lives, younger interviewees felt stifled by the region's association with the Shining Path. They complained of censorship and government restrictions on political activity and areas of study due to violence, which they had not personally experienced.

[15] Manuel Mayorga, UNSCH, Anthropology Department, interview by author, Ayacucho, Peru, November 5, 2010. At the time of the research, the government had banned lecturers at the UNSCH from teaching disciplines that had an association with the Shining Path's former presence at the university, including political science, sociology, and philosophy.

[16] Lisa J. Laplante, "Negotiating Reparation Rights: The Participatory and Symbolic Quotients," *Buffalo Human Rights Law Review* 19 (2012–2013), pp. 217–250.

[17] State officials working in collective reparations also raised this symbolic function, emphasizing the importance of providing communities with official documentation of government sponsorship. As a government reparations official in Ayacucho stated: "It's important for people to know that they [reparations] came from the state rather an international organization, and that this is meant to acknowledge violence, rather than

reparations, such as building schools or roads, as fulfilling what the state already owed them as their right to development. For a twenty-two-year-old Ayacuchan anthropology university student and ANFASEP Juventud member, collective reparations reinforced a problematic discourse of victimhood by focusing on the "generalized repair of destruction" over the direct repair of wrongdoing: "'Victim' connotes helplessness and charity; what communities want is justice and recognition."[18] Afectados commonly argued that individual reparations directly acknowledged wrongdoing, thereby serving as a form of justice.[19]

Historical Memory and Solidarity

> *What does historical memory have to do with reconciliation? What happens when the families affected by political violence live in a cycle of pain? What happens when they don't feel understood by the rest of society, resulting in practically a broken cord between generations of adults, who directly experienced the political violence, and those who indirectly experienced it, but can't really empathize, and don't take it as obligatory or important? If there existed more [projects for historical memory], as an affected person, I would believe that at least someone understands me. I would feel at least that the history that I have, I have shared with others. But without these places of memory, I would definitely feel that my pain is my own, that my past is my own. The function of historical memory is therefore to ensure that this pain, this remembering, is not just my own. Make it everyone's – yes, everyone's – so that we are all aware, so that we all would prevent such violence again, so that we all feel empathetic, so that we all will help lobby and fight for victims' rights. Because otherwise, we will continue to be fractioned. Some of us will belong to organizations for those affected by political violence like this one, and we'll keep fighting for the truth,*

represent one more government project." Officials working in reparations in Ayacucho and Lima argued that the legacies of the conflict were collectively shared and that communities were interconnected to the extent that a crime against one individual or family had collective repercussions. Because of the number of indirect victims, and the problems in identifying those who should receive individual reparations, they made a case that reparations should be collective and that individual reparations could further divide commissions. See Felix Palomino Alarcón Quispe, SER, interview by author, Ayacucho, Peru, October 19, 2010; Jairo Rivas, member of the Consejo de Reparaciones, interview by author, Lima, Peru, December 19, 2010.

18 ANFASEP Juventud member and anthropology student, age twenty-four, ANFASEP Juventud Focus Group, Ayacucho, Peru, October 16, 2010.

19 Some *aftectados* did not understand that the CVR was only able to make recommendations and did not itself have the legal ability to monitor and deliver reparations. Some felt directly betrayed by the CVR, referring to the CVR as a "*Comisión de Mentiras*" (Commission of Lies). After his frustration by the government's lack of progress in implementing reparations, Lerner cited criticisms that the CVR did not deliver its promise of reparations as one of his biggest disappointments. Lerner, interview. ANFASEP Juventud members stressed the importance of an integral approach, starting with individual victims and affected families, and then repairing the collective regional effects of the conflict.

for justice, for reparation, for dignity, and we'll feel alone, while others won't understand why we're fighting.

–Twenty-four-year-old female university student and member of ANFASEP Juventud, Ayacucho[20]

As I set out in Chapter 6, the CVR emerged as part of a larger emphasis on human rights and transparency following the discovery of massive corruption at the hands of the Fujimori regime. The Commission presented itself as an instrument of accountability, meant to bring justice to victims and counter impunity. In this regard, the CVR successfully put victims and the marginalization of rural and indigenous populations into the public eye and played a key role in furthering criminal justice.[21] Interviewees of varying social backgrounds and on all parts of the political spectrum broadly agreed with its root causes of the conflict, citing, in particular, political and economic marginalization, underdevelopment, and a crisis in education.[22]

Failure to implement the Commission's recommendations and the continuation of structural inequalities and injustices severely compromised its overall impact. Social understandings of reconciliation and of the CVR's contribution varied markedly. CVR participants frequently found the experience of giving testimony to be positive – relaying that it restored a measure of dignity and honor to victims.[23] Hearings highlighted the strength and agency of survivors.[24] The CVR's first hearing with Ascarza gave her a platform to speak about her missing son and paid tribute to her courage and campaigns on behalf of missing persons. In another of the CVR's early hearings, Magdalena Monteza Benavides, who was wrongly arrested and then raped by military soldiers, testified

[20] Female communications student at the UNSCH and ANFASEP Juventud member, age twenty-four, focus group, Ayacucho, Peru, November 6, 2010.

[21] In the post-CVR period, victims' experiences assumed a more prominent role in the public sphere, reflected in films and exhibitions about the conflict and the attention given to victims' campaigns in electoral politics.

[22] Public opinion polls during the CVR's operation showed that Peruvians were in favor of the CVR and moved by the testimony of victims. They also indicated significant popular support for carrying out the CVR's recommendations, particularly in criminal justice and reparations. See Carlos Iván Degregori, *Qué Difícil es Ser Dios: El Partido Comunista del Perú – Sendero Luminoso y el Conflicto Armado Interno en el Perú: 1980–1999* (Lima, Peru: Institute of Peruvian Studies, 2010); Eduardo Gonzales Cueva, "The Peruvian Truth and Reconciliation Commission and the Challenge of Impunity," in *Transitional Justice in the Twenty-first Century*, ed. Naomi Roht-Arriaza (Cambridge: Cambridge University Press, 2006), pp. 70–93.

[23] Kimberly Theidon, *Entre Prójimos: El Conflicto Armado Interno y La Política de la Reconciliación en el Perú* (Lima, Perú: Instituto de Estudios Peruanos, 2004). See also Lisa J. Laplante and Kimberly Theidon, "Truth with Consequences: Justice and Reparations in Post-truth Commission Peru," *Human Rights Quarterly* 29 (2007), pp. 228–250.

[24] Laplante and Theidon, "Truth with Consequences."

with her young daughter who was born of the assault. She detailed her personal journey and love for her child.[25] As members of ANFASEP Juventud stated, public testimony and its inscription into official memory markers provided a medium through which victims could feel less atomized and generated solidarity and social interest.[26]

The lack of follow-up to the CVR's work often undermined this positive impact. The Commission's short time frame and its high-profile proceedings stood in contrast to the lack of changes to individuals' lives. Interviewees emphasized corruption and the lack of justice – that not enough military officials have faced trial and the slow progress in reparations – and the continuation of socioeconomic problems, notably poverty and the lack of upward mobility.[27] As a member of ANFASEP Juventud put it, "Yes, we have democratic procedures now, which we deserve for our efforts, but we have no opportunities or dignity and the region remains forgotten."[28]

Understandings of reconciliation have varied widely. In affected communities in Ayacucho, survivors described reconciliation as an intimate and personal process, defining reconciliation as peace and tranquility and internal healing.[29] For an eighty-year-old woman from Cangallo whose son was killed by the military: "Reconciliation is being able to sleep tranquilly at night."[30] Most identified mental health and the passage of time as important drivers of reconciliation. Some referred to "reconciliation" as a "*palabra impuesta*" (imposed word) that does not exist for rural populations, where victims live in a "forced coexistence" with former perpetrators.[31] In focus groups in Colca, village women agreed that reconciliation was possible – and relevant – at the individual, interpersonal, and communal levels, but not with the state.[32]

[25] Benavides found the experience to be largely positive in affording social recognition and solidarity. Interview, Lima, Peru, February 23, 2011.
[26] ANFASEP Juventud Focus Group, Ayacucho, Peru, November 6, 2010.
[27] UNSCH Law Student Focus Group, Ayacucho, Peru, October 21, 2010.
[28] Participant in his twenties from Cayara, ANFASEP Juventud Focus Group, November 6, 2010.
[29] Colca Adult Focus Group, Colca, Peru, October 15, 2010.
[30] García Calderón, interview.
[31] Colca Adult Focus Group, Colca, Peru, October 15, 2010. See also interview with José Coronel Aguirre.
[32] Colca Adult Focus Group. In a workshop with thirty high school students in the village of Colca, participants stated that they believed that reconciliation was possible at many levels (the individual, inter-personal, and communal levels), but never with the state (national reconciliation). Youth participants defined reconciliation as "a way of living in harmony, peace, tranquility and equality," and "adopting a culture of peace." Some also described reconciliation as "forgetting bad experiences related to the war," as well as a "pact" and "understanding" between two groups. Colca Youth Focus Group (ages 16–18), Colca, Peru, October 15, 2010.

For educated sectors in Ayacucho – young people, academics, students, and civil society – national reconciliation often carried a stigma. While the CVR played an important role in putting collective memory into the public sphere and strengthening civil society, it also exposed a lack of political will to implement its recommendations. They often presented reconciliation as a "misnomer," and implying a "conciliation" which never existed. Echoing the sentiments of other students at the university, for an anthropology student at the UNSCH:

> The state looks for media, channels to transmit reconciliation. It's psychological propaganda to channel the discontent. And they do research and say that we all want reconciliation, but it's not what we said. For Peruvians in Lima the whole world is Lima, and the rest of us don't exist, or we are backwards and red [subversive]. They've been trying to bring us in for a long time, with their "modernization schools," trying to make us like them and we don't even know who we are anymore, but they still resent us.[33]

For this group the state was the primary barrier to reconciliation, and reconciliation would require concrete changes in state policies, especially in social justice and economic opportunities.[34] For a young member of ANFASEP Juventud: "What needs to be done for reconciliation? Well it's very clear to me. I understand that there are plenty of economic resources in this country, and they haven't given any to us. Once there is some investment in this forgotten region and its people, we can talk about reconciliation."[35]

The conception of justice as a prerequisite for reconciliation was a consistent theme for affected communities. They conceived of reconciliation as contingent upon social, economic, and political provisions, including an open understanding of citizenship and official support of multiculturalism. For Carlos Infante at the UNSCH, "Reconciliation for politicians is that the Indian or '*cholo*' [a derogatory term used for those of indigenous descent] accepts with happiness his donation." Reconciliation requires nation-building, not in the "fascist sense," but as a sociopolitical process of "value pluralism and mutual respect."[36] Nation-building would

[33] UNSCH anthropology student, age twenty-four, originally from Cayara, Ayacucho, Peru, October 21, 2010.

[34] In two focus groups conducted with eight university students at the UNSCH, six participants said national reconciliation has not advanced in Peru, and two believed it was impossible with the state. These included four law and four anthropology students. UNSCH Focus groups, Ayacucho, Peru, October 21, 2010.

[35] ANFASEP Juventud Focus Group.

[36] Interview with Carlos Rodrigo Infante Yupanqui, Ayacucho, Peru, November 4, 2010. Infante is a faculty member at the UNSCH and director of the monthly journal *Con Sentido*. His father, journalist Octavio Infante García, was murdered in the Uchuraccay massacre.

require meaningful engagement with the Shining Path as one of the main actors in the conflict: "We cannot forget that at one point it [the Shining Path] mobilized thousands of people. What happened to these people? Who represents them?" Citing the military's capture and killing of nineteen-year-old Ayacuchan ex-Shining Path woman Edith Lagos in 1982:

> Never before had Ayacucho been so mobilized. Thousands of people literally poured into the streets for her funeral. It is as if all the collective pain and suffering of this region and our people were encapsulated in this one event. Today, it is as if this history is swept under the rug; people pretend it never existed. Nobody talks about Sendero Luminoso [Shining Path] or their role in this society.[37]

Some portrayed the CVR's conception of national reconciliation between state and society as "abstract," and failing to integrate principal protagonists. Other civil society officials in Ayacucho shared similar views, stating that the CVR should have included a Shining Path commissioner and that government actors had sidelined critical issues surrounding the status of ex-Shining Path prisoners and military disappearances.

Civil Society and Memory Politics in Post-CVR Peru

Victims' campaigns and memory work preceded the CVR, providing an important backdrop to its work. On January 26, 1983, in the village of Uchuraccay in a remote mountain region of northern Ayacucho, the murder of seven journalists from Lima and their Ayacuchan guide marked an early turning point in a contentious process of civil society campaigns to investigate political violence. Three days earlier, after media allegations surfaced of indiscriminate murders in Huaychao, the journalists had traveled to the village to investigate the killings of Shining Path militants. Outcry over the murders led President Fernando Belaúnde to establish an investigation to look into the massacre. Headed by the acclaimed Peruvian novelist and political figure Mario Vargas Llosa, the Commission concluded that the villagers had killed the journalists in self-defense after mistaking them for Shining Path militants.[38] The report contextualized the murders within the greater tragedy of political violence in Peru, stating that the murders were vigilante acts where the military had encouraged villagers to protect themselves from Shining Path attacks.

Twenty years after the killings, while the CVR determined that the Investigatory Commission had provided a good account of the "tension

[37] Ibid. For a discussion of Lagos as a cultural rather than political figure, see Degregori, *Qué Difícil es Ser Dios*.

[38] Llosa has been an active figure in Peruvian politics, losing to Fujimori in presidential elections on June 11, 1990.

and general violence" that led to the confrontations, Peruvian civil society and academics have heavily criticized the Commission. Degregori points out that the report presented the killings as a "misunderstanding," depicting Uchuraccay as "backwards and violent" and its inhabitants as living in "pre-Hispanic times." He criticizes the "indigenism" of the report for further entrenching an image of cultural mysticism and violence in the Andes.[39]

Debates surrounding the Uchuraccay Commission are an early example of an intense politics of memory and representation, which continues into the present. Although the killings of the journalists marked an important turning point in bringing the conflict to national and international attention, residents of the village, who had faced attacks for decades, abandoned Uchuraccay during the conflict under growing violence at the hands of the military and Shining Path. Over two decades later, as the journalists' families and colleagues continue to call for investigations,[40] victims' groups in Ayacucho have lamented the lack of attention to the many peasant deaths in Uchuraccay before and after their arrival.[41]

While civil society activism helped set the stage for the CVR, the CVR also provided an important impetus for advocacy groups, as in the case of ANFASEP. In 1983, after military soldiers kidnapped her nineteen-year-old son, Arquímedes, from their home, Angélica Mendoza de Ascarza became a representative and symbol for victims of political violence in Peru. Generating domestic and international attention, "Mamá Angelica," as she is known in Ayacucho, founded ANFASEP in 1983 with other indigenous rural women as an organizing forum and refuge for family members of missing persons. Mostly run by relatives of victims of military abuses, Ascarza and other women searched mass graves for the

39 In an interview with the journal *Caretas*, Llosa elaborated on the notion of "the two Perus," consisting of "men who participate in the twentieth century and men such as these villagers of Uchuraccay who live in the 19th century, or perhaps even the 18th. The enormous distance that exists between the two Perus is what lies behind this tragedy." *Caretas* (April 2, 1990) in Maria Elena García, *Making Indigenous Citizens: Identity, Development and Multicultural Activism in Peru* (Stanford, CA: Stanford University Press, 2005), p. 43. Theidon faults the commission for reinforcing an image in the capital of an "Andean rage," where the inhabitants of the Sierra are portrayed as "endemically violent" and explosive. Kimberly Theidon, "Histories of Innocence: Post-War Stories in Peru," in *Localizing Transitional Justice: Interventions and Priorities after Mass Violence*, ed. Rosalind Shaw, Lars Waldorf, and Pierre Hazan (Stanford, CA: Stanford University Press, Studies in Human Rights, 2010), pp. 96–97.

40 Infante denies the official account, explaining that his father knew the peasants and they would have recognized him. He believes the military is responsible for the deaths and that the assignation of blame to the peasants is a cover-up. Infante, interview.

41 A site of several memorials to the former journalists and a peace park, the village receives few visitors today.

Figure 7.1 Santuario de la Paz y Reconciliación (Memorial to commemorate the murder of eight journalists and their guide in Uchuraccay, Peru). Photo taken by author in October 2010.

bodies of their missing children, frequently traveling to Lima to campaign on behalf of their family members. During the conflict, ANFASEP also served as a refuge, running a soup kitchen and cafeteria to feed orphans and children with missing family.

The history of ANFASEP exemplifies a complex dynamic between the CVR and local advocacy groups.[42] The post-CVR period saw a wave of NGO activity. Many in the NGO community referenced the CVR's findings, referring to the Commission as their *punto de referencia* (reference point).[43] ANFASEP played an important role in the history of the CVR. CVR officials sometimes referred to *Ascarza* as an inspiration for the CVR; Ascarza was the first individual to testify at the CVR hearings in Ayacucho. At the same time, the CVR helped ANFASEP grow as an

[42] Ponciano Del Pino, "Introducción: Memorias para el reconocimiento" (Introduction: Memories for acknowledgment), in *No hay mañana sin ayer. Batallas por la memoria y consolidación democrática en el Perú* (There is no tomorrow without yesterday: Battles for memory and democratic consolidation in Peru), ed. Carlos Iván Degregori, Tamia Portugal, Renzo Aroni, and Gabriel Salazar (Lima, Peru: Instituto de Estudios Peruanos, 2015).

[43] ANFASEP official Yuber Alarcón Quispe, for example, shares his deep respect for Salomón Lerner, to whom he refers as a personal inspiration. Interview.

organization by providing it with resources and raising its public profile.[44] With the CVR's support, ANFASEP established the Museo de la Memoria (Museum of Memory) above its offices in Ayacucho, detailing the history of political violence in Ayacucho and the story of ANFASEP as an organization. The museum features a replica of mass graves and the *Los Cabitos* military base and torture center, material artifacts of the disappeared, and a photographic mural of ANFASEP members, the majority of whom are indigenous women. Today, ANFASEP has approximately 200 members, and new wings, including ANFASEP Juventud (ANFASEP Youth) that consists of young professionals and students, many of whom lost relatives in the conflict, and who are committed to taking the organization's aims forward.[45] ANFASEP has also expanded its advocacy to other areas, notably reparations and addressing and raising attention to the legacies of state violence in the Amazon. On October 16, 2005, on the second anniversary of the CVR's final report, the Museo de la Memoria opened as a major media event, with hundreds of people in attendance, including former commissioners, political officials, and human rights advocates. From the Fujimori and García administrations' historical branding of the organization as a terrorist group, ANFASEP's political clout has markedly increased as state leaders pay attention to the organization.

The CVR also played a direct role in inspiring new organizations. In Lima, a number of former CVR staff now work at IDEHPUCP (Instituto de Democracia y Derechos Humanos de la Pontificia Universidad Católica del Perú, Institute of Democracy and Human Rights of the PUCP). Headed by Lerner, the institute conducts research on human rights, transitional justice, and forensic anthropology in Peru.[46] The CVR also helped inspire new organizations in Ayacucho,

[44] The García and Fujimori administrations routinely referred to the organization as "aligned with Sendero." Following her trip to Europe in 1985, Fujimori called *Ascarza* a Shining Path ambassador.

[45] ANFASEP provided for some of these youth during the war, cooking daily meals for children with missing family members. Some of the Juventud have become well-known activists and spokespersons for their communities for human rights and victims' campaigns. ANFASEP Juventud member Heeder Soto Quispe has become a human rights and community activist, working for EPAF, and an art therapist for indigenous women. His art features in the museum and he has traveled to peace conferences abroad to speak about victims' rights and the conflict. Heeder Soto Quispe, interview by author, Ayacucho, Peru, October 11, 2010. Also important is Daniel Roca Sulca from Cangallo. After his family's displacement by Shining Path violence, Sulca served in the army before becoming a human rights activist in Ayacucho. Today, he works for the victims' organization, CONAVIP (Coordinadora Nacional de Organizaciones de Afectados por la Violencia Política). Daniel Roca Sulca, interview by author, Ayacucho, Peru, November 9, 2010.

[46] IDEHPUCH now offers a masters' program in transitional justice and forensic anthropology and is a base for visiting scholars focusing on human rights and transitional justice.

some of which staff individuals who worked for the CVR and seek to continue its objectives. The mental health organization COSMA's (Comisión de Salud Mental de Ayacucho) recently retired director, psychiatric nurse and Carmelite nun Sister Anne Carbon, founded the organization in 2003 as a follow-up to the CVR's mental health reparations program to treat victims of political violence and their families. Today, the clinic doubles as one of the main providers of mental health services in Ayacucho and serves as a handicraft center for patients to engage in art therapy and acquire a means to sell their work.[47] COSMA has also generated more attention and solidarity for victims, attracting staff and a regular rotation of visiting doctors, staff, and interns from other parts of Peru and abroad.

At the same time, the CVR generated a significant critical backlash and has been at the center of a heated memory politics. Important advocates have challenged aspects of the CVR's work, particularly its historical findings. The majority of ANFASEP members disagree with the CVR's conclusion that the Shining Path caused more deaths than the state, maintaining that the figure for military-related violence should be higher.[48] As in Sierra Leone, affected communities in Ayacucho have also criticized the CVR's centralized character in Lima. In Ayacucho, *memoria histórica* (historical memory) is an important focus area for civil society, with community commemoration initiatives providing a voice to those who did not take part in the CVR.[49]

Significantly, in Peru, memory politics have also extended to sectors that did not participate in the CVR. In February 2011, the military released its counter-report, "*En Honor a la Verdad*" (In Honor of the Truth). The report agrees with the importance of historical memory,

[47] Carbon estimates that 50 percent of the patients today are dealing with legacies of political violence, while the other 50 percent deal with broader mental health issues. Given the conflict's long-ranging effects on society she, like others working in mental health in the region, finds it hard to untangle the two. Mental health staff frequently noted that alcoholism and domestic violence have become worse, an outgrowth of general disillusionment, lack of opportunity, and a scarred society. Sister Anne Carbon, interview by author, Ayacucho, Peru, October 1, 2010.

[48] As opposed to the Shining Path, who intentionally left their victims in the open to inflict terror, the military's tactic of disappearances and deliberate burning and mutilation of bodies left victims missing or unidentified. The Peruvian forensic anthropology organization EPAF suspects that more than 15,000 missing persons remain, of which only 1,500 bodies have been recovered and 600 have been identified. Tanya Molina Morote, forensic anthropologist and regional coordinator of EPAF, interview by author, Ayacucho, Peru, October 5, 2010. See also Joseph P. Feldman's discussion of ANFASEP, "Exhibiting Conflict: History and Politics at the Museo de la Memoria de ANFASEP in Ayacucho, Peru," *Anthropological Quarterly* 85 (2012), pp. 487–518.

[49] These community leaders and local NGOs focus on documenting historical memory through villagers' own mediums and voices.

emphasizing a collective duty to learn from history to prevent future abuses and administer justice for past wrongs. It identifies giving a voice to the armed forces, particularly the military, as its objective.[50] A common assertion is that the military would like a "do over" and to see a commission established with a military commissioner on board.[51]

While the airing of alternative memories and contestation of the past evidences deep divisions in Peruvian society, it also represents a larger discursive shift about what debates belong in the public sphere and the claims that the past generates. In a broader sense, the CVR put civil society in a stronger position to mobilize against the state, acting as a political resource through which advocacy groups can counter censorship and denial. As the *Chalina de la Esperanza* (Scarf of Hope) exposition in Lima illustrates, while the controversies surrounding the event reflected deep divisions within Peruvian society, the politics surrounding its censorship also attest to heightened awareness for the *afectados* and their increased political standing.

At the same time, memory politics have also involved painful trade-offs, particularly for the *afectados*. More so than in Sierra Leone, the NGO community in Ayacucho now turns to Lima to pursue its campaigns. This process has to an extent become self-reinforcing, as greater integration into democratic politics has changed the orientation of civil society organizations.[52] ANFASEP Juventud sees political advocacy in the capital and national integration as the main ways forward while retaining the relevance of the organization and fulfilling its aims.[53] Greater political integration, however, has created tensions within organizations and between organizations and their constituents. For ANFASEP, the organization's greater visibility in the post-CVR period has raised new concerns over the extent to which it should work through the centralized political process versus hold on to its traditional role of critiquing the

[50] Marco Merino Amand, Ejército del Perú, *En Honor a la Verdad* (Lima, Perú: Comisión Permanente de Historia del Ejército del Perú, 2010), p. 7. In interviews, military officials often expressed their interest in telling their version of events. Officials who were critical of the CVR still often respected the idea of an official truth-seeking process.

[51] According to several CVR commissioners, it is important to bear in mind that military officials were more willing to talk than is often acknowledged, and that conversations with lower-ranking military officials still took place off the record. While the military has disputed the CVR's figure for victims and its percentage of military-related deaths as too high, military members often stressed that they would also like to tell their story and that they felt their voice was missing in debates.

[52] During the field research, I sat in on weekly weekend sessions with ANFASEP Juventud and a "marketing trainer" they had hired from Lima. The sessions evaluated how ANFASEP could better promote itself and channel its work through the political process.

[53] ANFASEP Juventud Focus Group (eight participants), held at ANFASEP, Ayacucho, Peru, November 6, 2010.

state. There is a fear within the organization that the state's integral reparations program may dampen ANFASEP's clout in other areas and is at odds with the organization's political views and aims. ANFASEP administrator – also *Ascarza*'s daughter – Maribel Ascarza Mendoza is critical of the rural populations' emphasis on reparations:

> I often say that the peasants are pragmatic people – too pragmatic. They are too sensible. They have this culture of resignation. Reparations are a tremendous risk. I tell them that they shouldn't be so quick to accept reparations until their greater concerns are met. What about the disappearances? What about justice and a change in overall state policies? Don't accept reparations until your voice is heard and your cause is achieved.[54]

For Ascarza, aged fifty-four, there is a tension between her cohort, whom the conflict "forced to grow up so quickly" and who "never had a youth," and the younger generation. While the CVR helped create a language of human rights and equality and fostered a more open atmosphere – "It [the CVR] has let us [ANFASEP] meet openly today" – the negative side of this "human rights culture" is the "individualism" of the younger generation. While she insists on the importance of respecting the alternative views of young people, Mendoza warns of the broader loss of community: "They [young people] don't want to remember. We used to believe in community and have solidarity. This has changed."[55]

For other senior community activists, civil society's strengthened position also yielded limited consequences. At a meeting for educators in Ayacucho, teachers described an "NGO boom," yet expressed uncertainty about the "point of all these NGOs." Paralleling an emphasis on local peace-building in Sierra Leone, Ayacucho has witnessed a certain revivalism of indigenous culture and traditions and interest in turning inward among sectors of civil society. While not uniform, some have raised the fear that political integration would come at a cost of further exploitation. For an agricultural engineer and development worker working with indigenous women in the Víctor Fajardo province, centralized state policies present an array of negative effects, ranging from problematic agricultural policies, which erode the soil, to food policies, raising concerns about the region's increasing reliance on imported foods and linking fears of dependency and malnutrition to the depreciation of the region's native foods.[56] She, like others in her organization, was critical of

[54] Maribel Ascarza Mendoza, ANFASEP administrator and lawyer, interview by author, Ayacucho, Peru, October 12, 2010.

[55] Ibid.

[56] Agrarian Engineer and IPAC official (Instituto de Promoción Agropecuaria y Comunal), interview by author, Huancapi, Peru, October 16, 2010.

Figure 7.2 Village women during a community event in Uchuraccay, Peru, during a visit with COSMA. Photo taken by author in October 2010.

the CVR, taking the view that talking about the past stifled productivity for rural women by opening past wounds. While she comes from the capital city of Ayacucho, the organization relocated to rural areas, focusing on the development of local sustainable agriculture and the promotion of cultural traditions.

The *afectados* sometimes challenged these more rigid positions of community leaders. In a group interview with ANFASEP Juventud, two young men in their twenties and thirties expressed their approval that the field research incorporated voices beyond the organization's directors: "First of all, I would like to congratulate you because these topics, which are spoken of many times, are referred solely to directors of affected communities, and not the actors themselves as the bases of youth or their own affected families."[57] In some cases, the *afectados* formed their own organizations and campaigns, distancing themselves from their ideologically staunch counterparts. Where ANFASEP remains an Ayacuchan organization, much of the younger generation is focused on political integration through the state, seeing participation in the democratic process and pragmatism as the only way to achieve the organization's aims.[58]

Responsibility and Omissions: Reconciliation without Belligerents?

While the CVR helped disseminate a wider interest in collective memory and public awareness, the Commission also exposed – and generated – strong social divisions. Although actors on various sides of the political spectrum were broadly supportive of a truth-seeking process and of the "idea of a CVR," stressing the importance of studying the past for future conflict prevention, many took issue with the CVR's findings and composition. In Ayacucho, some considered the CVR to be too "academic" and "intellectual," with interviewees pointing out that most commissioners were educated, left-leaning white males from Lima, and that only one spoke Quechua.[59] Perceptions of victimization and underrepresentation affected individuals' willingness to engage with the CVR as individuals of varying political orientations accused the Commission of bias.[60]

Social views have been especially polarized over perceptions of responsibility. In rural parts of Ayacucho, although interviewees consistently identified the state as bearing primary responsibility for the conflict, disagreements arose over individual accountability. While some cited the extradition and prosecution of Fujimori as a victory for justice, others were grateful to the former president for "pacifying the country" and visiting the villages.[61] In Lima and along the coast, critics have faulted the CVR for being "too soft" on the Shining Path.

57 ANFASEP Juventud Focus Group, Ayacucho, Peru, October 16, 2010.

58 Many members of ANFASEP Juventud work for human rights NGOs with offices in Lima, frequently traveling to and working with their counterparts in the human rights community in the capital.

59 See also Cynthia E. Milton, ed., *Art from a Fractured Past: Memory and Truth-telling in Post-Shining Path Peru* (Durham and London: Duke University Press, 2014).

60 In almost all interviews, individuals who dismissed the commission had not read the report. This sometimes resulted in conspiratorial accusations that commissioners were pursuing their own political interests through the commission after having failed in the domestic political process, now with the aid of the international community. CVR president Salomón Lerner Febres has been subject to death threats and serious harassment.

61 Some stated that they felt a closer tie to Fujimori due to his immigrant Japanese background, referring to him as "*El Chino*" (the Chinese), and his hard-working, practical mentality. As a widow in Cayara stated, "He [Fujimori] was the only president who ever

Members of the military and former state actors have reacted particularly strongly. A mobilized coalition of military and conservative sectors has publicly accused the CVR of pursuing its own political agenda and promoting an inherent bias against the military.[62] The military's counter-report, issued in 2011, acknowledges "excesses," but denies institutional sanctioning of violence against civilians.[63] The report urges consideration of the contexts within which abuses took place as mitigating circumstances, focusing on the loss of agency during wartime and the emotional strain on soldiers. Military officials often extended this narrative to society at large, claiming that the middle classes turned a blind eye and gave the military a *carte blanche* to defeat terrorism, and now that the Shining Path was no longer a threat, pushed for trials.[64] In the view of a retired colonel from Lima who had been stationed in Ayacucho, "Peruvians were happy to support Fujimori. They supported him to do 'whatever it takes' to defeat terrorism. Now they want to prosecute him."[65] Military interviewees pointed out that they fought against a campaign of terror on behalf of a democratically elected state and took offense at the portrayal of the counter-insurgency as an "armed conflict" between two internal parties.[66] They highlighted the difficulty of identifying targets, describing a context of ambush and betrayal, and the difficulties of fighting an enemy who "wears no uniform" and uses civilians, including children, as human

visited us, cared for us, and came to talk to us." Interview by author, Cayara, Peru, October 13, 2010. On the impact of Fujimori's populist political style on the poor, see Oliart, "Albert Fujimori."

62 A common sentiment is that the CVR scapegoated the military and was trying to bring down the military corps. See publications by the Instituto Paz, Democracia y Desarollo (Institute of Peace, Democracy and Development). While none of the military officials interviewed had read the CVR's report, all stated that they "knew its position" by virtue of knowing the identity of the commissioners. They also felt the CVR's figures for victims and military-related deaths were too high, and critiqued what they saw as the "political interests" of the CVR. Interview with former military colonels from Lima who were stationed in Ayacucho during the conflict, Lima, Peru, January 16, 2011, and February 16, 2011.

63 The report asserts its commitment to civilian–military relations and training, citing psychological strain and personal reprisals, racism, cultural and language barriers, superiors' lack of control of subordinates, and poor recruitment policies during the conflict's quick escalation as factors that augmented abuses.

64 For many military members, the general population was indifferent and remained willfully ignorant about the conflict until the Shining Path reached Lima.

65 Interview with former military colonels from Lima who were stationed in Ayacucho during the conflict, Lima, Peru, January 16, 2011, and February 16, 2011.

66 Military officers point out that they received little in return for their service. They cite the absence of veterans' benefits and pensions, and high rates of PTSD. Interviewees representing ANFASEP and faculty and students at the UNSCH often took issue with the CVR's depiction of a two-sided conflict, stressing that counter-insurgency mischaracterized the power asymmetries in the state's commission of political violence and downplayed state terrorism.

shields.[67] Exacerbating factors were the tired state of their soldiers, who were generally young and uneducated and drawn from the coast, and the challenge of fighting a counter-insurgency campaign in the harsh and unfamiliar Andean terrain, where they did not speak the language of the local population.[68]

Also important, however, is what is left out of the public discourse. While the CVR recommended the rehabilitation of militants after their prison terms, to date – with the exception of individual pastoral work in jails and Evangelical outreach in rural areas – Peru lacks an official reintegration policy.[69] Social taboos surrounding the Shining Path have not ameliorated over time; to the contrary, the current involvement of Shining Path splinter cells in drug trafficking has further reinforced its image as a criminal – terrorist group. Open discussion is particularly delicate for lower-level former militants, many of whom recently left prison or never served jail time. While most former militants in the capital cities hide their identities, the relatively few who publicly came forward tend to be more politically active and committed to their ideological agenda, further entrenching a view of ex-fighters as unrepentant and fundamentalist.[70] Ex-insurgents also sometimes endorsed the view of current fighters as ideologically bereft, referring to the current involvement in the drug trade as an abandonment of ideology.[71] For a female ex-MRTA militant from Lima, the depoliticization of the MRTA was already noticeable when she was enlisted. In her recollection, the MRTA began attracting a larger number of "delinquents" looking for personal profit.[72] These individuals were "rogues," as opposed

[67] According to the former military official, the CVR "destroyed the military's honor and prestige." The official, who was sent to Cayara after the massacre, describes the village as a "ghost town" which was left dejected after prolonged violence by the Shining Path and the military. He contrasts Cayara to other villages where he had been stationed. In his view, Cayara was doomed due to its "cursed" strategic location in the fighting between the military and the Shining Path, and a standoff with the peasants was inevitable.

[68] Ibid. [69] Pilar Coll Torrente, interview by author, Lima, Peru, February 3, 2011.

[70] For Torrente, who has worked with hundreds of ex-Shining Path and MRTA female prisoners, this is the case for most ex-combatants. Some ex-Shining Path, however, have returned to politics on platforms advocating amnesty and reconciliation with the Shining Path. One example is Vasty Lescano Ancieta, who ran for local elections in Puno on a MOVADEF platform after serving a sixteen-year jail term. For a discussion of the presence of Shining Path in other regions, e.g., Puno, see José Luis Rénique, *La Batalla Por Puno: Conflicto Agrario y Nación en Los Andes Peruanos 1866–1995* (Lima, Peru: Institute of Peruvian Studies, 2004). See also the CVR report on Puno, Volume 5, Chapter 2.17, "El PCP-SL y La Batalla Por Puno."

[71] Former female Shining Path from Huánuco, interview with author, Lima, Peru, February 23, 2011. She joined the Shining Path as a twenty-year-old sociology student.

[72] The interviewee was an anthropology student at the PUCP in Lima from a middle-class family when she joined the MRTA. She dropped out of university and cut all ties with her family for ten years to serve in the MRTA, rising to the position of bodyguard to a senior leader before their joint arrest. Interview by author, Lima, Peru, February 26, 2011.

to the students from her generation, who joined for ideological reasons and made personal sacrifices, abandoning educational and professional opportunities and cutting ties with family members.[73]

Where truth commissions seek to increase solidarity by providing a forum to better understand individual motivations and agency during violence, this objective assumes a coherence and reflexivity in relation to testimony. During an interview with a high-ranking female ex-MRTA combatant, twenty years after her prison sentence, Marta (name changed) was able to provide a clear narrative of why she joined the MRTA. She highlighted, in particular, her interest in social justice from a young age, her close relationship with her "socially conscious" grandfather, and her growing political awareness as an anthropology student at the Catholic University of Peru (PUCP) in Lima. These culminated in her eventual attendance of MRTA meetings, which she felt was attractive for its more ideologically rigorous and principled image than the Shining Path. Yet, as she points out, although the majority of her cohort was politically active and sympathetic to the left, most did not join insurgency groups and none reached her rank.[74] While she has found some peace through her current work with street children and her dignified treatment by police women in prison, the stigmatization of ex-militants and the lack of open dialogue with others who have shared similar experiences are barriers to making sense of this chapter of her life.[75]

While the CVR had a mandate to raise awareness and contribute to social knowledge, the Commission was also a product of its environment. In a setting where public discussion of the Shining Path and MRTA remains sensitive and the CVR's relationship with former antagonists grew increasingly strained, the Commission heavily focused its efforts on engaging and providing acknowledgment for the *afectados* rather than militants. As Theidon notes, the result was a Commission that focused on victimization rather than on the conflict's protagonists,

[73] Although both women regretted their participation in the conflict, they shared their struggles to come to understand their involvement. Both had spoken to the CVR in private (and to focus groups) while in prison.

[74] The interviewee described the "test" process through which she rose up in the MRTA. She identified her arrest as the moment she realized her level of ideological commitment was not what she thought it was. A leak had led the police to surround the heavily armed safe house where she was hiding with the commander. When the commander instructed that both should kill themselves with grenades, she realized that her loyalty was insufficient to take her life.

[75] In her view, any answers she could give to such questions are "predetermined," and she has spent the last ten years trying to work out the reasons for her involvement in the MRTA with a psychologist.

leaving the question of what motivated thousands of individuals to take part and support the insurgencies largely unanswered.[76]

Conclusions

As in Sierra Leone, contextual factors in Peru played a critical role in shaping and constraining local perceptions of transitional justice. The CVR operated in a highly polarized environment. In Ayacucho, a backdrop of underinvestment and discrimination in indigenous and rural areas profoundly colored local justice and peace-building experiences. A heavy-handed military presence and decades of political violence took an additional toll, reinforcing a fear of authority structures and heightening a sense of regional and ethnic persecution. At the same time, a long legacy of state neglect and military violence left a deep distrust of political authority and politics. The military's use of disappearances during the conflict perpetuated an ongoing cycle of disappointment in the state, keeping families from filing claims for reparations. The ethnic undertones of the conflict further magnified these legacies, contributing to a sense of regional persecution and degradation of indigenous lives. Together, these factors generated mistrust and suspicion, posing barriers to popular participation and engagement with transitional justice institutions. The demographics of victimization and insurgent participation and the concentration of violence in remote areas further undermined social solidarity.

In the post-CVR period, reconciliation has had important temporal dimensions. The limited implementation of the CVR's recommendations and slow progress in reparatory justice further weakened political capital and undermined its momentum. Additionally, while the CVR generated dialogue about the past, class and regional differences strongly affected individuals' experiences of the Commission and perceptions of the conflict. Former protagonists' struggles to come to terms with their own pasts reflect these tensions, especially in a context of stigmatization and censorship. Although the CVR generated awareness for *afectados* and brought attention to state violence, its investigations became part of a contentious memory politics, which continues into the present. Individuals' experiences during the conflict and present situations strongly influenced their openness with the Commission and willingness to engage with its work. Unsurprisingly, those with the most to lose – actors affiliated with the

[76] Kimberley Theidon,"Histories of Innocence: Post-war Stories in Peru," in *Localizing Transitional Justice: Interventions and Priorities after Mass Violence*, ed. Rosalind Shaw, Lars Waldorf, and Pierre Hazan (Stanford, CA: Stanford University Press, 2010), p. 110.

former regime, the military, and the Shining Path – were often the most critical, vigorously disputing the CVR's findings and claims.

Rather than stall justice and reconciliation efforts, however, in both Sierra Leone and Perum I charted a complex and dynamic set of processes in which formal justice mobilized local actors, sometimes in agreement, but often in criticism and resistance. In each case, transitional justice institutions and civil society activism adopted distinct and varying foci and orientations. Where the Sierra Leonean TRC became part of a larger politics of reintegration and reconciliation, the CVR generated attention for the marginalization of rural and indigenous populations and to state violence, and fostered an interest in historical memory. In a context of severe stigmatization of insurgent groups and political and social censorship, it put less emphasis on reintegration and reconciliation with protagonists, focusing instead on victims' rights and redress.

Nevertheless, transitional justice in Peru also had significant, albeit unexpected, indirect effects. The CVR had important contributions in the civic sphere. This process was not linear and took on distinct dynamics over time. While the CVR helped raise awareness for the *afectados* and of state culpability and provided an important forum for advocacy groups, its investigations have generated intense debate and contestation.

Returning to procedural reconciliation, on their own, the controversies surrounding the CVR do not undermine its work. In important respects, Peru's highly charged memory politics strengthened democratic norms by channeling conflict into the public sphere and providing a space for competing narratives. For Rolando Ames Cobián, "This is not a job that makes you popular. We knew that from the start."[77] Reátegui comes to a similar conclusion: "If everyone criticizes you, you can say you have done your job."[78] By creating a discourse about rights and responsibilities, the CVR fostered a more pluralistic political process, reinforcing a framework through which groups could channel their grievances.

Taking a broader long-term view, these dynamics have generated distinct cumulative effects over time.[79] By putting collective memory into the public eye and stimulating debate about responsibility and guilt, the CVR was an important catalyst for alternative memories, particularly within affected communities and among marginalized groups. Truth-

[77] Rolando Ames Cobián, interview. [78] Félix Reátegui, CVR Researcher, interview.

[79] This stands in contrast to recent comparative impact assessment literature, which has found that, compared to trials, truth commissions have little effect on democracy. See Tricia D. Olsen, Leigh A. Payne, and Andrew G. Reiter, *Transitional Justice in Balance: Comparing Processes, Weighing Efficacy* (Washington, DC: United States Institute of Peace Press, 2010).

seeking in Peru has also extended beyond victims' groups, civil society, and those who participated in the CVR's proceedings, drawing in protagonists, notably the Peruvian military. While memory politics in Peru evidence deep-rooted societal divisions, they also represent a larger discursive shift regarding the claims generated by the past and who has a responsibility to address them. While not uniform, importantly, advocacy organizations now often direct their campaigns toward Lima, thereby working through and strengthening the democratic process. Significantly, however, procedural reconciliation has not addressed Peru's deep divisions and structural injustices, a tension which I will now examine in greater detail in the Conclusions.

8 Conclusions

Context, Transformation, and Holism in Transitional Justice

In this book, I examined two important recent experiences of transitional justice and peace-building. The case studies of Sierra Leone and Peru are significant because of the varying procedures and orientations of formal and informal mechanisms in each instance. As I will detail in this Concluding chapter, they also highlight in different ways the importance of context in shaping the experiences and trajectories of transitional justice. In recent decades, some of the worst outbreaks of violence have occurred within protracted social conflicts. Protracted social conflicts tend to be deep-rooted in economic, political, and social structures. They often feature multiple and recurring experiences of violence, at both the macro and micro levels, and at the hands of a range of actors. Civilians are frequently on the frontlines of protracted conflicts, sometimes as perpetrators of violence, and often as witnesses and targets. While transitional justice processes have increasingly sought to facilitate broad aims of conflict transformation, more research is needed to assess their role in conflict transitions and their contribution to peace-building and reconciliation. In the rest of the chapter, I will again take up the importance of context, before turning to an analysis of the promises and limitations of procedural reconciliation conceptually and in practice.

Transitional Justice as Contextually Bound

Transitional justice today is a rapidly growing and expanding global project, both in terms of the actors promoting and managing it and the contexts within which it operates. While transitional justice developed as a set of practices in response to Cold War regime transitions, in the last two decades transitional justice processes have emerged in complex and fragile conflict transitions. In these settings, transitional justice and peace-building processes have grappled with a wide and thorny range of issues, often in fragile circumstances, where the root causes of conflict persist and violence remains a strong possibility.

In this book, I argued that academic theory and practice have insufficiently appreciated and taken stock of these varying and multifaceted challenges. The establishment of transitional justice in conflict transitions has been fraught in practice, often colliding with competing understandings and processes.[1] Not infrequently, as both the Peruvian and Sierra Leonean experiences illustrate in different ways, formal justice processes have generated further tensions and politics, including countermovements and rejection of formal institutions and aims.

A central contribution of the book is its careful attention to contextual variation. In Chapter 2, I offered an overview of settings in which transitional justice mechanisms have emerged. I noted variances in types of conflicts, global and domestic normative inclinations, strategic considerations, and practical impediments. I concluded the chapter with a discussion of the specific challenges that arose when applying transitional justice to conflict transformation in conflict transitions.

In the empirical chapters, I went further and looked at how contextual factors affected not only the establishment of transitional justice mechanisms but also their broader orientations, procedures, and domestic receptions. In both cases, I stressed endogeneity, arguing that the wider circumstances surrounding and justifying the establishment of formal mechanisms, particularly truth commissions, also weakened their impact and reception over time. In Peru, agents involved in the conflict and the military remained powerful, and they retained a middle-class support base. As I argued in Ayacucho, the state's long-term marginalization of rural and largely indigenous parts of the country and a prolonged dirty war at the hands of military agents and insurgency groups had already eroded political trust and faith in authority. The ethnic undertones of the conflict had a particularly harmful impact, reinforcing a broader sense of victimization among affected (largely indigenous) populations while simultaneously distancing the conflict from the emotional identifications of the middle classes along the coast. While the Commission sought to generate civic trust and solidarity, insufficient follow-up, particularly in reparations, further augmented suspicion, reinforcing apathy in politics and institutions and social isolation and marginalization.[2] Although many

[1] Societies with long histories of subordination and violence often have particularly developed informal conflict resolution and customary law. Rosalind Shaw, Lars Waldorf, and Pierre Hazan, "Introduction," in *Localizing Transitional Justice: Interventions and Priorities after Mass Violence*, ed. Rosalind Shaw, Lars Waldorf, and Pierre Hazan (Stanford, CA: Stanford University Press, 2010), p. 11. See also Rosalind Shaw, *Memories of the Slave Trade: Ritual and the Historical Imagination in Sierra Leone* (Chicago: University of Chicago Press, 2002).

[2] Lisa Laplante and Kimberly Theidon argue that, while giving testimony had cathartic effects for their interviewees in Ayacucho, the lack of concrete follow-up later undermined

participants found testifying at the CVR to be positive, they also resented the state's insufficient political response to the CVR's work.

In Sierra Leone, public tolerance toward the RUF was higher and reconciliation found some resonance within communal restorative justice traditions. Sierra Leone's fragile peace and the enormous challenges of underdevelopment and post-war reconstruction additionally facilitated a more pragmatic approach toward the reintegration of ex-combatants. Here, however, as well, a long history of marginalization of affected regions, political corruption, and negative international interference generated suspicion and wariness toward formal processes.[3] Mismanagement and an uneven global commitment accentuated these challenges, augmenting a lack of local buy-in for formal processes. As in Peru, disenchantment was particularly acute vis-à-vis slow progress in reparatory justice. Tensions also emerged within affected communities and between stakeholders. Victims, in particular, resented the TRC's emphasis on the reintegration of ex-combatants and felt sidelined from reconciliation efforts.

In each case, I argued that transitional justice institutions did seek to respond to these pressures. Both commissions adopted distinct and varying foci and orientations. Both Commissions encountered unexpected challenges and readjusted their normative commitments in part in response to social and political pressures. As I argued in Chapter 4, this was particularly the case in Peru, where the CVR elevated certain aspects of its mandate over others. I highlighted choices that the CVR made, especially in its engagement with ex-combatants. Although the CVR initially sought to offer an inclusive platform that would provide an opportunity for individuals and groups on various sides of the conflict to testify, in a context of deeply entrenched societal polarization and stigmatization, the CVR chose to prioritize victims' rights, criminal justice, and raising awareness among middle and coastal classes. The CVR focused, in particular, on the macro root causes of violence, identifying the state's long-term marginalization of the Andean Sierra and those of indigenous descent as a key underlying cause of conflict. Unlike other participatory commissions, it put less emphasis on eliciting ex-combatants' participation, and on providing a platform to air their

these positive advances. Lisa J. Laplante and Kimberly Susan Theidon, "Truth with Consequences: Justice and Reparations in Post-Truth Commission Peru," *Human Rights Quarterly* 29 (2007), pp. 228–250.

[3] The lack of local buy-in for globalized transitional justice in Sierra Leone comes out strongly in Tim Kelsall's work as well. Tim Kelsall, *Culture under Cross Examination: International Justice and the Special Court for Sierra Leone* (Cambridge: Cambridge University Press, 2013).

viewpoints and rationales for taking part in political violence. Significantly, this orientation grew stronger over time. Although commissioners in this context were more rooted in a normative disposition in favor of human rights and punitive justice, the CVR's approach to ex-combatants became more firmly entrenched in response to stigmatization and tensions with combatants and significant political and social pressures.

In Sierra Leone, the TRC, in some regards, went in the opposite direction, particularly given the Commission's difficult relationship with the SCSL. As time passed, the TRC took a more approving stance on confidentiality and even-handedness in order to reassure ex-combatants that their participation would not incriminate them at the Court. As in Peru, this orientation grew more entrenched over time as the TRC struggled with its public image and with how to achieve its mandate in the face of unexpected challenges and pressures.

Procedural Reconciliation amid Ongoing Conflict

Rather than finding only stalled justice and reconciliation however, in light of the difficulties outlined above, I charted a complex and dynamic set of processes in which formal justice mobilized local actors, sometimes in agreement, but often in criticism and resistance. Procedural reconciliation, as I defined it, is a recognizable and mutually accepted widening of nonviolent normative and discursive parameters through which aggrieved parties can articulate and pursue their aims. Looking at reconciliation as a self-reflective and open-ended process,[4] I suggest that procedural reconciliation does not necessitate historical agreement or direct contact between antagonistic groups. Rather, it provides a space for competing, and often tense and irreconcilable, narratives and identities. Procedural reconciliation can take place through different media: discursively, through common language and rhetoric; normatively, through beliefs, culture, and values; and politically, through shared political structures and public spaces. Significantly, it is forward-looking in its establishment of new relationships and mechanisms of engagement. Finally, and also importantly, procedural reconciliation does not require cognitive reevaluation or cultivation of trust. It occurs when parties believe they have more to gain by pursuing their grievances through a shared process than outside of it.

[4] Claire Moon, "Prelapsarian State: Forgiveness and Reconciliation in Transitional Justice," *International Journal for Semiotics of Law* 17 (2004), pp. 185–197; Adrian Little, "Disjunctured Narratives: Rethinking Reconciliation and Conflict Transformation," *International Political Science Review* 33 (2012), pp. 82–98.

Conceptually, the understanding of procedural reconciliation highlights the longer-term and often indirect effects of transitional justice and the dynamic nature of reconciliation. I map out a fraught process in which transitional justice may cause further division and strife, yet nevertheless reinforced a limited form of procedural reconciliation. Importantly, procedural reconciliation rests on and accepts compromise and conflict as part of the political process. Truth-seeking and transitional justice facilitate procedural reconciliation to the extent that they further societal discussion and mobilize actors through common media. While individuals and groups may hold on to divisive viewpoints and conflict-related grievances, procedural reconciliation occurs to the extent that there is a longer-term consolidation of language and types of claims. Procedural reconciliation reflects a widening of engagement and shifts in actors' strategies, priorities, language, and political behavior.

Taking a broader, long-term view, in both Sierra Leone and Peru, the politics of reconciliation and truth had distinct cumulative effects over time. In both countries, formal justice had significant, albeit unexpected, indirect effects. In the Peruvian context, the CVR was an important catalyst for alternative memories, both within affected communities and among marginalized groups. I argued that one of the CVR's primary contributions was to raise public awareness of the marginalization of rural and indigenous populations and of state violence, and reinforce an interest in historical memory. By putting collective memory into the public eye and stimulating debate about responsibility and guilt, truth-seeking in Peru has extended beyond victims' groups and civil society, drawing in protagonists, notably the Peruvian military. While memory politics in Peru are indicative of deep-rooted societal divisions, they also represent a larger discursive shift regarding the claims that the past generates and who has a responsibility to address them. Although civil society in Peru also favored localism particularly in the emphasis on alternative community memorialization, Peruvian civil society's rights-based engagement was especially pronounced. Importantly, I outlined how advocacy organizations now largely direct their campaigns toward Lima, thereby working through and strengthening the democratic process.

Somewhat differently in Sierra Leone, the TRC reinforced a critical interest in local reconciliation and peace-building, which took on its own momentum over time. As I argued in Chapters 4 and 5, in the Sierra Leonean context, the emergence of Fambul Tok is part of a greater turn toward localism and decentralization of peace-building and reconciliation. While community-level restorative justice preceded the establishment of formal mechanisms, a politicized context and dissatisfaction with globalized justice also spurred its development. Activism surrounding the Sierra Leonean TRC became part of a larger politics of reintegration and reconciliation.

As I argued in the book, in both Peru and Sierra Leone, procedural reconciliation has been a double-edged process. On the one hand, the CVR, in particular, provided a forum that helped integrate civil society and victims' groups into politics. It also contributed to an important, albeit uneven, process of rationalization and acknowledgment that went beyond its immediate participants.

On the other hand, the analysis of procedural reconciliation highlights a complicated relationship between reconciliation and conflict. Although procedural reconciliation may lead to deeper reconciliation and alter perceptions, it may equally create further antagonism, fuel grievances, and harden identities. As I outlined in Chapters 5 and 7, unresolved grievances often drove individuals' political activism and public participation.

Empirically, the Peruvian and Sierra Leonean experiences also bring attention to the partial and often uneven nature of procedural reconciliation. Eric Wiebelhaus-Brahm suggests that truth commissions face a paradox: the more effective they are in generating attention, the more opposition they incur among subgroups, posing a risk to democracy.[5] The Peruvian and Sierra Leonean experiences also illustrate a different challenge. In divided societies with unresolved and acute conflict, truth-seeking measures generate particular debate and attention. Where the nature and causes of political violence are especially polarizing in Peru, the CVR had a strong impact on the public sphere. The Commission was at the center of a widespread and vigorous debate about the past, involving both numbers and facts about the conflict and legitimacy – who had the right to fight. Although this contestation offers a type of dialogue and engagement, the contours of the debate remain narrowly defined. Much of the military's discourse concerns the legitimacy of actors to carry out violence and whether civilian deaths were a necessary part in the conflict – whether the ends justify the means and whether civilian deaths were the result of systematic policies or "excesses." It is also a debate where groups do not recognize each other, reflected in the absence of the Shining Path from the public sphere and its routine categorization as a terrorist or criminal, rather than political, group. Indeed, where actors do engage in memory politics, this discussion is often less about disputing numbers and charges – although this is part of it – than about making a case for one's right to exist and demanding respect and recognition. The military's

[5] Eric Brahm, "Uncovering the Truth: Examining Truth Commissions Success and Impact," *International Studies Perspectives* 8 (2007), p. 28.

narrative pertains to the armed forces' self-understanding as moral agents and their service as performing an essential function in society. Debates over memory serve as part of a broader politics of recognition, delineating legitimacy and inclusion in present-day Peru.[6]

Both in Sierra Leone and Peru, procedural reconciliation has been precarious and has emerged in fits and starts. In each case, post-war democratization sometimes increased intergroup tensions.[7] In Sierra Leone, democracy deepened interethnic rifts as politicians mobilized on ethnic platforms during electoral campaigns. While the Peruvian state has banned MOVADEF from registering as a political party, in Sierra Leone the RUF party eventually merged with the APC in July 2007. Significantly, these parties have gained support among a disenchanted rural youth demographic reminiscent of both insurgencies' support bases.[8] In Peru, the 2012 electoral victory of President Ollanta Moisés Humala over Keiko Fujimori starkly resurfaced deeply entrenched historical grievances as politicians accused each other of being soft on terrorism and Humala's reference to Shining Path members in jail as "political prisoners" caused public controversy. Shortly after the election, tense and vocal debates over the CVR mounted again with the capture of the Shining Path's head of command.[9] Debates over the fate of the jailed Fujimori have arisen again in Peru's most recent election, by Pedro Pablo Kuczynski over Keiko Fujimori. These present-day politics evidence the fragile nature of procedural reconciliation, where some groups refuse to acknowledge each other and militants remain stigmatized. In both cases, the persistence of root causes is especially concerning. Where historical marginalization and economic disparities underpinned both conflicts, deep-rooted structural injustice has magnified the legacies of political violence, serving as a continued source of everyday suffering and victimization.

[6] See Charles Taylor, ed., *Multiculturalism and the Politics of Recognition* (Princeton: Princeton University Press, 1994).

[7] It is important to keep in mind that Peru was a democracy when the Shining Path emerged.

[8] Many of these people did not directly experience the conflict, but are from a similar demographic background to those who joined the movements during the conflicts. In Sierra Leone, the Revolutionary United Front Party won 2.2 percent of popular votes on May 14, 2002. Thereafter, it received its highest support in Kailahun, at 7.8 percent, in the parliamentary election.

[9] After at least one commissioner conceded a mistake made by the CVR – of not engaging military participants – Lerner responded publicly that engaging the actors of the conflict was never the point of the Commission. See Lerner's interview with *Caretas*. Lerner argues that critics of the CVR keep memory alive. *Caretas*, Entrevista by Enrique Chavez, "Lerner Febres Contraataca" (September 28, 2012).

Implications of Procedural Reconciliation: Revisiting Holistic Justice

Through its analysis of context and reconciliation, the book also raises significant conceptual tensions and issues for further consideration. Although theorists and practitioners have increasingly argued that transitional justice should contribute to long-term conflict transformation and peace-building,[10] I have maintained that in, practice, how transitional justice should transform conflict is far from clear. Research on the causes of conflict, on the one hand, and literature on transitional justice, on the other, tend to be atomized from each another. Scholarship on the drivers of conflict is also polarized, and does not easily lend itself into producing policy guidelines. Does a transformative and contextually relevant approach mean addressing one particular understanding of conflict at the micro or macro level, or a multipronged strategy that addresses various dimensions of conflict? Do various approaches to addressing conflict complement each other or are they at odds?

In the book, I highlighted what I perceive to be continuing questions and tensions regarding the relationship between transitional justice and conflict transformation. A first is between the process or social experience of transitional justice and its outcomes. Since its foundations, much of transitional justice theory and practice has focused on the social experiences of transitional justice. In other words, scholars have focused on transitional justice as an immediate and participatory process – which they seek to evaluate for its direct impact on social learning, for instance, or the recognition and dignification of victims.[11] Early critical accounts likewise often faulted formal processes on these terms. A critique of the South African TRC, notably, is that its focus on the direct perpetrators of apartheid ignored indirect beneficiaries.[12] This tendency has changed somewhat with the passage of time and the emergence of more community-based studies, which highlight local preferences. Where scholars and practitioners previously focused largely on process and popular participation, they have since put greater emphasis on outcome and longer-term structural change. Recent critiques of the South African TRC reflect this

[10] See Wendy Lambourne, "Transitional Justice and Peace-building after Mass Violence," *International Journal of Transitional Justice* 3, no. 1 (2009), pp. 275–284; Paul Gready and Simon Robins, "From Transitional to Transformative Justice: A New Agenda for Practice," *The International Journal for Transitional Justice* 8, no. 3 (2014), pp. 339–361.

[11] Martha Minow, *Between Vengeance and Forgiveness: Facing History after Genocide and Mass Violence* (Boston, MA: Beacon Press, 2000); Mark Osiel, *Mass Atrocity, Collective Memory, and the Law* (New Brunswick, NJ: Transaction, 1997).

[12] Mahmood Mamdani, "The Truth According to the Truth and Reconciliation Commission," in *The Politics of Memory, Truth, Healing and Social Justice*, ed. Ifi Amadiume and Abdullahi An-Naim (New York: Zed Books, 2000), p. 25.

orientation, drawing attention to the country's lack of progress in reparatory justice and the persistence of stark socio-economic disparities along racial lines.

These normative orientations are significant. As I detailed in Chapters 4 and 6, in the last few decades, truth commissions have also increasingly focused on the macro level. Both the Sierra Leonean TRC and the Peruvian CVR put emphasis on contextually specific structural and historical root causes. The CVR focused, in particular, on the macro root causes of violence, identifying the state's long-term marginalization of the Andean Sierra and those of indigenous descent as a key underlying cause of conflict. Unlike other participatory commissions, it engaged very little with ex-combatants' motivations and rationales. In Sierra Leone, the TRC offered a more inclusive platform, refusing to pass judgment on the legitimacy of the RUF and soliciting ex-combatants' participation. However, in this case, as well, the Sierra Leonean TRC distanced itself from the South African TRC, focusing on national reconciliation. It also made an effort to contribute to contextually defined root causes, notably, in this case, the marginalization of youth.

While transitional justice's greater focus on the structural causes of conflict is a welcome development, I am concerned that the current emphasis of formal mechanisms on macro transformation and societal reconciliation has also come with costs and raises new questions. A first is implementation and institutional overstretch. While, as I have discussed, social justice tends to be a key concern of survivors in protracted social conflicts, implementation of reparatory justice is often beyond the remit of transitional justice institutions, which have limited funding and clout. Although most truth commissions have tied themselves to some form of reparations, as others have noted, the implementation of reparations has tended to be poor.[13] This is also a problem for global and hybrid justice mechanisms, where global agents frequently leave after the official termination of operations. The continuation of deep-rooted structural injustices also raises important questions about global responsibility and accountability for conflict. The Sierra Leonean TRC, notably, has come under fire for editing out and underplaying the economic causes of the war and the responsibility of international financial institutions.[14]

[13] See the UN Secretary General, "The Rule of Law and Transitional Justice in Conflict and Post-Conflict Societies – Report of the Secretary General," UN Security Council (2011), p. 7; Priscilla B. Hayner, *Unspeakable Truths: Facing the Challenge of Truth Commissions* (New York, NY: Routledge, 2002), p. 8.

[14] Yasmin Sooka and Chris Mahony, "The Truth about the Truth: Insider Reflections on the Sierra Leonean Truth and Reconciliation Commission," in *Evaluating Transitional Justice: Accountability and Peace-building in Postconflict Sierra Leone*, ed. Kirsten Ainley,

Tensions within truth commissions, however, have also emerged more subtly in each case. In particular, I found that as truth commissions focused on outcome and incentives, participants later faulted them on their own terms. Tying into a larger literature in preferences,[15] Lisa Laplante and Kimberly Theidon take a somewhat Maslowian orientation – that class positions determine needs and priorities. In their words, testimony is a "contract": the sharing of intimate experiences brings with it a jurisdictional expectation of appropriate redress and obligation to act.[16] As I mentioned earlier, in my research, as well, disappointment over the slow implementation of reparations was the most common and bitter criticism of truth commissions among affected communities. Individuals who testified often felt especially betrayed and isolated as a result. The association between reconciliation and structural justice also emerged more diffusely, as indicated by the widespread sentiment in Ayacucho that "conciliation" should precede reconciliation – that reconciliation could only emerge through concrete government policy changes and improvements in everyday life.

Incentives are thus fundamental in shaping local experiences of transitional justice. In both Sierra Leone and Peru, individual incentives clearly catalyzed participation. In Sierra Leone, the TRC was tied to amnesty and securing the future status of the RUF. When comparing the TRC to Fambul Tok, communities frequently raised the concrete and ongoing benefits derived from community reconciliation. In Kailahun, grassroots reconciliation resonated through Fambul Tok, where it linked to collective labor and practices of reciprocity. Similarly, but in the converse, in Peru, the absence of individual benefit helps explain the lack of ex-combatant participation in the CVR. The military had more to lose than to gain from participation, especially where the CVR supported prosecutions. The same applies to Shining Path militants, who had strong motivations to lay low in a still stigmatized social context.

Nevertheless, it is important to caution against a wholly instrumental understanding of reconciliation. Transitional justice institutions in Sierra Leone and Peru mobilized on ideological and normative platforms in contexts of severe social disruption. In Sierra Leone, ex-combatants testified at the TRC despite the perceived risk of self-incrimination. For many, the opportunity to testify provided a chance to positively further their societal reintegration and contribute to society. Unsurprisingly, in

Rebekka Friedman, and Chris Mahony (London: Palgrave Macmillan, 2015), pp. 241–264.

15 See Rosalind Shaw and Lars Waldorf, *Localizing Transitional Justice: Interventions and Priorities after Mass Violence* (Stanford, CA: Stanford University Press, 2010).

16 Laplante and Theidon, "Truth with Consequences," p. 229.

both contexts, severe loss of momentum and frustrated expectations emerged as significant themes in local experiences of transitional justice. Criticisms of the TRC thus also reflect disillusionment with its insufficient realization of its own normative agenda. Where survivors regarded reparations, in particular, as symbolic forms of justice and acknowledgment, the lack of follow-up signaled continued indifference and vulnerability, and served as a missed opportunity to gain social and political capital. Sierra Leonean amputee and prominent victims rights campaigner Sunni Savinam described "broken trust" after "speaking his heart" at the TRC. In the same conversation, he brought up the SCSL's verdict against RUF commander Issa Sesay – at whose trial he also testified – repeating the date and time of day that the verdict was announced. While Savinam was not a proponent of the Court or of a criminal justice approach per se, the crucial difference, in his view, was that the SCSL followed up, while the TRC "did nothing."

Tying into a wider debate on transitional justice and economics, more work is needed on tensions between the aims and procedures of transitional justice. A lingering concern is that shifting focus on social and economic justice and development will undermine the contribution of transitional justice to accountability.[17] There is a danger that the focus on preferences and present-day suffering has shifted policy attention to "needs," rather than economic and social rights.[18] As affected communities frequently emphasized in Ayacucho, collective reparations can problematically subsume justice within general development. Collective reparations risk depoliticizing repair and undermining the symbolic effects of reparations.[19] Where some of the recent transitional justice

[17] Christine Bell, "Transitional Justice, Interdisciplinarity and the State of the 'Field' or 'NonField'," *International Journal of Transitional Justice* 3 (2009), p. 7. Lars Waldorf has been critical of linking transitional justice and economic development, arguing that transitional justice will lose its distinctiveness as a field and become analytically watered down. Lars Waldorf, "Anticipating the Past: Transitional Justice and Socio-Economic Wrongs," *Social and Legal Studies* 21, no. 2 (2012), p. 171.

[18] See Evelyne Schmid and Aoife Nolan, "'Do No Harm'? Exploring the Scope of Economic and Social Rights in Transitional Justice," *The International Journal of Transitional Justice* 8, no. 3 (2014), pp. 362–382. Phuong Pham, Patrick Vinck, Marieke Wierda, Eric Stover, and Adrian di Giovanni, *Forgotten Voices: A Population Based Survey of Attitudes about Peace and Justice in Northern Uganda* (New York: International Center for Transitional Justice and Human Rights Center, 2005).

[19] Zinaida Miller provides a useful discussion. She warns that "confining economics to reparations" might only narrowly redistribute wealth and focus society on reparations politics – on questions of who owes how much and to whom – rather than increase solidarity with the marginalized. Zinaida Miller, "Effects of Invisibility: In Search of the 'Economic' in Transitional Justice," *The International Journal of Transitional Justice* 2 (2008), p. 284. Yet she also stresses the importance of not outsourcing economic repair to development or reconstruction. "As a definitional project, transitional justice cannot

literature has moved closer to development in its emphasis on economic needs and structural justice, as the Peruvian case makes clear, for *afectados*, reparations are also important as a form of recognition and justice. The prioritization of individual over collective reparations reinforces the importance of acknowledgment as an end of transitional justice, as do the criticisms that individuals did not have access to the CVR's final report and did not hear from the CVR after testifying.

There is also a risk of sidelining the affective dimensions of transitional justice. In both Sierra Leone and Peru, truth commissions mobilized in contexts of prolonged marginalization and violence. Significantly, individuals testified before reparations were on the agenda. This, however, led to strong disappointment later on, as participants and affected communities stressed that they had testified in good faith to have a voice and contribute to a positive change for their communities. Many later reevaluated their participation in light of their present-day economic and social marginalization.

The risk that incentivizing reconciliation will undermine the social experiences of transitional justice also applies to the broader public. In Sierra Leone, the tying of ex-combatant testimony to reintegration often gave rise to criticisms, especially among victims, that ex-combatants were strategically motivated and disproportionately benefited from reconciliation. Formal mechanisms therefore should think carefully about their priorities and whether and how tying their work to wider ends beyond their control will undermine these. If it remains the case as many involved in the commissions alleged that the primary function of truth commissions is to provide a voice to the marginalized and a critical historical memory, then it may be prudent for punitive justice and reparations to run as wholly separate from truth-seeking processes.

Conclusions

Around the world, societies, communities, and individuals face the challenge of rebuilding homes, communities, and livelihoods in contexts of ongoing upheaval, often in proximity to perpetrators of atrocities. Transitional justice mechanisms have emerged as an increasingly formal and wide-ranging set of practices to address past atrocities, often with varying degrees of global support. In both Sierra Leone and Peru, I highlighted the frequent politicization of transitional justice and its vulnerability to the circumstances surrounding its establishment.

stand aside from the distributional consequences of its inclusion or exclusion of particular questions." Ibid., p. 291.

In settings of prolonged violence and long-term social, economic, and political marginalization, I detailed how damaged social and political capital became a prism through which individuals and communities experienced peace-building and reconciliation, polarizing justice and truth-seeking efforts.

Given the contexts in which transitional justice processes operate, the emergence of varying degrees of procedural reconciliation in both Sierra Leone and Peru is, in many ways, remarkable. Following long-term impunity, invisibility, and marginalization, procedural reconciliation represents an important normative and discursive development, which can lead to distinct cumulative effects over time. My study of procedural reconciliation in Sierra Leone and Peru is testament to individuals' and communities' willingness to engage with alternative pathways to deal with conflict notwithstanding deep-seated grievances and unaddressed injuries. At the same time, on its own, procedural reconciliation is not enough. If anything, procedural reconciliation serves as a barometer for lingering conflict. There is also a danger that procedural reconciliation can mask and legitimize the continuation of injustices by absorbing and transferring conflict into non-violent channels. Ultimately, procedural reconciliation can only be a first step. Lasting peace and reconciliation require parallel justice processes, economic opportunities and reparations, and the transformation of societal identifications and relationships. This requires significant dedication, goodwill, imagination, and investment into a just and equitable future.

Annex 1 Chronology of the Conflict in Sierra Leone

1787	Freetown is founded as a city for repatriated ex-slaves. British abolitionist Granville Sharpe establishes the Committee for the Relief of Black Poor. This brings formerly enslaved Afro Britons to Sierra Leone under "Province of Freedom," a predecessor of the Sierra Leone Company, as an initiative to repatriate slaves from the United States.
1896	Sierra Leone becomes a British colony.
1949	Sir Milton Augustus Strieby Margai founds the SLPP, and becomes the first prime minister of Sierra Leone. He is an important figure in setting out the country's post-colonial constitution and independence struggle.
April 27, 1961	Sierra Leone wins independence.
1964–1967	After the death of Sierra Leone's first prime minister, Sir Milton Margai, Milton's half-brother, Sir Albert Michael Margai, becomes the second prime minister of Sierra Leone.
1967	The APC comes into power under Siaka Stevens, who became president in 1971, and in 1978 made the APC the sole political party. Margai supports a series of coups and attempted coups. Elected brigadier John Bangura reinstates Stevens in a counter-coup after his temporary ousting under martial law., Stevens rules until 1984 and is known for corruption and use of politics for personal gain.
1985–1992	Stevens selects Major General Joseph Momoh as the sole candidate. He becomes president and largely continues the status quo.
March 23, 1991	Conflict breaks out in neighboring Liberia. The RUF with support of Charles Taylor's National Patriotic Front of Liberia intervenes in Sierra Leone to overthrow the Momoh government.
April 1992	The National Provisional Ruling Council wages a coup against the Momoh Regime. Twenty-five year-old Captain Valentine Strasser comes to power.
March 1995	The South Africa-based private military company Executive Outcomes enters Sierra Leone.

1996	The civilian government is reinstated and signs the Abidjan Peace Accord with the RUF.
March 1997	RUF leader Foday Sankoh is arrested in Nigeria.
May 1997	Corporal Tamba Gborie wages a military coup with a group of seventeen SLA soldiers, establishing the AFRC and sending Kabbah into exile. The RUF unites with the AFRC to capture Freetown. Johnny Paul Koroma becomes the new president and announces the war to be officially over. Samuel Hinga Norman leads the Kamajors and stays loyal to Kabbah.
October 1997	Following a period of looting and abuses in Freetown, Nigerian mission ECOMOG intervenes. ECOMOG gains control of the capital but fails to secure the remainder of the country. Under the Conakry Peace Plan, ECOMOG moderates a temporary agreement with the RUF.
January 1999	The RUF wages "Operation No Living Thing" on Freetown, killing approximately 7,000 people.
March 27, 1999	International intervention to bring about the Lomé Peace Accord gives the vice presidency and control of diamond fields to Sankoh in exchange for an RUF ceasefire and agreement that UNPK forces will monitor disarmament. President Kabbah resumes the presidency.
October 1999	UN peacekeepers intervene, leading to a hostage crisis as the RUF kidnaps approximately 500 forces.
2000	The RUF's failure to uphold Lomé and its subsequent advance on Freetown lead the British to intervene under Operation Palliser.
February 10, 2000	The Truth and Reconciliation Commission Act lays out the mandate of the TRC.
January 18, 2002	President Kabbah announces the end of the war.
November 2002	The TRC begins its investigation, handing over its findings to the Sierra Leonean government on October 5, 2004.
January 16, 2002	The UN and the government of Sierra Leone set up an agreement for the Special Court for Sierra Leone, after President Kabbah's letter to the UNSG Kofi Annan, asking the UN to prosecute those responsible.
July 2007	The RUF political party gains popular votes in the 2002 elections but no seats, receiving the highest support in Kailahun. It forms a coalition with the APC in July 2007.

Annex 2 Chronology of the Conflict in Peru

1948–1956	General Manuel A. Odría becomes president through military coup, under pressure from the oligarchy after a mutiny. He later takes a populist course in an administration marked by corruption and the suspension of civil rights.
1956	Odría calls for new elections, and Manuel Prado is elected.
1963	Fernando Belaúnde becomes president, embarking on a series of social reforms and development projects.
Late 1960s	Abimael Guzmán founds the Shining Path during his tenure at the UNSCH.
1968	General Juan Francisco Velasco Alvarado overthrows Belaúnde in a coup.
Early 1970s	The Shining Path establishes a presence in universities across the country, including in Lima.
1975	Francisco Morales Bermúdez Cerruti becomes the new president, holding the first elections in 1980.
April 1980	Following a period of depression, the military allows the restoration of constitutional rule, leading to the election of Belaúnde and the return of civil liberties.
May 17, 1980	The Shining Path burns ballot boxes in Chuschi, Ayacucho, on the evening of presidential elections. It also establishes *escuelas militares* (military schools) and begins its relocation to the provinces.
Early 1980s	Victor Polay Campos and Néstor Cerpa Cartolini found the MRTA, waging their first attack on May 31, 1982. Shining Path violence in rural areas increases, leading to a series of massacres, notably Lucanamarca in 1983.
1981	Fernando Belaúnde Terry announces a state of emergency and orders military intervention. He suspends constitutional rights in Ayacucho.
1983–1985	Extrajudicial disappearances, rape, disappearances, and torture are widespread, with the highest number of deaths occurring from 1983 to 1984.
1985–1990	Dr. Alan García Pérez of the APRA becomes president. The García administration is responsible for the highest number of disappearances under any incumbency during the conflict, and some of the worst counter-subversive activities, notably the El Frontón prison massacre in 1986.

1989	The military starts a more targeted counter-insurgency campaign, beginning to change the armed forces' relationship with the peasant population.
1990–2000	Independent candidate Alberto Fujimori wins the presidency, against novelist Mario Vargas Llosa. In 1991, Fujimori issues a law to give legal status to the *rondas*. The same year, the La Colina forces, a death squad operating under Fujimori and National Security Director Vladimiro Montesinos, carry out a number of massacres, notably Barrios Altos and the La Cantuta university massacre. The Inter-American Court later used the La Colina massacres as grounds to call for Fujimori's extradition from Japan.
April 5, 1992	Fujimori absolves the Congress of Peru and abolishes the constitution in an "*auto golpe*" (self-coup). He announces Peru's withdrawal from the Inter-American Court of Human Rights and places the judiciary under executive control. The administration establishes new antiterrorism legislation and the Repentance Law, giving reduced punishment to individuals accused of terrorism and treason, who name Shining Path or MRTA members.
1992	The Shining Path begins its "strategic equilibrium," moving to the cities, planting a bomb in the Miraflores district on Tarata street.
September 12, 1992	The police capture Abimael Guzmán in a safe house in Lima. Oscar Ramírez takes over the Shining Path.
December 1996	The MRTA takes over the Japanese embassy, occupying it for more than four months.
1999	The police capture Oscar Ramírez.
2000	Valentín Panuiga becomes interim president, working to restore democracy. He revokes Fujimori's withdrawal from the Inter-American Court and establishes the CVR.
June 2001	Alejandro Toledo is elected. The TRC begins operation, formally concluding its work on August 28, 2003.
August 2003	The Peruvian government submits a request for Fujimori's extradition from Japan.
October 13, 2006	Guzmán receives a life sentence in prison. Some Shining Path attacks continue.
December 2007	Fujimori is extradited to face criminal charges in Peru.
April 2009	Fujimori faces twenty-five years for kidnappings and killings committed under La Colina, marking the first extradition, trial, and conviction of a head of state back to his home country. Fujimori subsequently goes to trial for corruption together with Montesinos.

Bibliography

Abdullah, Ibrahim, ed. *Between Democracy and Terror: The Sierra Leone Civil War*. Dakar, Senegal: Codesria, 2004.

Abraham, Arthur, "War and Transition to Peace: A Study of State Conspiracy in Perpetuating Armed Conflict." In *Africa Development*. Dakar, Senegal: Codeseria, 1997, pp. 101–116.

Abrams, Jason S. and Priscilla B. Hayner. "Documenting, Acknowledging and Publicizing the Truth." In *Post-Conflict Justice*. Edited by M. C. Bassiouni. Ardsley, NY: Transnational Publishers, 2002.

Ainley, Kirsten. "Evaluating Success in Sierra Leone and Beyond." In *Evaluating Transitional Justice: Accountability and Peace-building in Postconflict Sierra Leone*. Edited by Kirsten Ainley, Rebekka Friedman, and Chris Mahony. Basingstoke, Hampshire, New York: Palgrave Macmillan, 2015, pp. 241–264.

Ainley, Kirsten A. "Responsibility for Atrocity: Individual Criminal Agency and the International Criminal Court." In *Evil, Law and the State: Perspectives on State Power and Violence*. Edited by John Parry. Amsterdam and New York: Rodopi, 2006, pp. 143–158.

Alie, Joe A. D. "Reconciliation and Traditional Justice: Tradition Based Practices of the Kpaa Mende in Sierra Leone." In *Traditional Justice and Reconciliation after Violent Conflict: Learning from African Experiences*. Edited by Luc Huyse and Mark Salter. Stockholm, Sweden: International Institute for Democracy and Electoral Assistance, 2008, pp. 123–146.

Allen, Tim. *Trial Justice: The International Criminal Court and the Lord's Resistance Army*. London: Zed Books, 2006.

Amnesty International. *Peru: The Cayara Massacre*. London: Amnesty International, September 1989.

Amnesty International. *Peru: The Truth and Reconciliation Commission a First Step Towards a Country without Injustice*. New York: Amnesty International, 2004.

Anderson, Benedict. *Imagined Communities: Reflections on the Origin and Spread of Nationalism*. London: Verso, 1977.

Arendt, Hannah. *Eichmann in Jerusalem: A Report on the Banality of Evil*. London: Faber & Faber, 1963.

Arendt, Hannah. *The Human Condition*. Chicago, IL: Chicago University Press, 1998.

Asmal, Kadar, Louise Asmal, and Ronald Suresh Roberts. *Reconciliation Through Truth: A Reckoning of Apartheid's Criminal Governance*. Cape Town: David Philip Publishers, 1997.

Auerbach, Yehudith. "The Role of Forgiveness in Reconciliation." In *From Conflict Resolution to Reconciliation*. Edited by Yaacov Bar-Siman-Tov. Oxford: Oxford University Press, 2004, pp. 149–176.

Aukerman, Miriam. "Extraordinary Evil, Ordinary Crimes: A Framework for Understanding Transitional Justice." *Harvard Human Rights Journal* 15 (2000), pp. 39–98.

Autessere, Séverine. "Hobbes and the Congo: Frames, Local Violence and International Intervention." *International Organization* 63, no. 2 (2009), pp. 249–280.

Autessere, Séverine. *Peaceland: Conflict Resolution and the Everyday Politics of International Intervention*. New York: Cambridge University Press, 2014.

Azar, Edward. *The Management of Protracted Social Conflict: Theory and Cases*. Dartmouth: Aldershot, 1990.

Bar-Tal, Daniel and Gemma H. Bennink. "The Nature of Reconciliation as an Outcome and as a Process." In *From Conflict Resolution to Reconciliation*. Edited by Yaacov Bar-Siman-Tov. Oxford: Oxford University Press, 2004, pp. 11–38.

Barahona de Brito, Alexandra, Carmen G. Enriquez, and Paloma Aguilar. *The Politics of Memory: Transitional Justice in Democratizing Societies*. New York: Oxford University Press, 2001.

Bassiouni, M. Cherif. "From Versailles to Rwanda in Seventy-Five Years: The Need to Establish a Permanent International Criminal Court." *Harvard Human Rights Journal* 10, no. 11 (1997), pp. 11–62.

Bassiouni, M. Cherif. "Searching for Peace and Achieving Justice: The Need for Accountability." *Law and Contemporary Problems* 59, no. 4 (1996), pp. 9–28.

Bell, Christine. "Transitional Justice, Interdisciplinarity and the State of the 'Field' or 'Non-Field.'" *International Journal of Transitional Justice* 3 (2009), pp. 5–27.

Bell, Duncan. "Memory, Trauma and World Politics." In *Memory, Trauma and World Politics: Reflections on the Relationship between Past and Present*. London: Palgrave Macmillan UK, 2006, pp. 1–29.

Berdal, Mats and David M. Malone, eds. *Greed and Grievance: Economic Agendas in Civil Wars*. Boulder, CO: Lynne Rienner, 2000.

Bergner, Daniel. *Soldiers of Light*. London: Penguin, 2005.

Boesten, Jelke. "Analyzing Rape Regimes at the Interface of War and Peace in Peru," *International Journal of Transitional Justice* 4 (2010), pp. 110–129.

Bloomfield, David. *On Good Terms*. Berghof Report 14. Berlin: Berghof Research Center for Constructive Conflict Management, October 2006.

Boraine, Alex. *A Country Unmasked: Inside South Africa's Truth and Reconciliation Commission*. Oxford: Oxford University Press, 2000.

Boraine, Alex. "Truth and Reconciliation in South Africa: The Third Way." In *Truth v. Justice: The Morality of Truth Commissions*. Edited by Robert I. Rotberg and Dennis Thompson. Princeton: Princeton University Press, 2000, pp. 141–157.

Boraine, Alexander. "Transitional Justice: A Holistic Interpretation." *Journal of International Affairs* 60, no. 1 (2006), pp. 17–27.

Borer, Tristan Anne. "A Taxonomy of Victims and Perpetrators: Human Rights and Reconciliation in South Africa." *Human Rights Quarterly* 25, no. 4 (2003), pp. 1088–1116.

Brahm, Eric. "Uncovering the Truth: Examining Truth Commissions Success and Impact." *International Studies Perspectives* 8, no. 1 (2007), pp. 16–35.

Braithwaite, John. *Crime, Shame, and Reintegration*. Cambridge: Cambridge University Press, 1989.

Braithwaite, John. "Restorative Justice: Assessing Optimistic and Pessimistic Accounts." *Crime and Justice* 25 (1999), pp. 1–127.

Braithwaite, John and Heather Strang, eds. *Restorative Justice and Civil Society*. Cambridge: Cambridge University Press, 2001.

Brooks, Roy Lavon. *When Sorry Isn't Enough: The Controversy over Apologies and Reparation for Human Injustice*. New York: New York University Press, 1999.

Burt, Jo-Marie. *Violencia y Autoritarismo en El Perú: Bajo La Sombra de Sendero y la Dictadura de Fujimori*. Lima, Peru: Institute of Peruvian Studies, 2009.

Call, Charles. "Is Transitional Justice Really Just?" *Brown Journal of World Affairs* XI, no. 1 (2004), pp. 101–113.

Chapman, Audrey R. and Patrick Ball. "Levels of Truth: Macro-Truth and the TRC." In *Truth and Reconciliation in South Africa: Did the TRC Deliver?* Edited by Audrey R. Chapman and Hugo Van Der Merwe. Philadelphia, PA: University of Pennsylvania Press, 2008, pp. 143–168.

Chapman, Audrey R. and Patrick Ball. "The Truth of Truth Commissions: Comparative Lessons from Haiti, South Africa, and Guatemala." *Human Rights Quarterly* 23, no. 1 (2001), pp. 1–43.

Chávez, Pereyra, Nelson Rojas, and Antonio Rolando Zapata Velasco. *Historia y Cultura de Ayacucho*. Edited by Antonia Zapata Velasco, Nelson Pereyra, and Rolando Rojas. Lima, Peru: Institute of Peruvian Studies, UNICEF, and DED Servicio Aleman de Cooperacion Social-Tecnica Programa Servicio Civil Para La Paz, 2008.

Chayes, Antonia and Martha Minow, eds. *Imagine Coexistence: Restoring Humanity after Violent Ethnic Conflict*. Cambridge, MA: Jossey-Bass, 2003.

The Chilean National Commission on Truth and Reconciliation Report. Available at: www.usip.org/files/resources/collections/truth_commissions/Chile90-Report/Chile90-Report.pdf.

Clark, Phil. *The Gacaca Courts and Post-Genocide Justice and Reconciliation in Rwanda: Justice without Lawyers*. Cambridge: Cambridge University Press, 2010.

Clark, Phil. "Hybridity, Holism and 'Traditional' Justice: The Case of the Gacaca Community Courts in Post-Genocide Rwanda." *George Washington International Law Review* 39, no. 4 (2007), pp. 765–838.

Cobián, Rolando Ames and Reátegui Félix. "Toward Systemic Social Transformation: Truth Commissions and Development." In *Transitional Justice and Development: Making Connections*. Edited by Pablo de Greiff and Roger Duthie. New York: Social Science Research Council, 2009, pp. 142–169.

Collier, Paul. *Economic Causes of Civil Conflict and their Implications for Policy*. Washington, DC: World Bank, 2000.

Collier, Paul and Anke Hoeffler. "Greed and Grievance in Civil War." *World Bank Working Paper* (1999), pp. 563–595. Available at: www.worldbank.org/research/conflict/papers/civilconflict.html.

Collier, Paul and Anke Hoeffler. "On Economic Causes of Civil War." *Oxford Economic Papers* 50, no. 4 (1998), pp. 563–573.

Collins, Cath. "Human Rights Trials in Chile: During and after the 'Pinochet Years.'" *The International Journal of Transitional Justice* 4, no. 1 (2009), pp. 67–86.

Comisión Permanente de Historia del Ejército del Perú. *En Honor a la Verdad.* Lima, Peru, 2010.

Conteh-Morgan, Earl and Mac Dixon-Fyle. *Sierra Leone at the End of the Twentieth Century: History, Politics, and Society.* New York: Peter Lang, 1999.

Cordero, Isabel Coral. "Women in War: Impact and Responses." In *Shining and Other Paths: War and Society in Peru, 1980–1995.* Edited by Steve J. Stern. Durham and London: Duke University Press, 1998, pp. 345–374.

Coulter, Chris. *Bush Wives and Girl Soldiers: Women's Lives through War and Peace in Sierra Leone.* Ithaca, NY: Cornell University Press, 2009.

Crocker, David A. "Reckoning with Past Wrongs: A Normative Framework" (June 2004), pp. 43–64. Available at: http://terpconnect.umd.edu/~dcrocker/Courses/Docs/Reckoning%20with%20past%20wrongs.pdf. Updated from David A. Crocker, *Ethics & International Affairs* 13 (1999).

Cueva, Eduardo Gonzales. "The Peruvian Truth and Reconciliation Commission and the Challenge of Impunity." In *Transitional Justice in the Twenty-first Century.* Edited by Naomi Roht-Arriaza. Cambridge: Cambridge University Press, 2006, pp. 70–93.

The CVR Hearing Videos, covering geographical areas of hearings, and thematic case studies, obtained through IDEHPUCP.

The CVR Report. Available at: www.cverdad.org.pe/ingles/pagina01.php.

CVR Working Group Minutes. Grupo de Filosofos. "Glosario de Terminos Para La Comisión de la Verdad" (July 12, 2003).

CVR Working Group Minutes. Grupo de Filosofos. "Glosario Operativo: Definiciones Epistemologico-Eticas CVR" (June 2, 2003).

Dancy, Geoff, Hunjoon Kim, and Eric Wiebelhaus-Brahm. "The Turn to Truth: Trends in Truth Commission Experimentation." *Journal of Human Rights* 9 (2010), pp. 45–64.

Datzberger, Simone. "Peace-building and the Depoliticization of Civil Society." *Third World Quarterly* 36, no. 8 (2015), pp. 1592–1609.

Daye, Russell. *Political Forgiveness: Lessons from South Africa.* New York: Orbis Books, 2004.

De Brito, Alexandra Barahona, Carmen Gonzalez Enriquez, and Paloma Aguilar, eds. *The Politics of Memory: Transitional Justice in Democratizing Societies.* Oxford: Oxford University Press, 2001.

De Grieff, Pablo. "Articulating the Links between Transitional Justice and Development: Justice and Social Integration." In *Transitional Justice and Development: Making Connections.* Edited by Pablo de Greiff and Roger Duthie. New York: Social Science Research Council, 2009, pp. 28–75.

De Grieff, Pablo. "Theorizing Transitional Justice." In *Transitional Justice*, Nomos, Volume L. Edited by Melissa Williams, Rosemary Nagy, and Jon Elster. New York: New York University Press, 2012, pp. 31–77.

De la Cadena, Marisol. "From Race to Class: Insurgent Intellectuals *de provoncia* in Peru, 1910–1970." In *Shining and Other Paths: War and Society in Peru, 1980–1995*. Edited by Steve J. Stern. Durham and London: Duke University Press, 1998, pp. 22–59.

De Mel, Neloufer. "The Promise of the LLRC: Women's Testimony and Justice in Post-war Sri Lanka," The International Center for Ethnic Studies Research Paper, 4. Colombo, Sri Lanka: Karunatatne & Sons (Pvt) Ltd, February 2013.

Degregori, Carlos Iván. "Harvesting Storms: Peasant *Rondas* and the Defeat of Sendero Luminoso in Ayacucho." In *Shining and Other Paths: War and Society in Peru, 1980–1995*. Edited by Steve J. Stern. Durham and London: Duke University Press, 1998, pp. 128–157.

Degregori, Carlos Iván. *Qué Difícil es Ser Dios: El Partido Comunista del Perú – Sendero Luminoso y el Conflicto Armado Interno en el Perú: 1980–1999*. Lima: Institute of Peruvian Studies, 2010.

Degregori, Carlos I., Javier Ciurlizza, and José Coronel. *Construyendo Justicia: Verdad, Reconciliación y Procesamiento de Violaciones de Derechos Humanos*. Lima, Peru: PUCP, 2003.

Del Puno, Panciano. "Family, Culture, and 'Revolution': Everyday Life with Sendero Luminoso." In *Shining and Other Paths: War and Society in Peru, 1980–1995*. Edited by Steve J. Stern. Durham and London: Duke University Press, 1998, pp. 158–192.

Denov, Myriam. *Child Soldiers: Sierra Leone's Revolutionary United Front*. Cambridge: Cambridge University Press, 2010.

Dewey, John. *Democracy and Education: An Introduction to the Philosophy of Education*. New York: Macmillan, 1916.

Dewey, John. *Experience and Education*. New York: Macmillan Company, 1938.

Digeser, Paul E. *Political Forgiveness*. Ithaca, NY: Cornell University Press, 2001.

Dougherty, Beth. "Searching for Answers: Sierra Leone's Truth and Reconciliation Commission." *African Studies Quarterly* 8, no. 1 (2004), pp. 39–56.

Du Toit, André. "The Moral Foundations of the South African TRC: Truth as Acknowledgement and Justice as Recognition." In *Truth v. Justice: The Morality of Truth Commissions*. Edited by Robert I. Rotberg and Dennis Thompson. Princeton, NJ: Princeton University Press, 2000, pp. 122–140.

Dwyer, Susan. "Reconciliation for Realists." *Ethics and International Affairs* 13, no. 1 (1999), pp. 81–98.

Dzur, Albert. "Restorative Justice and Civic Accountability for Punishment." *Polity* 36, no. 1 (2003), pp. 3–22.

Elshtain, Jean Bethke. "Politics and Forgiveness." In *Burying the Past: Making Peace and Doing Justice after Civil War*. Edited by Nigal Biggar. Washington, DC: Georgetown University Press, 2001, pp. 45–64.

Elster, Jon. *Closing the Books: Transitional Justice in Historical Perspective*. Cambridge: Cambridge University Press, 2004.

Fanthorpe, Richard. "On the Limits of Liberal Peace: Chiefs and Democratic Decentralization in Post-War Sierra Leone." *African Affairs* 105, no. 418 (2005), pp. 27–49.

Farah, Douglas. *Blood from Stones: The Secret Financial Network of Terror*. New York: Broadway Books, 2004.

Farah, Douglas. "They Fought for Nothing, and That's What They Got." *Washington Post* (September 1, 2001).

Febres, Salomón Lerner. *La Rebelión de la Memoria: Seleccion de Discursos, 2001–2003*. Lima, Peru: CEP, IDEH-PUCP, Coordinadora Nacional de Derechos Humanos, 2004.

Febres, Salomón Lerner. "Por Qué Incomoda la Memoria?" *La Republica* (September 16, 2012).

Feldman, Joseph P. "Exhibiting Conflict: History and Politics at the Museo de la Memoria de ANFASEP in Ayacucho, Peru." *Anthropological Quarterly* 85, no. 2 (2012), pp. 487–518.

Fletcher, Laurel E. and Harvey M. Weinstein. "Violence and Social Repair: Rethinking the Contribution of Justice to Reconciliation." *Human Rights Quarterly* 24, no. 3 (2002), pp. 573–639.

Fletcher, Laurel E., Harvey M. Weinstein, and Jamie Rowen. "Context, Timing and the Dynamics of Transitional Justice: A Historical Perspective." *Human Rights Quarterly* 31, no. 1 (2009), pp. 163–220.

Forgues, Rolando. *Perú: Entre el Desafío de la Violencia y el Sueño de lo Posible*. Lima, Peru: Liberia Editorial Minerva, 1993.

Freeman, Mark. *Truth Commissions and Procedural Fairness*. Cambridge: Cambridge University Press, 2006.

Freeman, Mark and Priscilla Hayner. "Truth-Telling." In *Reconciliation after Violent Conflict: A Handbook*. Edited by David Bloomfield. Stockholm: International Institute for Democracy and Electoral Assistance, 2003, pp. 122–144.

Friedman, Rebekka. "Culturally-Mediated Grieving: Women's Experiences in Northern Sri Lanka." In *Bridging Theory and Practice: Gender and Transitional Justice*. Edited by Roslyn Warren and Mayesha Alam. Washington, DC: Georgetown Institute for Women, Peace and Security Occasional Paper Series (Spring 2016), pp. 20–34.

Friedman, Rebekka. "Implementing Transformative Justice: Survivors and Ex-Combatants at the Comisión de la Verdad y Reconciliación in Peru," Ethnic ad Racial Studies" (2017)."

Friedman, Rebekka. "Restorative Justice: Promises and Limitations." In *Evaluating Transitional Justice: Accountability and Peace-building in Post-Conflict Sierra Leone*. Edited by Kirsten Ainley, Rebekka Friedman, and Christopher Mahony. Basingstoke, UK: Palgrave Macmillan, 2015, pp. 55–76.

Friedman, Rebekka and Andrew Jillions. "The Pitfalls and Politics of Holistic Justice." *Global Policy* 6, no. 2 (2015), pp. 141–150.

Fujii, Lee Ann. "Shades of Truth and Lies: Interpreting Testimonies of War and Violence." *Journal of Peace Research* 47, no. 2 (2010), pp. 231–241.

Fullard, Madeleine and Nicky Rousseau. "Truth-Telling, Identities and Power in South Africa and Guatemala." Research Brief, International Center for Transitional Justice (June 2009), pp. 54–86.

Gambetta, Diego. "Can We Trust Trust?" In *Trust: Making and Breaking Cooperative Relations*. Edited by Diego Gambetta. Oxford: Oxford University Press, 2000, pp. 213–237.

García, Maria Elena. *Making Indigenous Citizens: Identity, Development and Multicultural Activism in Peru*. Stanford: Stanford University Press, 2005.

Gberie, Lansana. *A Dirty War in West Africa*. Bloomington, IN: Indiana University Press, 2005.

Geddes, Barbara. "How the Evidence You Use Affects the Answers You Get: Rigorous Use of the Evidence Contained in Case Studies." In *Paradigms and Sand Castles: Theory Building and Research Design in Comparative Politics*. Ann Arbor, MI: University of Michigan, 2003, pp. 131–173.

George, Alexander L. and Andrew Bennett. *Case Selection and Theory Development in the Social Sciences*. Cambridge, MA: Belfer Center for Science and International Affairs, 2005.

Gibson, James L. *Overcoming Apartheid: Can Truth Heal a Divided Nation*. New York: Russell Sage Foundation, 2004.

Goldstone, Richard J. "Justice as a Tool for PeaceMaking: Truth Commissions and International Criminal Tribunals." *NYU Journal of International Law and Politics* 28 (1996).

Goodwin, Jeff and Theda Skocpol. "Explaining Revolutions in the Contemporary Third World." *Politics and Society* 17, no. 4 (1989), pp. 489–509.

Gorriti, Gustavo. *The Shining Path: A History of the Millenarian War in Peru*. Chapel Hill: University of North Carolina Press, 1999.

Grandin, Greg. "The Instruction of Great Catastrophe: Truth Commissions, National History, and State Formation in Argentina, Chile and Guatemala." *American Historical Review* 110, no. 1 (2005), pp. 46–67.

Gready, Paul. *The Era of Transitional Justice: The Aftermath of the Truth and Reconciliation Commission in South Africa and Beyond*. New York: Routledge, 2011.

Gready, Paul and Simon Robins. "From Transitional Justice to Transformative Justice: A New Agenda in Practice." *The International Journal for Transitional Justice* 8, no. 3 (2014), pp. 339–61.

The Guatemalan CEH Report. Available at: http://shr.aaas.org/guatemala/ceh/report/english/conc3.html.

Gurr, Ted Robert. *Why Men Rebel*. Princeton, NJ: Princeton University Press, 1970.

Gutmann, Amy and Dennis Thompson. "The Moral Foundations of Truth Commissions." In *Truth v. Justice: the Morality of Truth Commissions*. Edited by Robert I. Rotberg and Dennis Thompson. Princeton, NJ: Princeton University Press, 2000, pp. 22–44.

Guttman, Amy and Dennis Thompson. *Why Deliberative Democracy?* Princeton, NJ: Princeton University Press, 2004.

Halpern, Jodi and Harvey M. Weinstein. "Rehumanizing the Other: Empathy and Reconciliation." *Human Rights Quarterly* 26, no. 3 (2004), pp. 561–583.

Hamber, Brandon and Grainne Kelly. "A Working Definition of Reconciliation." "What is Reconciliation?" In *Reconciliation(s): Transitional Justice in Post Conflict Societies*. Edited by Joanna Quinn. Montreal and Kingston: McGill-Queen's University Press, 2009.

Hamber, Brandon and Gunnar Theissen. "A State of Denial: White South Africa's Attitudes to the Truth and Reconciliation Commission." *Indicator South Africa* 15 (1998), pp. 8–12.

Hamber, Brendon and Hugo Van der Merwe. "What Is this Thing Called Reconciliation?" *Reconciliation in Review* 1, no. 1 (1998), pp. 12–23.

Harris, David. *Hatun Willakuy*, abbreviated version of the CVR. Lima, Peru: Comisión de Entrega de la Comisión de la Verdad y Reconciliación, February 2004.

Harris, David. *Sierra Leone: A Political History*. Oxford: Oxford University Press, 2013.

Hayner, Priscilla B. "Fifteen Truth Commissions-1974–1994: A Comparative Study." *Human Rights Quarterly* 16, no. 4 (1994), pp. 597–655.

Hayner, Priscilla B. "Past Truths, Present Dangers: The Role of Official Truth Seeking in Conflict Resolution and Prevention." In *International Conflict Resolution after the Cold War*. Edited by Paul C. Stern and Daniel Druckman. Washington, DC: National Academy Press, 2000, pp. 338–382.

Hayner, Priscilla B. "The Sierra Leone Truth and Reconciliation Commission: Reviewing the First Year." *The International Center for Transitional Justice* (2004).

Hayner, Priscilla B. "Truth Commissions." *NACLA Report on the Americas* 32, no. 2 (1998).

Hayner, Priscilla B. *Unspeakable Truths: Facing the Challenge of Truth Commissions*. New York: Routledge, 2002.

Hinojosa, Iván. "On Poor Relations and the Nouveau Riche: Shining Path and the Radical Peruvian Left." In *Shining and Other Paths: War and Society in Peru, 1980–1995*. Edited by Steve J. Stern. Durham and London: Duke University Press, 1998, pp. 60–83.

Hirschman, Albert. "Against Parsimony: Three Easy Ways of Complicating Some Categories of Economic Discourse." *American Economic Review* 1, no. 1 (1984), pp. 11–28.

Hite, Katherine and Cath Collins. "Memorial Fragments, Monument Silences and Re-awakenings in 21st-Century Chile." *Millennium: Journal of International Studies, Violence and Memory Forum* 38, no. 2 (2009), pp. 379–400.

Hoddie, Matthew and Caroline Hartzell. "Signals of Reconciliation: Institution-building and the Resolution of Civil Wars." *International Studies Review* 7 (2005), pp. 21–40.

Humphreys, Macartan and Jeremy M. Weinstein. "Who Fights? The Determinants of Participation in Civil War." *American Journal of Political Science* 52, no. 2 (2006), pp. 436–455.

Huntington, Samuel. *The Third Wave: Democratization in the Late Twentieth Century*. Norman: University of Oklahoma Press, 1991.

Ignatieff, Michael. "Articles of Faith." *Index on Censorship* 25, no. 110 (1996), pp. 110–122.

The Institute for Justice and Reconciliation. "The South African Reconciliation Barometer Dialogue Report" (2010). Available at: www.ijr.org.za/publications/recbar2011.php.

The International Center for Transitional Justice. "What is Transitional Justice?" (2008). Available at: http://ictj.org/sites/default/files/ICtransitionaljustice-Global-Transitional-Justice-2009-English.pdf.

Irving, Helen, Jacqueline Mowbray, and Kevin Walton, eds. *Julius Stone: A Study in Influence*. Sydney: Federation Press, 2010.

James-Allen, Paul, SheKu B. S. Lahai, and Jamie O'Connell. "Sierra Leone's Truth and Reconciliation Commission and Special Court: A Citizen's Handbook." In *National Forum for Human Rights and the International Center for Transitional Justice*. New York, 2003.

Jaspers, Karl. *The Question of German Guilt*. New York: Dial Press, 1948.

Jelin, Elizabeth. "Public Memorialization in Perspective: Truth, Justice and Memory of Past Repression in the Southern Cone of South America." *The International Journal of Transitional Justice* 1, no. 1 (2007), pp. 138–156.

Jelin, Elizabeth. *State Repression and the Labors of Memory*. Minneapolis, MN: University of Minnesota Press, 2003.

Kaldor, Mary. *New and Old Wars: Organized Violence in a Global Era*. Cambridge: Polity Press, 1999.

Kaplan, Robert D. "The Coming Anarchy." *The Atlantic Monthly* (1994).

Karl, Terry Lynn and Philippe Schmitter. "Modes of Transition in Latin America: Southern Europe and Eastern Europe." *International Social Sciences Journal* 128 (1991), pp. 269–284.

Kay, Bruce H. "Violent Opportunities: The Rise and Fall of 'King Coca' and Shining Path." *Journal of Interamerican Studies and World Affairs* 41, no. 3 (1999), pp. 97–127.

Kaye, Mike. "The Role of Truth Commissions in the Search for Justice, Reconciliation and Democratisation: The Salvadorian and Honduran Cases." *Journal of Latin American Studies* 29, no. 3 (1997), pp. 693–716.

Keen, David. *Conflict and Collusion in Sierra Leone*. Oxford: James Currey Ltd, 2005.

Kelsall, Tim. *Culture Under Cross Examination: International Justice and the Special Court for Sierra Leone*. Cambridge: Cambridge University Press, 2009.

Kelsall, Timothy. "Truth, Lies, Ritual: Preliminary Reflections on the TRC in Sierra Leone." *Human Rights Quarterly* 27, no. 2 (2005), pp. 361–91.

Kerr, Rachel and Erin Mobekk. *Peace and Justice: Seeking Accountability after War*. Cambridge: Polity Press, 2007.

Kim, Hun J. *Expansion of Transitional Justice Measures: A Comparative Analysis of Its Causes*. Minneapolis, MN: University of Minnesota, 2008.

Kim, Hunjoon and Kathryn Sikkink, "Explaining the Deterrent Effect of Human Rights Prosecutions for Transitional Countries," *International Studies Quarterly* 54, no. 4 (2010), pp. 939–963.

Kirk, Robin. *The Monkey's Paw: New Chronicles from Peru*. Amherst, MA: University of Massachusetts Press, 1997.

Kiss, Elizabeth. "Moral Ambition with and Beyond Political Constraints." In *Truth v. Justice: The Morality of Truth Commissions*. Edited by Robert I. Rotberg and Dennis Thompson. Princeton, NJ: Princeton University Press, 2000, pp. 68–98.

Kriesberg, Louis. "Changing Forms of Coexistence." In *Reconciliation, Justice and Coexistence: Theory and Practice*. Edited by Mohammed Abu-Nimer. Lanham, MD: Lexington Books, 2001, pp. 47–64.

Kriesberg, Louis. "Coexistence and the Reconciliation of Communal Conflicts." In *The Handbook of Interethnic Coexistence*. Edited by Eugene Weiner. New York: Continuum, 2000, pp. 47–64.

Kriesberg, Louis. "Reconciliation: Aspects, Growth, Sequences." *International Journal of Peace Studies* 12, no. 1 (2007), p 1.

Kriesberg, Louis and Bruce W. Dayton. *Constructive Conflicts: From Escalation to Resolution*. Lanham, MD: Rowman and Littlefield Publishers, 2011.

Kritz, Neil J. *Transitional Justice: How Emerging Democracies Deal with Former Regimes*. Washington, DC: United States Institute of Peace, 1995.

Krog, Antjie. *Country of My Skull*. London: Vintage Books, 1999.

Lambourne, Wendy. "Transitional Justice and Peace-building after Mass Violence." *International Journal of Transitional Justice* 3, no. 1 (March 2009), pp. 28–48.

Laplante, Lisa J. and Kimberly Susan Theidon. "Truth with Consequences: Justice and Reparations in Post-Truth Commission Peru." *Human Rights Quarterly* 29, no. 1 (2007), pp. 228–250.

Lederach, John Paul. *Building Peace: Sustainable Reconciliation in Divided Societies*. Washington, DC: US Institute of Peace, 1997.

Lederach, John Paul. "Civil Society and Reconciliation." In *Turbulent Peace: The Challenges of Managing International Conflict*. Edited by Chester A. Crocker, Fen Osler Hampson, and Pamela Aall. Washington, DC: US Institute for Peace, 2001, pp. 841–854.

Lederach, John Paul. *The Moral Imagination: The Art and Soul of Building Peace*. Oxford: Oxford University Press, 2005.

Leebaw, Bronwyn. *Judging State Sponsored Violence: Imagining Political Change*. Cambridge: Cambridge University Press, 2011.

Leebaw, Bronwyn. "Legitimation or Judgment? South Africa's Restorative Approach to Transitional Justice." *Polity* 36, no. 1 (2003), pp. 23–51.

Lessa, Francesca. *Memory and Transitional Justice in Argentina and Uruguay: Against Impunity*. New York: Palgrave, 2013.

Linz, Juan and Alfred Stefan. *Problems of Democratic Transition and Consolidation*. Baltimore, MD: Johns Hopkins Press, 1996.

Little, Adrian. "Disjunctured Narratives: Rethinking Reconciliation and Conflict Transformation." *International Political Science Review* 33, no. 1 (2012), pp. 82–98.

The Lomé Peace Accord. Available at: www.sierra-leone.org/lomeaccord.html.

Mac Ginty, Roger. "Gilding the Lily? International Support for Indigenous and Traditional Peacebuilding." In *Palgrave Advances in Peace-building*. Edited by Oliver Richmond. Basingstoke, UK: Palgrave, 2010, pp. 347–366.

Mac Ginty, Roger. "Hybrid Peace: The Interaction between Top-down and Bottom-up Peace." *Security Dialogue* 4, no. 41 (2010), pp. 391–412.

Maconachie, Roy and Tony Binns. "Beyond the Resource Curse? Diamond Mining, Development, and Post-Conflict Reconstruction in Sierra Leone." *Resource Policy* 32 (2007), pp. 104–115.

Mahoney, James and Terrie P. Larkin. "Comparative-historical Analysis in Contemporary Political Science." In *The Oxford Handbook of Political Methodology*. Edited by Janet M. Box-Steffensmeier, Henry E. Brady, and David Collier. Oxford: Oxford University Press, 2008.

Mahony, Chris. "A Political Tool? The Politics of Case Selection at the Special Court for Sierra Leone." In *Evaluating Transitional Justice: Accountability and*

Peacebuilding in Post-Conflict Sierra Leone. Edited by Kirsten Ainley, Rebekka Friedman, and Chris Mahony. London: Palgrave, 2015, pp. 77–100.

Maier, Charles S. "Overcoming the Past? Narrative and Negotiation, Remembering and Reparation: Issues at the Interface of History and the Law." In *Politics and the Past: On Repairing Historical Injustices*. Edited by John Torpey. Lanham, MD: Rowman & Littlefield Publishers, 2003, pp. 295–304.

Mainwaring, Scott. "Transitions to Democracy and Democratic Consolidation: Theoretical and Comparative Issues." In *Issues in Democratic Consolidation: The New South American Democracies in Comparative Perspective*. Edited by Scott Mainwaring, Guilermo O'Donnell, and Samuel Valenzuela. Notre Dame, IN: University of Notre Dame Press, 1992, pp. 317–26.

Mallon, Florencia E. "Chronicle of a Path Foretold? Velasco's Revolution, Vanguardia Revolucionaria, and 'Shining Omens' in the Indigenous Communities of Andahuaylas." In *Shining and Other Paths: War and Society in Peru, 1980–1995*. Edited by Steve J. Stern. Durham and London: Duke University Press, 1998, pp. 84–127.

Mamdani, Mahmood. "The Truth According to the Truth and Reconciliation Commission." In *The Politics of Memory, Truth, Healing and Social Justice*. Edited by Ifi Amadiume and Abdullahi An-Naim. New York: Zed Books, 2000, pp. 176–183.

Mani, Rama. *Beyond Retribution: Seeking Justice in the Shadows of War*. Cambridge and Maldon, MA: Polity Press, 2007.

Manrique, Nelson. "The War for the Central Sierra." In *Shining and Other Paths: War and Society in Peru, 1980–1995*. Edited by Steve J. Stern. Durham and London: Duke University Press, 1998, pp. 193–223.

Marks, Tom. "Making Revolution with Shining Path." In *The Shining Path of Peru*. Edited by David Scott Palmer. London: C. Hurst & Co. Ltd., 1992, pp. 209–223.

Marks, Zoe. *The Internal Dynamics of Rebel Groups in War: The Politics of Material Visibility and the Organizational Capacity in the Revolutionary United Front*. PhD Thesis, Oxford University, 2014.

McClintock, Cynthia. "Theories of Revolution and the Case of Peru." In *Shining Path of Peru*. Edited by David Scott Palmer. London: C. Hurst & Co. Ltd., 1992, pp. 243–258.

Mendeloff, David. "Truth-seeking, Truth-telling and Postconflict Peace-building: Curb the Enthusiasm." *International Studies Review* 6 (2004), pp. 355–380.

Mendez, Juan E. "Accountability for Past Abuses." *Human Rights Quarterly* 19, no. 2 (1997), pp. 255–282.

Mendez, Juan E. and Javier Mariezcurrena. "Unspeakable Truths: Facing the Challenge of Truth Commissions." *Human Rights Quarterly* 24 (2003), pp. 237–256.

Millar, Gearoid. " 'Ah Lef Ma Case Fo God': Faith and Agency in Sierra Leone's Post-war Reconciliation." *Peace and Conflict: Journal of Peace Psychology* 18, no. 2 (2012), pp. 131–143.

Millar, Gearoid. "Assessing Local Experiences of Truth-telling in Sierra Leone: Getting to 'Why' Through a Qualitative Case Study Analysis." *The International Journal of Transitional Justice* 4 (2010), pp. 477–496.

Millar, Gearoid. "Between Western Theory and Local Practice: Cultural Impediments to Truth-Telling in Sierra Leone." *Conflict Resolution Quarterly* 29, no. 2 (2011), pp. 177–199.

Millar, Gearoid. *Millennium: Journal of International Studies*, Special Forum on Memory and Grief, 38, no. 2 (2009).

Millar, Gearoid. "Peace-building Plans and Local Reconfigurations: Frictions between Imported Processes and Indigenous Practices." *International Peacekeeping* 20, no. 2 (2014), pp. 137–143.

Milton, Cynthia E. "Defacing Memory: Untying Peru's Memory Knots." *Memory Studies* 4, no. 2(2011), pp. 190–205.

Minow, Martha. *Between Vengeance and Forgiveness: Facing History after Genocide and Mass Violence*. Boston, MA: Beacon Press, 2000.

Mitrany, David. *A Working Peace System*. Chicago, IL: Quadrangle Books, 1966.

Mitton, Kieran. "A Pragmatic Pact: Reconciliation and Reintegration in Sierra Leone." In *Evaluating Transitional Justice: Accountability and Peace-building in Post-Conflict Sierra Leone*. Edited by Kirsten Ainley, Rebekka Friedman, and Christopher Mahony. Basingstoke: Palgrave Macmillan, 2015, pp. 217–240.

Mitton, Kieran. *Rebels in a Rotten State: Understanding Atrocity in the Sierra Leone Civil War*. Oxford: Oxford University Press, 2015.

Moon, Claire. *Narrating Political Reconciliation: South Africa's Truth and Reconciliation Commission*. Lanham, MD: Lexington Books, 2008.

Moon, Claire. "Prelapsarian State: Forgiveness and Reconciliation in Transitional Justice." *International Journal for Semiotics of Law* 17, no. 2 (2004), pp. 185–197.

Murphy, Jeffrie G. and Jean Hampton. *Forgiveness and Mercy*. Cambridge: Cambridge University Press, 1988.

Nagy, Rosemary. "Reconciliation in Post-Commission South Africa: Thick and Thin Accounts of Solidarity." *Canadian Journal of Political Science* 35, no. 2 (2002), pp. 323–346.

Neumann, William. "Peru Forced to Confront Deep Scars of Civil War." *New York Times* (May 26, 2012), p. 6.

Ní Aoláin, Fionnuala and Colm Campbell, "The Paradox of Transitions in Conflicted Democracies." *Human Rights Quarterly* 27, no. 1 (2005), pp. 172–213.

Nino, Carlos Santiago. *Radical Evil on Trial*. New Haven, CT and London: Yale University Press, 1996.

Norval, Aletta J. "Memory, Identity, and the (Im) possibility of Reconciliation: The Work of the Truth and Reconciliation Commission in South Africa." *Constellations* 5, no. 2 (1998), pp. 250–265.

Ntsebeza, Dumisa B. "The Uses of Truth Commissions: Lessons for the World." In *Truth v. Justice: The Morality of Truth Commissions*. Edited by Robert I. Rotberg and Dennis Thompson. Princeton, NJ: Princeton University Press, 2000, pp. 158–169.

Nunn, Nathan and Leonard Wantchekon. "The Slave Trade and the Origins of Mistrust in Africa." *American Economic Review* 101 (2011), pp. 3221–3253.

Okello, Moses Chrispus. "Afterword: Elevating Transitional Local Justice or Crystallizing Global Governance." In *Localizing Transitional Justice:*

Interventions and Priorities after Mass Violence. Edited by Rosalind Shaw, Lars Waldorf, and Pierre Hazan. Stanford, CA: Stanford University Press, 2010, pp. 275–284.

Oliart, Patricia. "Albert Fujimori: 'The Man Peru Needed?'" In *Shining and Other Paths: War and Society in Peru, 1980–1995*. Edited by Steve J. Stern. Durham and London: Duke University Press, 1998, pp. 415–421.

Olonisakin, Funmi. *Peacekeeping in Sierra Leone: The Story of UNAMSIL*. London: Lynne Rienner Publishers, 2008.

Olsen, Tricia D., Leigh A. Payne, and Andrew G. Reiter. *Transitional Justice in Balance: Comparing Processes, Weighing Efficacy*. Washington, DC: United States Institute for Peace, 2010.

Orentlicher, Diane F. "Settling Accounts: The Duty to Prosecute Human Rights Violations of a Prior Regime." *The Yale Law Journal* 100 (1991), pp. 2537–2615.

Osiel, Mark. *Mass Atrocity, Collective Memory, and the Law*. New Brunswick, NJ: Transaction, 1997.

Palmer, David Scott, ed. *The Shining Path of Peru*. London: C. Hurst & Co. Ltd., 1992.

Pankhurst, Donna. "Issues of Justice and Reconciliation in Complex Political Emergencies: Conceptualising Reconciliation, Justice and Peace." *Third World Quarterly* 20, no. 1 (1999), pp. 239–255.

Patron, Rosemary Lerner Rizo. "Between Conflict and Reconciliation: The Hard Truth." *Human Studies* 30, no. 2 (2007), pp. 115–130.

Payne, Leigh A. *Unsettling Accounts: Neither Truth Nor Reconciliation in Confessions of State Violence*. Durham and London: Duke University Press, 2008.

Peters, Krjin. "From Weapons to Wheels: Young Sierra Leonean Ex-Combatants Become Motorbike Taxi Drivers." *Journal of Peace, Conflict and Development* 10 (2007), pp. 1–23.

Peters, Krijn. *War and the Crisis of Youth in Sierra Leone*. Cambridge: Cambridge University Press, 2011.

Peters, Krijn and Paul Richards. "Why We Fight: Voices of Youth Combatants in Sierra Leone." *Africa: Journal of the International Africa Institute* 68, no. 2 (1998), pp. 183–210.

Pham, John-Peter. *Child Soldiers, Adult Interests: The Global Dimensions of the Sierra Leone Tragedy*. New York: Nova Science Publishers, 2005.

Philpott, Daniel. *Just and Unjust Wars: An Ethic of Political Reconciliation*. Oxford: Oxford University Press, 2012.

Philpott, Daniel. "Reconciliation: An Ethic for Peace-building." In *Strategies of Peace*. Edited by Daniel Philpott and Gerard Powers. Oxford: Oxford University Press, 2010, pp. 91–114.

Popkin, Margaret. "The Salvadoran Truth Commission and the Search for Justice." In *Truth Commissions and Courts: The Tensions between Criminal Justice and the Search for Truth*. Edited by William Schabas and Shane Darcy. Dordrecht, Netherlands: Kluwer Academic Publishers, 2004, pp. 105–124.

Portocarrero, Gonzalo, *Razones de sangre: Aproximaciones a la violencia política*

Post-conflict Reintegration Initiative for Development and Empowerment (PRIDE). "Ex-Combatant Views of the Truth and Reconciliation Commission and the Special Court in Sierra Leone." Freetown, Sierra Leone, PRIDE in partnership with the International Center for Transitional Justice, 2002.

Quinn, Joanna. "Constraints: The Un-Doing of the Ugandan Truth Commission." *Human Rights Quarterly* 26, no. 2 (May 2004), pp. 401–427.

Quinn, Joanna, ed. *Reconciliation (s): Transitional Justice in Post-Conflict Societies.* Montreal and Kingston: McGill-Queen's University Press, 2009.

Rahn, Wendy M. and John E. Transue. "Social Trust and Value Change: The Decline of Social Capital in American Youth, 1976–1995." *Political Psychology* 19, no. 3 (1998), pp. 545–565.

Renan, Ernest. "What is a Nation?" In *Becoming National: A Reader.* Edited by Geoff Eley and Ronald Grigor Suny. New York and Oxford: Oxford University Press, 1996, pp. 41–55.

Renique, José Luis. *La Batalla Por Puno: Conflicto Agrario y Nación en Los Andes Peruanos 1866–1995.* Lima, Peru: Institute of Peruvian Studies, 2004.

Reno, William. *Corruption and State Politics in Sierra Leone.* New York: Cambridge University Press, 1995.

Richards, Paul. *Fighting for the Rainforest.* The International African Institute in association with James Currey/Heinemann, 1996.

Richards, Paul. "To Fight or To Farm? Agrarian Dimensions of the Mano River Conflicts (Liberia and Sierra Leone)." *African Affairs* 104, no. 417 (2005), pp. 571–590.

Richmond, Oliver P. "A Post-Liberal Peace: Eirenism and the Everyday." *Review of International Studies* 35, no. 3 (2009), pp. 557–580.

Robins, Simon. "Challenging the Therapeutic Ethic: A Victim-Centred Evaluation of Transitional Justice Process in Timor Leste." *International Journal of Transitional Justice* 6, no. 1 (2012), pp. 83–105.

Root, Rebecca. Transitional Justice in Peru. New York: Palgrave Macmillan, 2012.

Rorty, Richard. "Human Rights, Rationality and Sentimentality." In *On Human Rights.* Edited by Stephen Shute and Susan Hurley. New York: Basic Books, 1993, pp. 111–34.

Rotberg, Robert I. "Truth Commissions and the Provision of Truth, Justice and Reconciliation." In *Truth versus Justice: The Morality of Truth Commissions.* Princeton, NJ: Princeton University Press, 2000, pp. 3–21.

Sachs, Albie. "The Task for Civil Society." In *The Healing of a Nation.* Edited by Alex Boraine, Janet Levy, and Kader Asmal. Cape Town: Justice in Transition, 1995.

Sarkin, Jeremy. "The Necessity and Challenges of Establishing a Truth and Reconciliation Commission in Rwanda." *Human Rights Quarterly* 21, no. 3 (1999), pp. 767–823.

Schaap, Andrew. *Political Reconciliation.* Oxford and New York: Routledge, 2005.

Schabas, William. "Conjoined Twins of Transitional Justice: The Sierra Leone Truth and Reconciliation Commission and the Special Court." *Journal of International Criminal Justice* 2, no. 4 (2004), pp. 1082–1099.

Schabas, William. "The Relationship between Truth Commissions and International Courts: The Case of Sierra Leone." *Human Rights Quarterly* 25, no. 4 (2003), pp. 1035–1066.

Schabas, William. "Truth Commissions and Courts Working in Parallel: The Sierra Leone Experience." *Proceedings of the 98th American Society of International Law* 98 (2004), pp. 189–95.

Schabas, William A. and Shane Darcy, eds. *Truth Commissions and Courts: The Tension between Criminal Justice and Truth.* Dordrecht: Kluwer Academic Publishing, 2004.

Schwan, Gesine. "The 'Healing' Values of Truth-Telling: Chances and Social Conditions in a Secularized World." *Social Research* 65 (1998), pp. 725–740.

Schwartz-Shea, Peregrine and Dvora Yanow. *Interpretive Research Design: Concepts and Processes.* New York: Routledge, 2012.

Shaw, Rosalind. "Displacing Violence: Making Pentecostal Memory in Sierra Leone." *Cultural Anthropology* 22, no. 1 (2008), pp. 66–93.

Shaw, Rosalind. "Linking Justice with Reintegration? Excombatants and the Sierra Leone Experiment." In *Localizing Transitional Justice: Interventions and Priorities after Mass Violence.* Edited by Rosalind Shaw and Lars Waldorf. Stanford, CA: Stanford University Press, 2010, pp. 11–132.

Shaw, Rosalind. *Memories of the Slave Trade: Ritual and the Historical Imagination in Sierra Leone.* Chicago, IL: University of Chicago Press, 2002.

Shaw, Rosalind. "Memory Frictions: Localizing the Truth and Reconciliation Commission in Sierra Leone." *The International Journal of Transitional Justice* 1 (2007), pp. 183–207.

Shaw, Rosalind. "Rethinking TRCs: Lessons from Sierra Leone." Special Report. United States Institute of Peace, 2005.

Shklar, Judith. *Legalism: Law, Morals, and Political Trials.* Cambridge, MA: Harvard University Press, 1986.

Shriver, Donald W. Jr. *An Ethic for Enemies: Forgiveness in Politics.* Oxford: Oxford University Press, 1998.

Sierra Leone Working Group on Truth and Reconciliation. "Searching for Truth and Justice in Sierra Leone: An Initial Study of the Performance and Impact of the Truth and Reconciliation Commission" (February 2006). Available at: www.fambultok.org/TRCStudy-FinalVersion.pdf.

The Sierra Leonean TRC Report. Available at: www.sierra-leone.org/TRCDoc uments.html.

Sikkink, Kathryn. *The Justice Cascade: How Human Rights Prosecutions are Changing World Politics.* New York and London: W.W. Norton and Company, 2011.

Sil, Rudra and Peter J. Katzenstein. *Beyond Paradigms: Analytical Eclecticism in the Study of World Politics.* New York and London: Palgrave Macmillan, 2010.

Simpson, John. *In the Forests of the Night: Encounters with Terrorism, Drug-Running and Military Oppression.* London: Random House, 1993.

Sisk, Timothy D. *Democratization in South Africa: The Elusive Social Contract.* Princeton, NJ: Princeton University Press, 1995.

"The Situation of Human Rights in Sierra Leone." U.N.Doc. E/CN.4/2001/35, at 13 H 41.53. Eleventh Report of the Secretary General on the United Nations Mission in Sierra Leone.

Sluzski, Carlos. "The Process Towards Reconciliation." In *Imagine Coexistence: Restoring Humanity after Violent Ethnic Conflict.* Edited by Antonia Chayes and Martha Minow. Cambridge, MA: Jossey-Bass, 2003.

Snyder, Jack and Leslie Vinjamuri. "Trials and Errors: Principle and Pragmatism in Strategies in International Justice." *International Security* 28, no. 5 (2003), pp. 5–44.

Sooka, Yasmine and Chris Mahony. "The Truth about the Truth: Insider Reflections on the Sierra Leonean Truth and Reconciliation Commission." In *Evaluating Transitional Justice: Accountability and Peacebuilding in Post-Conflict Sierra Leone*. Edited by Kirsten Ainley, Rebekka Friedman, and Chris Mahony. London: Palgrave, 2015, pp. 241–264.

The South African TRC Report. Available at: www.info.gov.za/otherdocs/1920 03/trc/.

The Special Court for Sierra Leone. *Decision on the Request by the TRC of Sierra Leone to Conduct a Public Hearing with the Accused*, SCSL-02-08-PT-101 (October 29, 2003). Available at: www.sl-sc.org.

Sriram, Chandra Lekha. *Confronting Past Human Rights Violations: Justice v. Peace in Times of Transition*. London and New York: Frank Cass, 2004.

Starn, Orin. "Maoism in the Andes: The Communist Party of Peru-Shining Path and the Refusal of History." *Journal of Latin American Studies* 27, no. 2 (1995), pp. 399–421.

Stern, Steve J. "Beyond Enigma: An Agenda for Interpreting Shining Path and Peru, 1980–1995." In *Shining and Other Paths: War and Society in Peru, 1980–1995*. Edited by Steve J. Stern. Durham and London: Duke University Press, 1998, pp. 1–21.

Stovel, Laura. *Long Road Home: Building Reconciliation and Trust in Post-war Sierra Leone*. Mortsel, Belgium: Interstentia, 2010.

Taylor, Charles. *Multiculturalism and the Politics of Recognition*. Edited by Charles Taylor. Princeton, NJ: Princeton University Press, 1994.

Teitel, Ruti G. *Transitional Justice*. New York: Oxford University Press, 2000.

Teitel, Ruti G. "Transitional Justice Genealogy." *Harvard Human Rights Journal* 16 (2003), pp. 69–94.

Tepperman, Jonathan D. "Truth and Consequences." *Foreign Affairs* 81, no. 2 (2002), p. 128.

Theidon, Kimberley. "Histories of Innocence: Post-war Stories in Peru," in *Localizing Transitional Justice: Interventions and Priorities after Mass Violence*, ed. Rosalind Shaw, Lars Waldorf, and Pierre Hazan (Stanford, CA: Stanford University Press, 2010), p. 110.

Theidon, Kimberly Susan. *Entre Prójimos: El Conflicto Armado Interno y la Política de la Reconciliación en el Perú*. Lima, Perú: Instituto de Estudios Peruanos, 2004.

Theidon, Kimberly Susan. Intimate Enemies: Violence and Reconciliation in Peru. University of Pennsylvania Press. 2013.

Theidon, Kimberly Susan. "Histories of Innocence: Post-War Stories in Peru." In *Localizing Transitional Justice: Interventions and Priorities after Mass Violence*. Edited by Rosalind Shaw, Lars Waldorf, and Pierre Hazan. Stanford, CA: Stanford University Press, Studies in Human Rights, 2010, pp. 92–110.

Theidon, Kimberly Susan. "Justice in Transition: The Micropolitics of Reconciliation in Post-War Peru." *Journal of Conflict Resolution* 50, no. 3 (2006), pp. 433–457.

Todorov, Tzvetan. *Hope and Memory: Lessons from the Twentieth Century*. Princeton, NJ: Princeton University Press, 2003.

The Truth and Reconciliation Commission Report for the Children of Sierra Leone. Available at: www.unicef.org/infobycountry/files/TRCCF9SeptFINAL.pdf.

Tsing, Anna L. *An Ethnography of Global Connection*. Princeton, NJ: Princeton University Press, 2005.

Tutu, Desmond. *No Future without Forgiveness*. Houghton, South Africa: Random House, 1999.

UN DDR Sierra Leone Country Programme Report. Available at: www.unddr.org/countryprogrammes.php?c=60.

UN High Commissioner for Refugees. "Sierra Leone: Lack of Aid Funds for Amputees, Rape Survivors, War Widows" (2009). Available at: www.unhcr.org/refworld/publisher, IRIN, SLE,49a660d01a,0.html.

UN High Commissioner for Refugees. "Sierra Leone: Lack of Aid Funds for Amputees, Rape Survivors, and War Widows" (2012). Available at: www.irinnews.org/Report/83100/SIERRA-LEONE-Lack-of-aid-funds-for-amputees-rape-survivors-war-widows.

UN Office for the Coordination of Humanitarian Affairs, IRIN Interview with Special Court for Sierra Leone Chief Prosecutor, David Crane (September 25, 2012). Available at: www.irinnews.org/InDepthMain.aspx?InDepthId=31&ReportId=70568.

UN Secretary General. "The Rule of Law and Transitional Justice in Conflict and Post-Conflict Societies – Report of the Secretary General" (2011).

United Nations. "What is Transitional Justice? A Backgrounder" (February 20, 2008). Available at: www.un.org/en/peace-building/pdf/doc_wgll/justice_times_transition/26_02_2008_background_note.pdf.

US Institute of Peace. "Truth Commissions: Digital Collection." Available at: www.usip.org/publications/truth-commission.

USAID/Peru. "Peru: Economic Growth" (February 2011). Available at: www.usaid.gov/pe.

Van Roermund, Bert. "Rubbing Off and Rubbing On: The Grammar of Reconciliation." In *Lethe's Law: Justice, Law, and Ethics in Reconciliation*. Edited by Emilios A. Christodoulidis and Scott Veitch. Oxford: Hart Publishing, 2001, pp. 175–190.

Villa-Vicencio, Charles. "Reconciliation." In *Pieces of the Puzzle: Keywords on Reconciliation and Transitional Justice*. Edited by Charles Villa-Vicencio and Erik Doxtader. Cape Town, South Africa: Institute for Justice and Reconciliation, 2004, pp. 3–9.

Villa-Vicencio, Charles. *Walk with Us and Listen: Political Reconciliation in Africa*. Washington, DC: Georgetown University Press, 2009.

Villa-Vicencio, Charles and William Vorwoerd, eds. *Looking Back, Reaching Forward: Reflections on the Truth and Reconciliation Commission of South Africa*. Cape Town, South Africa: University of Cape Town Press, 2000.

Vinjamuri, Leslie and Michelle Sieff. "Reconciling Order and Justice? New Institutional Solutions in Post-Conflict States." *Journal of International*

Affairs, Special Edition on International Institutions and Justice 52, no. 2 (1999), pp. 757–779.

Weinstein, Harvey M., Laurel E. Fletcher, and Patrick Vinck. "Stay the Hand of Justice: Whose Priorities Take Priority?" In *Localizing Transitional Justice: Interventions and Priorities after Mass Violence*. Edited by Rosalind Shaw and Lars Waldorf. Stanford, CA: Stanford University Press, 2010, pp. 27–48.

Williams, Sarah. "Amnesties in International Law: The Experience of the Special Court for Sierra Leone." *Human Rights Law Review* 5, no. 2 (2005), pp. 271–309.

Wilson, Richard A. *The Politics of Truth and Reconciliation in South Africa: Legitimizing the Post-Apartheid State*. Cambridge: Cambridge University Press, 2001.

Wood, E. J. "The Social Processes of Civil War: The Wartime Transformation of Social Networks." *Annual Review of Political Science* 11, no. 1 (2008), pp. 539–561.

Yin, Robert K. *Case Study Research: Design and Methods*, 4th edition. Thousand Parks, CA: Sage, 2009.

Young, Iris Marion. "Communication and the Other: Beyond Deliberative Democracy." In *Democracy and Difference*. Edited by Seyla Benhabib. Princeton, NJ: Princeton University Press, 1995, pp. 295–311.

Zack-Williams, A. B. "Child Soldiers in the Civil War in Sierra Leone." *Review of African Political Economy* 87, no. 73 (2001), pp. 73–82.

Zack-Williams, A. B. "Sierra Leone: The Political Economy of Civil War, 1991–1998." *Third World Quarterly* 20, no. 1 (1999), pp. 143–162.

Zalaquett, José. "Introduction." *Report of the Chilean Commission of National Truth and Reconciliation*. Available at: www.usip.org/files/resources/collections/truth_commissions/Chile90-Report/Chile90-Report.pdf.

Zehr, Howard. *Changing Lenses: A New Focus for Crime and Justice*. Scottsdale, PA: Herald Press, 1990.

Zehr, Howard. "A Restorative Framework for Community Justice Practice." In *Criminology, Conflict Resolution and Restorative Justice*. Edited by Kieran McEvoy and Tim Newburn. New York: Palgrave Macmillan, 2003, pp. 135–152.

Zehr, Howard. "Restorative Justice: When Justice and Healing Go Together." *Track Two* 6, no. 3–4(1997), p. 20.

Zehr, Howard. "Restoring Justice in God and the Victim: Theological Reflections on Evil, Victimization, Justice, and Forgiveness." In *Neighbors Who Care*. Edited by Lisa Barnes Lampman and Michelle D. Shattuck. Washington, DC: William B. Eerdmans Publishing Company, 1999, pp. 131–159.

Index

CPSIA information can be obtained
at www.ICGtesting.com
Printed in the USA
LVOW13*1945281217
561099LV00010B/157/P

9 781107 185692